The Community
as Classroom

The Community as Classroom

Integrating School and Community Through Language Arts

Candida Gillis

University of Idaho

Boynton/Cook Publishers
HEINEMANN
Portsmouth, NH

Boynton/Cook Publishers, Inc.
A Subsidiary of
Heinemann Educational Books, Inc.
361 Hanover Street, Portsmouth, NH 03801
Offices and agents throughout the world

The following have generously given permission to use copyrighted work:

Page 29: "My Views" scale. © CTIR, University of Denver, 1978.
  Reprinted with permission.

Every effort has been made to contact the copyright holders and
students for permission to reprint borrowed material. We regret any
oversights that may have occurred and would be happy to rectify them
in future printings of this work.

Library of Congress Cataloging-in-Publication Data
Gillis, Candida.
    The community as classroom: integrating school and community
  through language arts/Candida Gillis.
      p.   cm.
    Includes bibliographical references.
    ISBN 0−86709−280−7
    1. Language arts (Elementary)−United States.   2. Language arts
  (Secondary)−United States.   3. Activity programs in education−
  United States.   4. Community and school−United States.   I. Title.
  LB1576.G452   1991   91−19073
  428′.007−dc20   CIP

#23868344

Cover design by Jenny Jensen Greenleaf
Printed in the United States of America.
92 93 94 95   9 8 7 6 5 4 3 2 1

for my mother and father

Contents

Preface

This book is for teachers and anyone else who works with children or adolescents in educational settings — schools, scout groups, Sunday schools, even camps — and who cares about making language arts education more exciting and purposeful. The book has two focuses. Primarily, it is a book of teaching ideas, a collection of language arts-based activities designed for K–12 teachers to help students become more familiar with and knowledgeable about the worlds outside of school. Secondarily, it is about helping the young become more familiar with elders.

We live in a world today that is increasingly specialized, and in which young people are frequently segregated from their larger communities. Children and adolescents spend the majority of their time with their age-mates in schools and in their neighborhoods with friends doing things that appeal to their common interests. Many young people have few regular or significant experiences with the diversity of people and places a community holds; they grow up with only vague notions or ignorant of aspects of the community that do not concern or interest them. Schools themselves are isolating, grouping young people by age, interest, and, often, socioeconomic background. Although the language arts — reading, writing, listening, and speaking — are the means by which we supposedly broaden our knowledge of the world, they are often taught in a setting removed from that world. This book takes the view that when students use language arts for the genuine purpose of interacting with their communities, they not only learn and strengthen those abilities but strengthen their identities as members of a larger society.

There are any number of ways teachers can integrate the communities and classrooms; they can invite a guest speaker occasionally, take the class on a field trip, show films, assign reading material, or engage in more complex, long-range units or projects. *The Community as Classroom* describes a more systematic (though by no means inflexible) method teachers can use to incorporate community study throughout the school year. The advantage of regular, focused integration is that it encourages students to see their communities as permanent educational resources and strengthens their roles as inquirers and explorers. The method consists of a number of teaching activities grouped into five phases. In the first phase, students become conscious of and explore their pre-existing attitudes toward whatever aspect of the community they are studying, whether the attitudes are positive or negative, hold misconceptions or biases. Next, students investigate the sources of their attitudes — the books, television programs, advertisements, and language that have influenced their\views. Third, students get acquainted with their subject in a variety of ways, including reading, writing, interviewing, and watching. Fourth, students engage in additional research and/ or projects suggested by their earlier discoveries. At various stages in their community study, young people have numerous opportunities for sharing information more formally through writing, acting, public speaking, composing displays, and other formats; this formal sharing, or publishing, is the fifth (but not necessarily last) phase.

My purpose in grouping activities into these five phases is to emphasize the potential depth and breadth of community explorations — to give teachers and students a means for going as deeply into one or more topics as they want. It is also meant to provide teachers with a general sequence for activities that can be helpful in planning lessons and projects. However, the five-phase organization is intended as a useful guide, not a rigid prescription. Activities in later phases may easily and profitably accompany activities in earlier phases. For example, some kinds of publishing are appropriate when students are beginning their community study. Also, students might examine their attitudes in the middle of a project, when they discover related topics.

What in a community might a class explore? Anything and anyone: a building or geographical feature, a local business or industry, members of an occupation, profession, or ethnic group. Students might investigate a transit system, a power plant, optometrists, dog trainers, people with Down's syndrome, an historic fort, or a nearby fish hatchery. Nearly any subject can be the focus of a short- or long-term project of reading, writing, listening, and speaking. To illustrate the ways the community and classroom can be integrated I have chosen the subject of elders and old age — a subject that I have long felt deserves more attention in our schools. Most of the work on aging education has been done in the social studies and for the elementary grades. However, it is an appropriate subject for language arts and secondary school English classes as well, considering the wealth of literature on the theme and the innumerable writing opportunities the subject affords. Old people comprise a large part of all communities, yet for many young people, elders are unfamiliar and perhaps even threatening. When the young become acquainted with the old, all generations benefit.

Most of the teaching ideas suggested in this book can be adjusted in complexity, depth, and duration for students of different ages and abilities. People in any grade can conduct interviews, write books of poems, examine images in literature, make informative displays, write persuasive letters, and do many of the other activities described (children in lower grades, obviously, will require more assistance). By making activities shorter, simpler, and more explicit, teachers can adapt them to elementary classes, or add depth, length, and rigor to suit high school groups. For example, to explore stereotypes in children's literature, third-graders can fill in short answers to specific questions about the text and pictures, while senior high students can write longer essays about the effects of artistic styles and uses of descriptive language. Some activities, however, are obviously more appropriate for older students: examining characterization in literature, conducting surveys of television commercials, creating reader's theaters, leading writing workshops or reading groups, publishing literary magazines. And others are more appropriate for younger grades: writing and performing puppet shows, writing and illustrating books about grandparents, creating new folk tales, and making models in the class and role-playing. Within each chapter are activities for all ages, with sufficient variations so that teachers may choose.

The activities in *The Community as Classroom*, whether taken as an entire, sequential program or used piecemeal, will help students learn that one purpose of language is to explore and understand our environments and that through language we shape and share our culture. When we expand our curriculum to include the people and places around us, we help to make that community a more rewarding part of our students' lives. We encourage young people to see that they are important members of that community and that by broadening their understanding, they enrich themselves.

Acknowledgments

I have many to thank for their help, direct or indirect, in this project. My appreciation goes first to the people whose suggestions and efforts helped me prepare the bibliographies: Diana Mitchell, Jacquelen Baucom, Colleen Ozora, Judith Keck, and many others who were kind enough to share their discoveries of favorite books; J. Christian Purvis, my research assistant, contributed tiresome hours checking bibliographic details. Next, my thanks go to Mike Carnell and Carolyn Tragesser and their students in Moscow Senior and Junior High Schools who used several of my activities in their classes, and to the many parents, teachers, students, and elders who contributed their ideas and shared their work with me, including Tina Woods, Jennifer Olson, and Ralph M. Zeigler. In addition, I am grateful to the people who have worked and published in the field of aging education: Francis E. Pratt, Richard O. Ulin, Catherine Townsend Horner, and the others whose works have drawn attention to the need to demythologize old age and given teachers the means to do it. I am indebted to University of Idaho Research Foundation for awarding me a grant for this research, and to the U. of I. Department of English for its ongoing support. Finally, recognition must go to the Michigan Councils for the Humanities and Arts, the Michigan State University Department of English and College of Arts and Letters, and all the people who supported and participated in the original Life-Writing Project in the 1970s. My special thanks to Dr. Linda Wagner-Martin, co-administrator and mother of that project, for introducing me to the subject of elders' writing and setting all of these wheels in motion.

Chapter One

Getting Together

From the time we entered school most of us entered a world that was more diverse than the world of our families. Yet even school had a certain sameness. For those twelve-plus years, we spent at least seven hours a day with other people who were our age doing similar things we liked or grumbled about, more or less. We learned about the world mainly from our teachers and books and the occasional field trip. If we were lucky we learned new things from each other, if our age-mates were different from us in ethnic background or in physical or mental ability. But for many of us, our classroom colleagues were more alike than different. In my elementary school we were predominantly white; some were Asian, a few, Hispanic. In my grade, half were Jewish, half Gentile—Catholics, Protestants, and undeclareds; one girl was from the South, another's family came from Italy, and the rest of us were Westerners. We were all from a generic middle class. For the most part, we were as alike as kickballs.

On field trips and family excursions I had glimpses of a world far different from the one I lived in. In this larger world I saw huge houses, old, tall buildings streaked with grime, fields with mysterious machines sitting in them, and people who looked different: old people, dark people, people in costumes I had never seen. I heard other languages and smelled new smells—all within twenty miles of my house. On these trips I learned how vastly different from my neighborhood and school my larger community was.

Junior and senior high school brought that larger community closer. Not only were there more students but they came from a wider range of economic and cultural backgrounds. This new-found diversity was mainly visible before and after school; in the class-

1

room we were alike. Except in gym, home economics, shop, music, and art, we were separated into classes according to our test scores and career plans. Thus, we spent most of our school time with others not only of our own age, but also of our own ability and general interests. The "dumb" kids were together in special ed or remedial classes. (Mainstreaming of these students into regular classes happened only in smaller or poorer districts—in other words, when the school could not afford special classes.) Kids who were "smart" were scheduled into honors classes. (In my school these classes were designated HH, for "high high.") Everyone in the schools was either college bound or voc-tech, and those in the voc-tech group were subdivided even further—business, auto, industrial arts. People in one group knew little of what the other students did in their classes. And we were separated according to our physical capabilities: no students in my classes were in wheelchairs, were visually or hearing impaired, or had cerebral palsy or other physical handicaps. Those students were in special classes or went to different schools.

Much has changed since I was in school. Classrooms today are more diverse in terms of the backgrounds, interests, and abilities of the students. Tracking is not so clear-cut; students with physical or learning disabilities are less segregated. Yet much remains alike in our classrooms. In many ways they are a world for young people that exists outside of the community mainstream. For six to seven hours a day children and adolescents spend their time in designated buildings and grounds with others of their ages in order to do a range of educational tasks. These tasks usually involve learning about the world vicariously. History is in a book, writing is learned through writing assignments, and frogs come ready for dissection, pre-pickled, in large jars. At three o'clock students re-enter the larger community—a community that has little relation to school. Instead of a majority of youngsters of the same age, the real community has babies, old people, middle-aged people. Instead of students, teachers, principals, counselors, a custodian or two, a nurse, and a librarian, the community includes butchers, bakers, barbers, biologists, and beauticians. Instead of a series of nearly identical rooms containing thirty desks each, a community contains pool halls, grange halls, Elks halls, and town halls, hospitals, offices, book shops, and body shops. The social structure of a community is far more complex than that of a school, whose status hierarchies are based on authority (who has it and who doesn't) and popularity (who is and who isn't). A community contains people in all stages of life, health, and possibly wealth, and its history is larger and richer than the history of any one institution within it. As a resource for learning, the community is a treasure trove of history, architecture, biology, art, music, languages, psychology, mathematics, sociology, and literature.

In some states and in some communities, educators and community members have joined in projects to bring the classroom and community closer together. A special issue of *Instructor and Teacher* (Winter, '85) describes a number of school-community projects. These projects and the movement behind them are called partnerships. A partnership project may consist of an adopt-a-grandparent program, of parents tutoring in an elementary classroom, or of a local business donating money and equipment for computer labs or sponsoring a writing contest. The goals of partnerships are to "create new learning experiences for kids and build broader connections with their community,"[1] and to enhance the community's commitment to the education of its young people — to extend the responsibility for learning and teaching beyond the school walls. According to *Instructor and Teacher*, 26 states have programs for school-community partnerships in which schools collaborate with a variety of civic organizations for the benefit of each. Here are some of the collaborations: A school runs a community center. A Junior League presents "Kids on the Block" puppet shows in schools. Local police serve as resource people for a school district and give "Officer Ollie" puppet shows in an elementary school. Attorneys conduct mock trials in a classroom. A group of elders runs a hotline for children called "Grandma Please." Local opera and theater companies give parts of performances in schools.[2] Whether the collaboration is as simple as local police officers talking about traffic safety or as complicated as children operating a recycling center, the benefit is enormous. Partnerships can "reinforce basic skills, as well as supplement the curriculum. They reunite the world of education with the surrounding environment."[3]

There are many more specific reasons why schools and communities should come together, but one of the strongest is the need to enhance students' language arts abilities.

The Community of Language

What is the one sound heard most often at school outside the classroom? Talk. Language. All the language arts — reading, composing, speaking — are social. They are pleasurable as well as functional. We human beings learn language by using it and use language to understand and navigate in our environments. The language arts are the media through which we interact with and develop within our communities. Think of how many ways we use language daily: we read and listen to news about our community, state, nation, and world. We respond to what we read and hear by talking about it to others, and sometimes by writing. We hear and/or look at hundreds of commercial messages daily, from newspaper ads to signs in shop windows. We learn to consume language as well as produce it. Language shapes our thought, and thought gives rise to language.

In *Explorations in the Teaching of Secondary English*, Stephen Tchudi and Diana Mitchell write, "Language learning is a process of wondering and exploring, of discovering the conventions of language in society so that people can use language fully for their own purposes."[4] Language is learned best when it is used "naturally and pleasurably."[5] When language is studied for its own sake — disconnected from human beings and their real purposes for using it — language becomes an artifact: complicated, abstract, pointless. Only by using language do people learn it, and only when they see a genuine need to learn. With hard work on the teacher's part, the classroom can become an environment in which language is used for a variety of natural reasons — a place where students formulate questions, organize and articulate ideas, create powerful, persuasive arrangements of words, and respond to the language of others. One of the ways teachers can make language learning more purposeful and relevant is to integrate the young person's world outside of school with the world of the classroom. A community is a mother lode of language.

When a child stops an ice cream truck, opens a bank account, asks a bus driver when to disembark, checks out a library book, or recites the Scout promise, the child is interacting with the community using language. And the child is strengthening his or her ability to use language instrumentally — as a means of accomplishing something. As children grow and their worlds extend beyond the neighborhood, the situations in which they use language become more complex. Adolescents, for example, are able to use discourse in a range of registers — levels of formality — and converse effectively in any number of social situations. Joking with the barber, reading the instruction book of a new video game, talking a parent into extending a curfew, applying for a summer job — each requires different language skills and a great deal of knowledge about how language operates in society. The person who can do all these is fluent indeed.

Language is the prime medium for learning — about the world and about language itself. Language arts study in the classroom has too often been devoid of the natural purposes for language use. Take writing: typically, children in school write in order to practice —

neatness in making letters, correctness in spelling, mechanical fluency — or in order to record information. Arthur Applebee, in his study of writing in secondary schools, found that the primary reason teachers had students write was to recall information in order to test what students had learned.[6] Outside school we write to record or share information, but rarely to show how much we know. In schools the audience for writing is usually the teacher, regardless of the assignment's stated purpose. For example, we ask students to write letters to friends, to members of the community, to newspaper editors. But even these assignments are primarily to enable us, the teachers, to determine whether children's writing has improved and also to assign grades. Regardless of how often we try to make the audiences for student writing realistic, our writing situations remain artificial. Most eighth-graders do not write letters of inquiry to prospective employers even though they practice this business-letter-writing skill in their English classes. The fourth-graders who write ghost stories for kindergartners probably will not get to read them to the younger children. Most school writing to audiences other than the teacher is "as if" writing. And although many letters do get mailed (thank-you letters, letters to editors, pen-pal letters), rarely do the recipients' responses count in our evaluation of writing quality. Writing effectiveness is not judged by the real audiences but by the teacher, who remains the primary reader and judge. In school a successful piece of writing is one that receives a good grade, not one that gets results.

Like writing, literature in schools is often academic. For many older students Literature exists as a separate genre — that body of work read aloud or silently for book reports and/or tests and class discussion. It is a genre that includes anything a teacher makes you read, anything in an anthology or reader, anything written by someone famous (and even better, dead), and anything you have to answer questions about after you finish reading. Books that are truly good are those read by flashlight under the covers or in the back seat of the car on long trips. They are the books you pick out yourself at the library, the books your friend lets you borrow, the books with dog-eared pages and crumpled covers. Literature has authority. Good books offer friendship.

Good books (or literature with a small *l*) are just about everywhere, not just in schools or libraries. Consider the range of literature that exists outside of school. Every community has writers — published and unpublished, young and old, educated and uneducated. These people write journals and memoirs, essays, poems, short stories, or song lyrics. Some meet regularly to share their work, others write only for friends, families, or themselves.

Communities also have local publications besides the local newspaper that contain stories, essays, poems, or articles: an automobile
club magazine, a humane society newsletter, a campus literary
magazine. And what about the wealth of local popular literature,
such as graffiti, billboards, advertisements, signs in local stores?
Little of the community's literature finds its way into classrooms. It
is no wonder, then, that students come to see literature as Literature,
mysterious and inaccessible—even threatening—by the time they
are in high school. Why not extend and expand the range of literature
in the classroom to include literature of the real world? Why not
use, in addition to the ads in *Newsweek*, the more familiar commercials and printed ads of local merchants to study the language
of advertising? Why not read aloud a poem written by the neighborhood grocer or study the transcript of a speech by a local civic
leader?

The art of speaking, too, is often disconnected from its natural
environment. We teach students how to write and deliver formal
speeches to their classmates (which few would do in reality), or to
classmates pretending to be an imaginary audience of strangers
(which they are not). We teach techniques of impromptu, persuasive,
entertainment speaking and perhaps principles of debate to classmates who pretend they have come to be entertained or persuaded.
We teach students not to say "ya know" or to punctuate their
speech with "ums" by punishing the speaker with a lower grade
instead of with fidgeting, falling asleep, yawning, or talking, which
a real audience might do. We teach informal speaking techniques—
how to conduct a discussion that stays on track, how to contribute
ideas without dominating, how to respond verbally to other people's
ideas, how to summarize, and how to ask for information or
clarification—by putting students in artificial situations and
expecting them to have genuine ideas, to be interested, to care. And
the outcome of productive discussion in the English classroom is
the same as the reward for articulate formal speech: not enthusiasm,
applause, or nods of agreement, but a grade.

In a community outside of school, effective communications
are those that get results. Speaking, listening, reading, and writing
are processes relevant to living and growing in a world beyond the
self. By using the community as a resource, young people can
expand and strengthen not only their language abilities but their
awareness and knowledge of other subjects as well. In their explorations of community resources—art, architecture, history, cultural
groups, institutions, businesses, and so on—students become
investigators, organizers, and publishers of what they learn. Language
arts become investigative tools and the media for recording and

sharing information. Reading, writing, listening, speaking are purposeful.

Extending the classroom walls is not a new idea in education, nor is the notion of integrating language arts activities with the study of other subjects. The idea had an early spokesperson in John Dewey, who wrote at the turn of the century (1899) that education should be active, based on experience, and prepare students for community life.[7] In 1935, the National Council of Teachers of English published the report of the Curriculum Commission, chaired by W. Wilbur Hatfield. The report, *An Experience Curriculum in English*, described a K−12 language arts curriculum based on John Dewey's emphasis on the individual student, on his or her growth and experiences. It was the point of view of the commission that language arts experiences should help students acquire communication skills necessary for work as well as social success, not simply for success in school. Instruction and materials should be relevant, should address the needs of individual learners, and should integrate, wherever possible, life situations. Language arts activities should go beyond the English class into classes in other subjects, and into the community itself. English teachers should create opportunities for students to use language realistically and should stress creative expression as a means of acknowledging and sharing experience. The primary objectives of English education should be social, and to develop children's capacity to value experience for its own sake.[8] This document marked a major change in the focus of English education, for it acknowledged the social dimensions of language arts education and the value of experience to learning. Parts of it would be considered modern by today's standards, but alas, the NCTE has not reprinted it.

"English for life" continued as a theme in successive books and articles on the teaching and learning of language arts, including Angela Broening's *Conducting Experiences in English*,[9] the companion book to Hatfield's, and Ruth Mary Weeks's *A Correlated Curriculum*,[10] which proposed ways of fusing the study of literature, writing, and speaking with other subjects and with extracurricular activities such as concerts, community publications, and art shows. During the years that followed World War II, the need to prepare children for life in a society that was more complex technologically and more competitive internationally became the theme of a number of NCTE publications. In *The English Language Arts*, Dora V. Smith and the NCTE Commission on the English Curriculum were among those who advocated a school curriculum that would teach students to be critical consumers of media and propaganda, to write for real reasons and purposes — a curriculum that constantly related learning to home and community.[11]

The 1960s and 1970s brought an even greater emphasis on relevance and experience to the classroom. Jerome Bruner's theories about the structure of the disciplines and the need for teaching students to learn through discovery became the foundation of a number of funded language arts projects aimed at developing curricula based on inquiry and discovery learning. John Dixon's *Growth Through English*, a report on the Anglo-American Seminar on the Teaching of English held in 1966 at Dartmouth College, helped to disseminate to American educators the British view that students' experiences in their daily lives should be at the English curriculum's core. The classroom should promote reading, writing, and speaking for genuine purposes, and stress talk, dramatics, personal writing, and literature as an expression of human experience.[12] Another proponent of experiential education was James Moffett, whose K−13 curriculum in English language arts conceived of growth in language as the ability to communicate about increasingly abstract subjects to increasingly impersonal audiences for more complex and formal purposes. His curriculum included classroom activities based on children's real language uses — storytelling, diaries, sharing, observing, and reporting.[13] Moffett's work and the work of James Britton, L. S. Vigotsky, Jean Piaget, and others have shed more light on the relationships among language, writing, speaking, and thought. This research has helped us pay attention to the ways in which writing and speaking are means of shaping and coming to terms with experience and not simply vehicles for communicating information.

Language arts instruction in the classroom has come a long way from the turn of the century, yet it faces many of the same criticisms as it did long ago. Although students no longer sit at desks bolted to the floor and copy themes, many complain that they still have to memorize and regurgitate trivial facts about authors' lives, do grammar drills, and write for no real reason about subjects they care little about. But innovations continue. Eliot Wigginton, whose philosophy echoes Dewey, Hatfield, Dixon, and others, is a current proponent of making learning more meaningful. His "Foxfire" method of teaching encourages students to formulate their own questions and to seek answers by carrying out research in the world beyond the classroom. Students work together on self-initiated projects to define problems and explore solutions; the teacher is only a partner, a guide. In a Foxfire project, students may investigate particulars in their local community — a unique person, an aspect of the town's history — or larger issues, such as soil erosion or child abuse, so long as the subject has significance beyond any one individual. The emphasis is on teamwork and collaboration, and the teacher is a guide, fellow collaborator, and evaluator of students' growth. The students' research must be geared toward accomplishing state-mandated educational objectives, however. Projects must be designed and executed in ways that ensure that students acquire and even exceed the particular skill levels or knowledge specified by state or school for their grade. Students are regularly and systematically evaluated during their work to ensure that they are meeting appropriate educational objectives. And the results must be shared with audiences beyond the students; one of the more typical projects is the production of a book.[14]

Clearly, the community is a rich resource in which students can learn any number of language arts and other skills, no matter who initiates the study, student or teacher, and no matter where the learning takes place, in or out of the classroom. Community study taps children's experiences with life and with language; it has purposes that are immediately apparent and produces knowledge that seems immediately relevant. Best of all, it helps to break down the artificial boundaries that separate children from the world around them, enabling children to feel comfortable as inquirers in either setting.

A Method for Integrating the Classroom and Community

Integrating community and classroom can be enormously complex or very simple. It can happen in a few minutes, occasionally during a school year, or occur throughout a child's twelve years of schooling. A typical form of integration is a unit of study based on one aspect of the community that takes place over one, two, or several weeks. The unit may combine more than one curricular subject — science, English, social studies, art, mathematics — in order to explore community, people, places, or professions. For example, seventh-grade teachers at a Michigan middle school situated next to a grove of sugar maples focused their classes on all aspects of the sugar bush for two weeks. Activities included reading (about the history of the grove, maple trees, and methods of making syrup), observing, calculating, and measuring (tapping the trees), and writing (information pamphlets, recipes with maple syrup, books of poetry about the experience). The maple tree study was a major project and required a great deal of coordination and preparation; but according to the teachers, their efforts more than paid off. The students were interested and eager, worked hard, and produced some lively writing.

Yet community study need not be so concentrated. It may be short-term or incidental, such as a trip to a local fire station during fire prevention week, a police officer's talk about street safety, a local poet's sharing her work with a class, or the reading aloud of a book about life in another culture. It may be the central focus of a project (an elementary class studies community architecture) or tangential to another subject (a high school class records interviews with migrant farm workers in conjunction with reading *The Grapes of Wrath*). Teachers can bring the community into the classroom through books, speakers, simulations, or community volunteers who participate in regular classroom activities, such as writing or reading. Teachers may also bring the classroom into the community, through field trips and individual projects that engage students in community research. Whatever method or methods teachers use, they will discover that the process of integrating the community yields some interesting and unexpected benefits.

Children's and adolescents' perceptions of the people, places, and things in the world beyond the school are to some degree already formulated. Thus, exploring our community involves not only finding out what we don't know but also discovering what we *do* know—the attitudes and preconceptions we have acquired, the elements in our culture that have shaped those attitudes, and how those attitudes influence our thought and behavior. Community study is a self-exploration, an examination of the extent and nature of our knowledge, assumptions, beliefs, and convictions. It is also a venture into the culture at large and the forces that influence our thinking. Even the simplest integration of class and community is potentially complex. For example, a talk by a doctor on mental retardation scheduled to enhance the class' understanding of Steinbeck's *Of Mice and Men* could be accompanied by a discussion of students' attitudes toward retardation and lead to an investigation into the myths and realities of a diversity of cognitive/educational handicaps, into the educational and professional opportunities for retarded people, and into a project to promote community awareness.

Because community study can be complex, teachers may wish to integrate the community into the classroom more systematically. Systematic approaches have several advantages. They enable teachers to focus activities on specific language arts goals—to make sure that certain reading, writing, listening, and speaking experiences are included (for example, writing a clear, persuasive letter or listening for the main point in a talk). In addition, they have the potential of heightening students' ongoing involvement with the community, particularly if they encourage students to explore their own perceptions and preconceptions while they learn. Finally, by integrating the community and classroom more purposefully, teachers can establish in more permanent ways the educational value and richness of the community. The community thus becomes a legitimate, regular resource, as familiar as the old literature anthology or basal reader, and definitely more exciting.

An effective way to undertake the study of any segment of the community or to bring the classroom and community together more systematically is through activities that I have arranged into five phases. These phases, described below, approximate the stages of a problem-solving approach to teaching. In the first phase are activities designed to elicit what young people already know, think, feel about the part of the community they will study. In the next, activities help students explore the sources of attitudes and whether their attitudes are based on myths or realities. Activities in the third phase help students learn facts about their subject in a variety of ways, from field research to watching films in class. Often, what students learn results in the identification of more specific problems, topics, issues, and questions that they want to explore more deeply. The fourth phase addresses more lengthy projects. Finally, in the fifth phase, I suggest a number of ways students can record and share what they have learned. Activities in all five phases are oriented to language arts — reading, writing, listening, speaking, and viewing — but it will be up to the teacher to assign specific goals to activities. The activities are not hierarchical or sequenced so that a teacher may do any of them in any order.

Phase One: Discovering Attitudes

The study of any subject in the community can begin with an exploration of the students' existing expectations, stereotypes, prejudices, fears about or biases toward that subject. Exploring these attitudes is especially important when students are going to investigate something in the community that may hold negative connotations. Many children fear doctors and hospitals because they associate them with pain. Law enforcement officers, too, can evoke fear in young people who are afraid that officers inflict punishment. Some students have learned to distrust people who speak or dress differently or who have physical or mental handicaps. But even when a child's or adolescent's preconceptions are not so fearful or negative, they may be full of misinformation. For example, many communities have homeless residents. These people are not all ignorant, uneducated, lazy, or drug/alcohol addicts, as many believe. Other communities have groups of recent immigrants. They, too, are not all ignorant, uneducated, or even poor. An initial stage of any community exploration might begin with activities that explore questions such as: "What do I feel about _____ ?" "What do I think _____ is?" "What is the purpose of _____ ?" "What do I already know about _____ ?" "What do I think _____ are like?" Activities can encourage young people to be honest, to admit and describe prejudices (negative as well as positive), to be comfortable with the fact that they may not know all they should. They should enable students to see that their views are not unique but are shared by others, and perhaps are reflections of larger social attitudes. The activities I describe in Chapter 2, including writing to prompts and pictures, filling in blanks in stories and cartoons, and assorted creative dramatics activities, are designed to accomplish these goals.

Phase Two: Where Do Attitudes Come From?

Where do our ideas and feelings about things in our communities come from? Do others share our attitudes? Are they realistic, or are they based on negative or positive stereotypes? Once students discover the nature and extent of their attitudes, beliefs, and opinions about a subject, they are ready to examine the cultural attitudes, myths, and stereotypes that influence their thoughts. This is the ideal time to look at the ways a subject is presented in our language, in folk tales, myths, and children's and other literature, by the press, television, and advertising. Why, for example, might we think of doctors as smart and athletes as stupid? Why do cemeteries seem scary, or schools dreary? What cultural attitudes about teachers, banks and bankers, law enforcement officers, people in wheelchairs, or auto workers are reinforced in our culture's literature or within our community? The activities described in Chapter 3 are designed to help young people explore the sources of their attitudes and the attitudes of their society. They ask students to take a close look at language and the way language influences thought. They engage students in close examinations of literature for children and young adults, film, television, and advertising—media that have the potential to shape attitudes as we grow up.

Phase Three: Getting Acquainted

Once students know what they feel about an aspect of the community and the attitudes that are prevalent in their culture and locally, they are ready to learn facts that will help them differentiate between realities and myths or misconceptions. The second-grade class that discovers that teachers are often portrayed as female, either mean, ugly, and old, or sweet, young, and beautiful, are ready to find out just how diverse in personality, looks, and interests teachers are. The tenth-grade class that learns that many young people think of a local factory as a sweatshop where people work like mindless robots on an assembly line are eager to visit the factory and talk to workers to find out what modern assembly lines are really like. Activities in this phase call for students to do research both in and out of the classroom. They are designed to help students get acquainted with their topic in the classroom by examining *realistic* portrayals in literature and film, by reading informative books, by listening to speakers, and by using language in new ways to reshape their thinking. In addition, activities outside class can help students learn about their subject firsthand.

Phase Four: Projects to Challenge Assumptions

When they investigate both the facts and myths about a subject, students may find situations that are less than ideal or uncover problems that are not yet solved. For example, students studying a community's law enforcement agencies might discover that they, as well as others, believe that traffic police pick on drivers simply to meet quotas. The facts reveal that quotas are nonexistent, that the belief is a myth held primarily by young drivers. How, then, can young people in the community become more aware of the legitimate reasons that officers give tickets? What can the class do to correct the misconceptions? For another example: students engaged in a study of a town's parks find that some people don't want parks in their neighborhoods because they believe that they attract large groups of rowdy teenagers, gangs, drug dealers, and stray dogs. A group of students decides to do additional research to find out if these concerns are valid, and if so, to identify measures the park commission and city council could take to promote more productive use of the parks, and if not, formulate strategies to help the city change the reputation of parks generally. A third example: students studying a local newspaper discover that unbiased reporting is more difficult than they thought. They decide to create a set of guidelines for good reporting and try them out by taking over the school newspaper for one edition, and to initiate a letter-writing campaign to promote objectivity in journalism.

Activities in this phase call for explorations into more specific aspects of a subject—explorations that require more depth, time, and often more commitment. In this phase, students may undertake group or individual projects that will yield additional knowledge or deeper understanding. They may decide to explore related fields or to learn more about one they are studying. They use what they have already learned to ask new questions and to discover answers.

Phase Five: Publishing

When students investigate community topics more deeply, they may find the occasion to share what they have learned with others. In the examples above, students might write an information pamphlet about traffic tickets that could be distributed to local teens, or a formal research report to the city council summarizing city park use over a two-week period. This kind of sharing I call *publishing*. I use the term broadly to include any more formal (polished) presentation of information. Publishing is sharing, but to an audience wider than the teacher and, perhaps, the classroom. While all the activities in the other phases involve informal sharing, publishing requires more preparation. A descriptive paragraph about a community building may be shared; a book of stories about the building is published. The possible forms of publication are many: a class anthology of stories and poems written by students and/or community members; a display of individually written biographies (of a building, of a person, of a business, of a street); a student-created display of students' art and writing; the production of a play; a puppet show; a display of photo-essays; the showing of a student-produced videotape. Publishing may be the culminating activity of a lengthy community study or it may occur following one project. The purpose of publishing is, of course, to preserve and extend knowledge. It is also a wonderful opportunity to deepen school-community understanding and commitment and to interest other young people in new investigations. Publishing need not be elaborate or expensive. But it should be informative, interesting, and fun to do.

Goals for Language Arts

But don't all these activities belong in the social studies? Will students really improve their language arts abilities by studying, say, the local steel mill? *Yes.* Many goals and objectives for language arts instruction can be accomplished when kids and the community get together. Here is a partial list of abilities that can be strengthened or learned by many of the projects and activities described in this book:

Speaking and listening
- listening for the main and related points

- conversation: how to listen, share, encourage others to contribute ideas, etc.
- ability to analyze an audience
- questioning: how to ask for information in any number of ways — on the telephone, with questionnaires, in letters
- interviewing: how to ask questions, listen for and transcribe answers; how to respond and give feedback; how to ask for clarification; how to probe; how to organize and summarize information for presentation
- using voice, face, and gesture to communicate meaning in a public speech
- techniques of pacing a story or speech for dramatic effect
- adding characterization to an oral reading through intonation and expression
- responding effectively to questions from an audience
- participating productively in a group discussion

Language and writing
- vocabulary: word meaning, usage, changes in usage, slang and jargon, etymology
- enhancing writing with concrete, accurate details
- organizing details in meaningful sequences: chronological, in order of significance, etc.
- sorting important information from the less important: arranging material in a way that has the greatest effect on a reader
- selecting and using language appropriate to an audience and purpose
- writing paraphrases and summaries
- analyzing the use and effects of language in advertising
- writing dialogue that tells a story and conveys character
- describing people and places so readers can visualize them
- using metaphor and sensory detail to convey meaning in writing
- supporting ideas with facts, statistics, citations of authority
- constructing logical arguments
- writing in one's own language
- narrating a story in sequence
- using devices of language — rhythm, rhyme, alliteration, etc. — to create effects in a poem

Reading and literature

- reading for the main point
- determining meaning from context clues
- deepening engagement with literature by relating events and people in literature to events and people in real life
- comprehending and retelling a story or essay
- identifying the dramatic elements in a story
- responding to a story in several ways
- making inferences
- becoming familiar with specific genres and authors
- identifying the dramatic elements in a story from real life or literature
- visualizing setting
- discerning author's purpose in essays
- making predictions based on foreshadowing, description, etc.
- identifying more than one level of meaning
- hearing rhythm and rhyme in poetry
- becoming familiar with characteristics of written forms, including magazines and newspapers

The list is as endless as any list of language arts objectives. Clearly, students can accomplish many goals in their community study. But the teacher must ensure that the learning of specific objectives does occur. Simply "doing something" does not guarantee that students will accomplish these objectives. If I interview a local artisan, I do not necessarily learn how to conduct better interviews. If I am assigned to write a persuasive speech, I may not know how to make my speech powerful. If teachers are conscious of an activity's potential for building language arts abilities, they will help make community study as productive as possible.

The Elders: Toward a Multi-Generational Community

One segment of the community that young people spend proportionately little time with is old people. In schools, where children live for the better part of five days a week, the elderly are a relative rarity. For several reasons, many children in the United States today have few, if any, intimate acquaintances with people over sixty-five except, perhaps, their grandparents, who probably do not reside with them. Older people today are more financially independent, healthier, and therefore more mobile than they were a hundred years ago. More older people live away from their children, often in retirement communities where children are allowed only as visitors. More retirees today own and use recreational vehicles, and/or spend much of their time either by themselves or with other seniors on special tours, cruises, vacations. Young people, too, tend to occupy their spare time with others of their age. Summer camps, both day and boarding, proliferate for children of all ages: computer camps, weight-loss camps, tennis camps—all provide enrichment of one kind or another and keep children together with other children for longer periods of time. Young people who do not attend camps spend a good part of the summer with each other in pools, playgrounds, parks, malls, arcades, empty lots, soccer fields, and basketball courts. Middle-class American society has become increasingly age-segregated. Children's and adolescents' views of older people are more likely to be formed not from firsthand knowledge but from brief encounters in airports, supermarkets, and church, and from images in the books they read, stories they hear, and portrayals they see on television.

At the same time, the number of people over sixty-five in the United States is increasing. Because of advances in medical technology and new knowledge about nutrition, today's children will probably be old for a longer time than will their grandparents. Young people need to know about being old and to develop realistic and positive attitudes about what may be one-third of their lives. In order to acquire these attitudes, young people need to get to know old people—either directly or through literature. They need to abandon the prejudices and stereotypes about being old and replace them with knowledge of and sensitivity to the psychological and physical realities of aging. If they are to have productive lives in their later years, children must feel comfortable with their own aging and with the old ages of others.

Every American community contains old people as well as young ones. They are one of a community's resources, though perhaps to many young people, an invisible one. For this reason, and because of the advantages to both young and old alike, I have chosen the elders as a focus for illustrating the many ways teachers can bring the community and classroom together through language arts.

Notes

1. *Instructor and Teacher* (Winter 1985), p. 5.

2. ———, pp. 30–31, 40–41.

3. ———, p. 5.

4. Tchudi, Stephen, and Diana Mitchell. *Explorations in the Teaching of Secondary English* (New York: Dodd, Mead, 1988), p. 47.

5. ———, p. 52.

6. Applebee, Arthur N. *Writing in the Secondary School: English and the Content Areas.* Research Report #21 (Urbana, IL: NCTE, 1981).

7. Dewey, John. *The School and Society.* (Chicago: University of Chicago Press, 1899).

8. *An Experience Curriculum in English: A Report of the Curriculum Commission of the NCTE.* W. Wilbur Hatfield, Chair. (Urbana, IL: NCTE, 1935).

9. Broening, Angela. *Conducting Experiences in English.* (New York: Appleton-Century-Crofts, 1939).

10. Weeks, Ruth Mary. *A Correlated Curriculum.* (New York: Appleton-Century-Crofts, 1940).

11. Smith, Dora V. *The English Language Arts.* (New York: Appleton-Century-Crofts, 1956)

12. Dixon, John. *Growth Through English.* (Urbana, IL: NCTE, 1967).

13. Moffett, James. *A Student-Centered Language Arts Curriculum, Grades K-13.* (Boston: Houghton Mifflin, 1968).

14. Wigginton, Eliot. *Hands On: A Journal for Teachers.* (Rabun Gap, GA: The Foxfire Fund, November, 1988).

Chapter Two

Discovering Attitudes

What do we feel about being old? How do we approach the prospect of our own aging? When we think about old people, what images do we see? Here are two views of old age:

I am stiff. I am in a hospital. I eat this black stuff. I have sloppy handwriting. I am very, very, very old. I am very, very, very, very, very smart.

— Stephanie Gilbert, grade 2

Untitled

I take catnaps from ten to one
And nap again in the setting sun.
I've lost my muscle, getting fat
With bones that creaked as I stood or sat.
Yet I like to argue — anything,
Like my drink, to talk or sing.
My hair's gone white, my eyes grown dim
But I'm still a good man for the shape I'm in.

— Ralph M. Zeigler, age 75

Compare the vitality in Zeigler's and Gilbert's writing to the four dreary images of old age described by these college students who were asked to write in response to "The old man ..." and "The old woman ..." before reading Bontemps's "A Summer Tragedy":

The old man walked behind the cemetery and it startled the two boys pushing the cart of hay. ... His clothes were old and tattered and he looked scared yet mysterious. Age had wrinkled his skin and his eyes were almost swallowed up into his head.

The lips were chapped and he had about three days of growth on his chin. ... A creature lost in time, wishing the days would end.

The old man sat in the chair looking out at the setting sun. It had been another day that passes uneventfully — that seemed to be the way most of his days past (sic) now. It didn't use (sic) to be like this — in fact he used to be so very active, involved in everything.

The old woman sat in a chair staring blankly at the T.V. She used to travel and ski, climb mountains.

The old woman stood at the ancient porcelain stove with a frayed and stained wooden spoon in her hand. ...

Although we may not envision old age itself in a positive light, many of us hope to or do in fact lead active, productive lives in our later years. The same students whose descriptions of old men and women were so bleak wrote about their own prospective old ages as full of energy and life:

I will still be playing golf.

I am going to still grow a garden. ... I will be one of those hip grandmas that wears the latest fashions and drives a sporty car.

I would dearly love to be irresponsible and run off with my grandchildren to the carnival leaving my own children to shake their head.

Most of all I see myself having some fun. I want to make sure life is worth living.

And here is a similar view from an eighth-grader:

When I'm 80, I don't want people to label me as an "old" person, a person that gets a reputation for being a great knitter. How boring.

I guess some old, tired people have no choice. So, hopefully, by the time I'm that old I'll still be doing the things I like, like running and skiing. I won't even own a rocking chair.

And with all the modern skin care creams that will be available by then, I won't have to worry about wrinkles. And my hair won't be grey either. I can just get it color treated.

After my big career as a news person, I'll have tons of money to throw around on trips around the world, and a boat to cruise around in.

But sometimes, I will just relax, read something, maybe this, and laugh.

—Beth Pollard

Not many children see life in old age as worth living. For Stephanie, old age has its drawbacks, but it has a positive side, too — intelligence. Obviously, the older one gets, the smarter one gets. For Beth, old age may bring wealth, leisure, pride, and a continuing sense of humor. But their optimism is not shared by all young people. Most children's and adolescents' attitudes about old age come from their limited experience (usually with their grandparents), and even more, from the attitudes expressed in language, literature, and the media. Their attitudes are also determined by their relative maturity. The research that has been done on children's attitudes about old age shows that many fear being old, although apparently what children know and feel varies according to their age, becoming more accurate and less stereotypical as they mature. Using a test designed to measure children's attitudes toward the elderly (CATE), Richard Jantz, Carol Seefeldt, and other researchers at the University of Maryland's Department of Early Childhood/ Elementary Education found that the children they interviewed did not want to be old. Wrinkles, gray hair, posture, gait, and the other physical features of old age were perceived as unattractive.[1] Children age six through eleven described old people and their interactions with them negatively. Other researchers have found that children tend to view elders as inactive, bored, unhappy, sick, out of touch with the times, and with no specific function other than to love their grandchildren. All the researchers note that children's attitudes are filled with stereotypes and reflect ignorance of the realities of aging. Old age is the time when one dies; children who fear dying (and most do) also fear being old.

Educators and psychologists agree that only by understanding the facts of aging can young people overcome their fear or revulsion. And before young people can explore the realities of old age and come to know older people more intimately, they must first find out what their thoughts and feelings are. They must confront their attitudes, their fears, and the extent of their knowledge about aging, however limited or false.

Methods of Tapping Children's Attitudes

Writing, talking, drawing, and even acting are media for exploring children's ideas about old people and being old. Specific activities may produce extended compositions, short-answer responses, or skits or plays. A teacher will want to choose activities that fit the students' ages, energy levels, and concentration abilities. All the activities described here can be adjusted for different age groups; they can be made more concrete or abstract, more or less structured. They are based on several assumptions—that our attitudes are often not conscious, that children and adolescents often cannot easily articulate what their attitudes are, and that sometimes the best way to find out one's attitudes is to sneak up on them.

Writing to Prompts

For older students who are able to compose easily in writing, writing in response to a series of prompts is an effective way to uncover the images and feelings associated with old age. Prompts are simply topics given verbally or in writing as opening lines: "The old man ...," "The old woman ...," "When I am 75. ..." The students continue the story any way they choose. When I use these I give only one prompt at a time and allow about eight minutes for writing after each. (The time will vary with the age and writing abilities of the students, of course.) I encourage the students to write whatever is on their minds and to write quickly in order to capture their immediate thoughts. I tell the students their writing will not be graded and that they should not worry about spelling or mechanical correctness. I want them to feel as free as possible to say what they want and not what they think I want to hear or what they think will earn a good grade. Children in lower grades who find the physical act of writing more time-consuming can also do this exercise, but they will need more time to compose, and like the older students, should do this writing as "sloppy copy," to be polished later. Children in kindergarten or the first grade who do not write much may dictate their responses to the teacher or aide.

Drawing to Prompts

Drawing is another way to discover one's feelings about a subject. And one does not need to be artistically gifted to do it. My son's second-grade class wrote to the prompt "If I were one hundred years old," and each child illustrated his or her response. (I have included several in this book.) The pictures say a great deal about the children's feelings—in some cases, more than the writing. Stephanie's picture, for example, is a delightfully imaginative rendering of the shaky, wrinkled aspects of old age. It highlights the physical infirmity she sees as one of old age's dominant characteristics.

Students of any age can draw their responses. Older students sometimes balk at the task, complaining that it is babyish. I find that with them, an activity I call free-drawing works better because it forces everyone to be sloppy, lessening self-consciousness. In free-drawing, students draw as fast as they can without stopping except to change implements. (I provide several crayons or markers for each person, or a box for a group.) Like free-writing, where the writer cannot lift the pen from the page and must keep writing regardless of what he or she is saying, free-drawing requires that the student keep the picture going. The rule is, "Don't stop to think about what you are composing." After ten minutes or so I call time. Then I ask students to write about their pictures: describe a scene or person in the picture; tell a story that is going on in part of the picture; explain the picture; become a part of the picture and write about the picture from your point of view; explain a conflict you see in the picture. The specific writing topic should be the student's choice.

Sharing is an important follow-up to these and all the other activities described in this chapter. Students should have the opportunity to share as a class or in groups their writing (and/or their pictures *if they choose*; the drawing is, after all, "free"), and to look for similarities and differences in their responses. Questions such as "What do the stories about the old woman have in common?" can lead to the conclusion that many of the images are negative, scary, passive, sad (whatever, depending largely on the maturity of the students). These discoveries will in turn lead students to a greater awareness of their own feelings, and that their feelings are not unique. Students in junior and senior high school, and even those in upper elementary grades, have no trouble finding similarities and differences among their responses. They will be able to point out that the stories and pictures show old people as bent over, wrinkled, mean, by themselves, sitting down, and so on. The stereotypes (which I describe in more depth in the next chapter) are so dominant that responses can be grouped in categories: the mean old man, the lonely old woman, the witch, etc. To help younger people identify the common images associated with aging, I recommend more concrete kinds of sharing activities. For example, ask children to make a list of at least five words that might be used in a book or story to describe an old woman or old man. Or, arrange the children's stories into groups with similar features and give each set to a group of students with the questions "What do the stories in your set have in common? What characteristics do these old people share? Make a list of the features that stand out." Another way to share is to have students in groups make composites from the individual responses of the people in the group. What a composite contains will depend on the nature of the individual stories and how different or similar they are. It may consist of a story about the meeting of the several old people described by the group members, or a description of one old person who exhibits the combined characteristics of each description. A composite might even be a collage made from each group member's drawings. Creating a composite allows students to share more actively, to pay careful attention to the features of each member's response, and to search for commonalities.

Writing to Pictures

Pictures—photographs or paintings—are another effective tool for helping students identify their attitudes. For younger children who find writing difficult, pictures are an effective prompt for storytelling, talk, or discussion. For older children and teens, pictures can stimulate a variety of writing. In one part of the CATE, Jantz et. al. showed children a picture with an old man in it and asked them what they would feel like if they were as old as the man.[2] Another approach is to have students make up and tell or write stories or provide information about old people in pictures. Children can do this individually, as a class, or in smaller groups. Grace Warren, a teacher at U.S. Grant High School in Van Nuys (California), uses a prewriting activity in which groups are given a picture of an old person and asked to brainstorm ideas about the person before writing a descriptive paragraph.[3] Concrete questions can help children get their stories or ideas flowing:

- Pretend that you know this person. Is the person a friend or enemy? Where did you meet the person, and what happened to make you become friends or enemies?
- Make up an imaginary fact sheet for the person: address, occupation, family, and so on.
- Write a letter from this person to a friend or to the person from a friend.
- Write an obituary for the person.
- Write an entry from the person's diary.
- Explain what kind of babysitter the person would be.
- Describe where the person lives and what he or she does during a typical day.
- Imagine that this person is you at an older age. What would you like or not like about being this person?

Magazines, newspapers, and photo albums are good sources of pictures. Students can even contribute pictures of their own elder family members for these activities. A danger in using pictures to stimulate discussion of attitudes, however, is that the pictures themselves can encourage stereotyping. If the person in the picture looks sad, lonely, is positioned away from other people, is in a wheelchair, is in a room full of old-fashioned things, is engaged in a stereotypically old person's activity (knitting, sitting on a porch swing), the picture will elicit very predictable responses, and may take over students' real feelings. Because one goal in teaching about old age is to discourage stereotypes, teachers must choose pictures carefully. Pictures also should feature the person in an inconspicuous context. If a picture is striking in some other way — for example, if the person in the picture stands in front of a famous landmark or is visibly engaged in an activity — it may evoke a response to something other than the person. Portraits work best.

The advantage of pictures is that they stimulate the imagination. Young people who have difficulty picturing an old man or old woman and find themselves with not much to write or talk about can be inspired by a photograph or drawing of an old person. Pictures can trigger memories, help children recall experiences with old people — grandparents, strangers, characters in books or films. When the time comes for sharing the responses, students, particularly younger children, may want to talk about these experiences and should be allowed to do so (within reasonable time limits).

Shortcuts: Lists, Free-Association, Scales, Fill-Ins, and Surveys

Activities that assess people's attitudes more quickly and easily than those described above include making lists, doing free-association, and filling out questionnaires on short-answer or checklist forms.

Lists. Making lists is an effective warm-up for other writing activities. Whether done more quickly, as in brainstorming, or more thoughtfully, list-making helps students get their ideas on paper prior to writing or discussing. The advantage of lists is that they are concrete. When students have trouble answering "What do you think about being old?" the problem may be that the question is too vague, too abstract, or too irrelevant. Any of these lists may draw out students' ideas:

- When you think about being old, what are four things you think about?
- Make a list of the worst things about being old. Next to your list, write down all the good things about it.
- What do you think of as the dominant physical traits of old age? Make a list.
- Make a list of five qualities you think you will have when you are 80.

- Your generation may live a long time. Make a list of reasons why living until you are 100 would be a good or a bad thing.

One activity, designed by Francis E. Pratt for high school social studies classes, encourages students to explore their attitudes toward aging in three steps, beginning with a list. First, students write down ten words they might use to describe people over sixty-five. Next, they put a plus, minus, or zero next to each adjective if it is positive, negative, or neutral. Last, students reflect on their lists and write a paragraph on what the list reveals about their attitudes.[4] This activity can be used effectively for junior high students and children in upper elementary grades. Children in lower grades also can be asked to list as many words as they can think of that describe old people, but the teacher might wish to use pictures to help the children get ideas. Instead of asking children to note positive, negative, or neutral terms, teachers can ask children to draw smiles, frowns, or straight-line mouths next to words that are nice, ugly, or neither, or to arrange the words in two columns— words they would like to be called when they are old, and words they would not like to be called. The children will have no trouble seeing that the negative words outnumber the positive or drawing the conclusion that as a group, they don't like old age. (This activity is also excellent for introducing the concept that language and thought are interconnected, a concept discussed in Chapter 3.)

Free-Association. List-making, if it is done quickly, is a form of free-association—writing (or saying, for younger students) whatever words, phrases, or images come to mind immediately in response to words or pictures. Free-associating is like writing to prompts, but the words or pictures are more specific than a general prompt and the responses are usually brief, sometimes disconnected phrases. I have had considerable success in my classes with free-association activities because they are concrete, fast-moving, and highly engaging. They require some verbal quickness and imagination, but little skill in writing. Everyone can become involved quickly, no answers are right or wrong. Discussions or writing that follow free-associations, therefore, are usually lively; everyone has something to contribute. I have used both pictures and words (or phrases) to elicit students' attitudes. In picture association, the teacher shows students a series of pictures of old people. As each picture is shown (for about twenty seconds), students write down the first thing or things that come to their minds. Again, the pictures must be carefully selected. They should be equally realistic (don't put one painting in a group of photographs) and contain an equal number of men and women and people of different racial and ethnic backgrounds.

(However, factors such as economic status, race, or ethnicity should not overshadow age. If the set of pictures is balanced — that is, includes several elders from various groups, other factors will subside in importance.) In a variation on this activity, the teacher places the pictures around the room and students circulate and look at them, then return to their seats and write as quickly as possible as many words or phrases that the pictures call to mind. The key to free-association is to work fast to capture first impressions. First impressions often tell more about our prejudices and feelings than do our carefully thought-out responses.

In word association the teacher says a word or phrase aloud, and the students write down their responses. Some of the words or phrases that denote the realities of aging, such as *gray hair, bald, cane, hearing aid, wrinkles, geriatric, social security, pension, retirement, cataracts, dentures, stroke, nursing home*, are neutral, yet they will evoke positive or negative attitudes. Words that have negative or positive connotations are less effective for this exercise. A word like *senile*, for example, is already negative and will elicit predictably negative associations. A word like *retirement* is not.

Word association is also an excellent way to find out what students do and don't know about the facts of aging. Like lists and longer written or verbal responses, free-association should be followed by sharing, either in small groups or as a class. The sharing will likely produce a list of adjectives — many derogatory — that students can arrange along a continuum from negative to positive. For example, the phrase *gray hair* may yield *old, stringy, ratty, soft, thin, dyed, blue*; the word *retirement* may elicit *old, grandpa, bored, fishing, gold watch, sad*. The word *dentures* may produce *toothpaste, bad breath, loose, gums, geezer*. The values of the words are clear when they are placed on a continuum:

− Negative	0 Neutral	+ Positive
geezer	*grandpa*	*soft*
stringy	*blue*	*fishing*
bad breath	*old*	
sad	*thin*	
ratty		
loose		
bored		

This activity is a variation of Pratt's adjective list, but it has the advantage of showing visually the predominance of negative associations.

Scales. A semantic differential is a list of pairs of words with opposite meanings, with numbers or marks in between to indicate degree of strength in one direction or the other. Students place a mark on the number that best indicates their feelings about a particular subject. The scale "My Views," developed by Gary R. Smith at the University of Denver and cited in Pratt, assesses attitudes about old people.[5] (See Figure 2–1.) It can be used effectively with students in all grades. While Smith uses "When I think of old people I think of people who are ..." as the prompt for the scale, teachers can easily use others, such as "When I think of an old man," "When I think about my grandmother," "When I think about my own old age," to draw out a variety of attitudes. This activity is a more concrete version of the prompted writing and a variation on free-association and list-making described earlier. What makes it different and useful is that it presents students with concepts they may not consciously associate with aging but which bear on their attitudes. For example, I might not write the word *honest* when asked to list terms that describe old people, yet I do tend to think of elders as honest. Thus, the scale helps children define their attitudes more fully.

Fill-Ins. Another easy way to assess attitudes is with a CLOZE-type procedure, in which students fill in blanks in a story with adjectives, nouns, verbs, and adverbs. For example:

> The old man walked (adverb) down the (adjective) street, holding the precious (noun) in his (adjective) hands. He was feeling (adverb) , because his (noun) had recently (verb) . He hoped that soon his (noun) would (verb) , because he was running out of (adjective)   (noun) .

Or omit the names of the parts of speech to give writers even greater freedom:

> The old woman _____ in her _____ yard. Her face looked _____ and _____. In two days, her _____ would _____. She felt _____. It was only yesterday that she found the _____ in her _____ and _____. Would she ever _____?

This activity has several variations. For people who cannot think of what words to insert, the teacher can provide a list of words and/or phrases (the week's spelling words?). The list should include a range of words to avoid biasing the responses (for example, don't overload the list with negative words like *lonely, sad, dejected*). Also, the teacher may vary the general structure of the stories, the topic, characters, and the position of the blanks. For example, the

Figure 2-1
My Views

(Please circle the number on the word scale that best expresses your feelings.) "When I think of old people, I think of people who are ..."

	1	2	3	4	5	6	7	
KIND	1	2	3	4	5	6	7	CRUEL
HEALTHY	1	2	3	4	5	6	7	UNHEALTHY
DISHONEST	1	2	3	4	5	6	7	HONEST
HAPPY	1	2	3	4	5	6	7	SAD
QUIET	1	2	3	4	5	6	7	LOUD
INACTIVE	1	2	3	4	5	6	7	ACTIVE
SEXY	1	2	3	4	5	6	7	NOT SEXY
POOR	1	2	3	4	5	6	7	RICH
STRONG	1	2	3	4	5	6	7	WEAK
FAST	1	2	3	4	5	6	7	SLOW
WISE	1	2	3	4	5	6	7	NOT WISE
SIMPLE	1	2	3	4	5	6	7	COMPLICATED
USELESS	1	2	3	4	5	6	7	USEFUL
TOLERANT	1	2	3	4	5	6	7	INTOLERANT
CHANGEABLE	1	2	3	4	5	6	7	RIGID
PUBLIC	1	2	3	4	5	6	7	PRIVATE
WORDS	1	2	3	4	5	6	7	DEEDS
FORWARD-LOOKING	1	2	3	4	5	6	7	BACKWARD-LOOKING

blanks can be all one part of speech, such as adjectives. A caution here: it is too easy to make up a story that will lead to stereotypical responses. The activity will be more meaningful if a variety of responses is truly possible.

Students generally will, without guidance, fill in the blanks predictably. The old woman's face will be *sad* and *tired*, the old man's hands *calloused*. Such responses can yield a lively discussion of our stereotypes of old people and old age. However, unpredictable responses that show old age in original, more favorable ways should be welcomed and even encouraged as a follow-up activity. ("The old man walked *quickly* down the *busy* street, holding the precious *lottery ticket* in his *eager* hands. He was feeling *overjoyed* because his *number* had recently *won*. He hoped that soon his *prize* would come because he was running out of *investment capital*." Or, "The old woman *stomped* up and down in her *back*yard. Her face looked *purple* and *furious*. In two days her *landlord* would *arrive*. She felt *overwhelmingly frustrated*. It was only yesterday that she found the *cockroaches* in her *cupboards* and *drawers*. Would she ever *get rid of the pests*?" Chapter 4 addresses in more depth other ways to help young people use language creatively to change their views of old age.

Another kind of fill-in activity utilizes cartoons. Cut out (or draw) a cartoon of a younger person and an old person, or a cartoon of several older people. Cartoons may be manufactured by pasting together on a page figures cut from several cartoons or sketches. Draw a balloon over each, and have children fill in the balloons. Be sure to avoid well-known cartoon characters with defined person- alities as well as ones that reflect stereotypes. Teachers can tailor

the cartoons to evoke various responses by placing the figures in different settings, making the figures male or female, and positioning them differently. What would two old women say to each other? What would an old woman say to an old man? What would two children say to an elder couple? Would the words be different if the children were close to the elders or far apart? A variation is to leave the mouth off and have the child draw in a mouth, and even draw in a setting. This exercise should be followed by writing and/or sharing aloud their responses to questions such as "Are the people happy or sad? Why?" "Where are these people? How did they get there?" "What is going to happen to them?" While some stories that emerge will be quite original, others will be characteristically negative or predictable. Old people will talk to each other about their poor health, being lonely, about their grandchildren, or other concerns, and to young people about cookies, puppies, or "behaving." Young people will call old people "gramps" or "granny," and may say something apologetic ("I'm sorry I broke your rocker."), or make requests for time or attention ("Will you take me to the zoo?"). Cartoons, and the responses they evoke, can be the beginning of interesting class-initiated research on the ways our culture expects young and old people talk to each other, on typical patterns of interaction, and on ways of widening our language experiences across generations.

True-False. How much do young people know about aging and its accompanying physical processes? According to the research, very little. Most young people's attitudes include a number of myths and false notions about what happens when we grow old. A good way to find out what children do and don't know, besides free-association, is a simple true-false test. Items might include ones such as these:

- All men lose their hair when they get old.
- Old people can't remember when they were young.
- Old people can't learn new things.
- Men live longer than women.
- Creativity declines with old age.
- People over 60 lose their sexual interest and potency.
- All old people become senile sooner or later.
- Old people sleep a lot.
- An old person who continually reminisces is getting senile.

Of course, all the above are false. Other facts about aging that contradict the myths are available from the National Council on

Aging, local agencies, and doctors, nurses, and gerontologists in any community. (The address for the National Council on Aging and other similar resources are contained in the bibliography.)

A true-false test is also a way to assess people's beliefs about the psychological and emotional aspects of being old. Here are some sample statements:

- Nursing homes speed up peoples' deaths.
- All old people are afraid of dying.
- Most old people are lonely.
- When I am old I won't have any friends.
- When I'm old, men/women won't find me attractive.
- Old people don't kiss.
- Old people wish they were young.
- Old people love children.
- Old people love animals.
- People get more religious as they age.
- Young people are smarter than old people.

Individual students may differ in their feelings about any one statement, particularly if their experiences with old people have shown them otherwise. Age, too, will be a factor in students' responses. An eight-year-old might agree with the second item because she, like many children her age, is afraid of death, and also like most eight-year-olds, cannot imagine feeling any different when she is older. A student who has seen his grandparents kiss will not agree with the sixth item. Many of my college students think that they are definitely smarter than old people, although young children, like Stephanie, believe the opposite. And some children know that not all elders love children. This test will bring out those diverse experiences and lead to interesting discussions of the realities of aging and, hopefully, to the conclusion that not all old people are alike.

Creative Dramatics

Sometimes young people, especially children, find it easier to express their feelings indirectly, with dolls, puppets, props, or cartoon characters. Here are a few activities that can help students identify their feelings and attitudes through dramatics.

Improvisations. Improvisations work with students of all ages, even adults. Collect props such as hats, lensless glasses, canes, even gray wigs and beards. Have students improvise skits in which they use these props. Or give each student a prop and ask him or her to make up a character that goes with it. The student must create a personality and background for the character—hobbies, habits, residence, family, etc. In another kind of improvisation, students pretend they are themselves when they are old and deliver improvised monologues about their lives. Or, several students can improvise elder characters in a skit based on a defined situation:

- sitting next to each other at a sports event
- in the lounge of a nursing home
- in the waiting room of a doctor's office
- on a bench in a park or shopping mall
- in an elevator
- on a crowded street waiting for the light to change
- in line at the market
- on a very crowded subway
- in an airplane in rough weather
- at the police station waiting to be booked
- watching a rodeo event

Adding a conflict may enhance the improvisation: the people at the sports event are cheering for opposing teams. The people in the nursing home lounge are waiting for dinner and are very hungry. In the doctor's office, only one chair is vacant when the characters enter. The subway train stalls. The street light is stuck and doesn't change. The person at the front of the grocery store line can't locate money. Situations can be adjusted to suit the age and experience of the class. Students who have done improvisations routinely are less shy and generally develop their characters more quickly.

Puppetry. Many times children find talking through a puppet, doll, or stuffed animal easier than expressing their feelings directly. Improvised puppet shows using hand puppets (made simply from small paper bags or large socks), stuffed animals, finger puppets made from paper, or even dolls are a good way to help young children explore their feelings. Any kind of hand puppet or marionette will work—animals, creatures, or people. To make a puppet old, attach cotton for white hair and beards and bend pipe cleaners into glasses. Children can invent their own stories for characters they create. Or, they can use situations such as those above to get an enactment started.

Guided Fantasy and Role Playing. Ask students (any age) to close their eyes and follow along with a fantasy: "Imagine that you are very, very, very, very old. You are sitting in a particular place. Where is this place? How long have you been here? How did you come to be here? You are alone now. What are you thinking about? Are you happy or unhappy? What has made you feel this way?" Go slowly and pause after each question to let people develop images in their minds and answers to the questions. After sufficient pause after the last question, begin again: "You will not be alone for long. Someone (or some people) is coming. Who is it? Why is the person coming? What will happen when the person comes?" Again, pause after each question, and provide a longer silence after the last question. From here, the teacher may proceed in several ways. I find free-writing an excellent next step for older students, and particularly asking them to write twice — once after each set of questions — for about eight minutes. (I also like to follow the free-writing by asking students to take ten minutes to prepare some writing to share.) Another follow-up activity is to ask for volunteers to become the old people they created in their minds, and as those people, to sit in front of the class and answer questions from the class, or improvise a scene. (These are more difficult tasks, and probably more suitable for ages twelve and up.) Or students might simply talk about their characters in small groups or in a class discussion.

Pantomime. The way children act out being old tells a great deal about the way they perceive old age and how much they know about it. An old person crossing a street, fixing something to eat, washing his or her face or brushing teeth, feeding a cat, driving a car, getting dressed, selecting groceries from a shelf are subjects that young people can pantomime and talk about. Pantomimes bring out impressions of a character's posture, agility, intelligence, and general demeanor. Is the person slow, bent over, shaky? Does she look sad? Is he grumpy, angry? The discussion that follows pantomime may focus largely on the physical aspects of old age — how hard it is to button a shirt, the way people clean false teeth, why people walk slowly or can't read labels.

Dramatic activities should always be followed by writing or discussion. Follow-up topics can focus on the portrayals, whether the characters were conceived as happy, sad, friendly, busy, lonely, smart, stupid, pretty, ugly, and so on. Did the dramatic situations have happy endings? What did the actors do with voice, gesture, or posture to make us see the character OLD? It is also interesting to talk about whether the students would like to resemble any of the characters when they are old, and why or why not. After a discussion, drawing or journal writing allows each child a private time to reflect on the dramatic activity and to think about his or her attitudes more fully. It enables students to recall experiences with or feelings about elder individuals they know well and to compare these people to the characters in the dramas. Students who have particularly strong feelings or memorable experiences will appreciate the chance to think about them.

Attitudes in the Community

The activities described above should illustrate to young people that their fears, feelings, prejudices, and ideas about old age are shared by others. Our attitudes are influenced and even shaped by our cultural as well as our personal experiences. The attitudes that exist among our friends, our peers, in our schools, neighborhoods, and nation will contribute to the values and orientations we hold. After examining their own perspectives and prejudices, students will profit from taking a look at the attitudes of people outside the classroom. To do this, students can adapt some of the activities described in this chapter. The "My Views" scale, the fill-in stories, the true-false tests, and cartoons can be copied and distributed to friends, parents, neighbors, or anyone else whose attitudes might be interesting to obtain. Older students can ask younger students to tell stories about pictures of elders and tape record the responses. A class may wish to determine how receptive the community is, generally, to older residents by questioning local business people, city and county officers, and elders themselves. (Do stores provide rest areas for elder shoppers? Ramps for wheelchair access? Does the public transportation system give seniors discounts? Does the local newspaper cover seniors' events?) If students suspect that the attitudes are negative, they may choose to investigate the problem in more depth. In Chapter 5, I describe some projects students might take in this direction.

When students see that their attitudes are not unique but have origins in the larger community, they are already on their way to exploring the sources of their views. The class discussions in many of the activities in this chapter may lead naturally to talk about the culture and the values expressed in the culture's literature and media—its books, television, music, advertising. What children see and hear (and what they don't see and hear) about old age tells them how the society values (or does not value) its elder population. If young people wish to discover the roots of their attitudes, they should begin by examining the influential language and literature that helped shape their thoughts. And this is the subject of the next chapter.

Notes

1. Jantz, Richard, Carol Seefeldt, Alice Galper, and Kathy Serock. *Curriculum Guide: Children's Attitudes Toward the Elderly.* (University of Maryland, Department of Early Childhood/Elementary Education and the Center on Aging, 1976), pp. 6–7.

2. _____, p. 6.

3. Ericson, Bonnie O., and Joanna McKenzie. "Idea Seeds: Grow Old Along with Me: Introducing Youth to Age." *California English* (January/February, 1988), p. 16.

4. Pratt, Francis E. *Teaching About Aging.* (Boulder, CO: ERIC Clearinghouse for Social Studies/Social Science Education, 1977), pp. 29–30.

5. Smith, Gary. *Aging.* (Denver, CO: Center for Teaching International Relations, Graduate School of International Studies), p. 2. Cited in Pratt, p. 31.

Chapter Three

Where Do Attitudes Come From?

> The old woman tried to walk down the aisle as smoothly as possible, clutching on to the backs of peoples' chairs to maintain her balance. Her shoulders have turned inwards and she is heavier than ever before. Her soft white hair is thinning and there are visible bald spots that she tries to cover. What little hair is left is pulled up on the sides with black bobby pins, sharply contrasting in her white hair.
>
> —college junior

Our attitudes about everything in our community are learned. We are not born with a fear of the dentist, with a sense of discomfort in the presence of someone with a physical handicap (perhaps different from one of our own), or with the belief that physical laborers are unintelligent. We acquire these attitudes, often in childhood. They come from what we hear at home, on television, in songs—from our culture's publications—and they may be reinforced or changed by our actual experiences.

When my son was three years old he inherited a book and record set called the *Seven Little Postmen*. The story goes like this: A little boy, Tommy, writes a letter to his grandmother. He mails the letter, which travels to his grandmother, thanks to the work of seven postmen (sic—all are men). The grandmother lives alone in the last house on the street, is lonely, and on the day the letter arrives, she has been wishing Tommy would visit. We see her sitting in her wicker rocking chair, knitting. Her feet are slippered and rest on a footstool. She is overweight, wears a sweater and wire-rimmed glasses. Her hair is white, parted in the middle, and pulled back in a bun. A plant in a wicker stand is on one side of her chair, and a lamp made from a three-legged stool is on the other. On this combination table and lamp is a picture of Tommy. From the ceiling hangs a bird cage. When Tommy's letter arrives, she says (to no one in particular and, according to the record, in a whiny, scratchy voice) "'Good Gracious! I wonder who sent me this fancy letter.'" Tommy's letter contains the good news that he is, in fact, coming to visit soon, and is bringing a kitten "'for your very own.'"[1]

Although the image of the grandmother is warm and loving, it also presents an undesirable picture of what it is to be old and female. Why has old age been portrayed so negatively in much of American society? While most Americans value old people individually, they do not value the general state of old age. Sociologists point out that over the last hundred years, American attitudes toward old age have become increasingly negative. They cite a number of reasons: the fact of being an industrialized society in which *many* people live longer and are therefore less revered; the turn-of-the-century emphasis on becoming a world power and its accompanying value of strength; the decline of the extended family as the primary kinship unit.[2] Our culture's diminished value of old age is reflected in the negative and/or stereotypical images of old people in its literature, cultural myths, and media. Many of the attitudes children have about being old come from the stories they hear, read, and see — the jokes, the fairy tales, the books, the television shows. Values and attitudes are also reflected in our language.

Attitudes in Language

The first and perhaps most subtle source of our attitudes is our language. Not only does our language reveal what we think and feel, but it also shapes, to an extent, our thoughts. Language and culture, like language and thought, are inextricably linked. What a culture values will be reflected in its words — by the number and kinds of words and phrases associated with things that are important. And these words and phrases can determine what impressions and attitudes young children acquire. When I first read my son some of my old storybooks, I was struck by the consistent use of the pronoun "he" to refer to doctors, scientists, and others in traditionally male occupations. Teachers and nurses were uniformly "she." This gender stereotyping is not so prevalent today. Because I don't want him to grow up with inaccurate expectations of work and gender, I now consciously use "he" and "she" interchangeably when I read to him from older books. Similarly, one of the ways we teach our children to respect people of different cultures is by using respectful rather than derogatory terminology. People who use racial slurs in front of their children shouldn't be surprised by the attitudes their children adopt.

A simple starting activity that explores language as a source of attitudes is a more specific version of the activity developed by Pratt described in the last chapter. Instead of having students list as many words or phrases as they can to describe old people, have the students list, first, as many nouns (or "namers" or "terms that stand for") as they can think of that refer to old man, old woman, and/or old person, and group them according to their connotative value.

− Negative	0 Neutral	+ Positive
crone	senior	elder (as a noun)
geezer	old person	ancient (as a noun)
fogey		
old bat		
old witch		
coot		
codger		
old hag		

Next, have students make similar lists of adjectives

− Negative	0 Neutral	+ Positive
wizened	aged	ripe
senile	geriatric	antique
cantankerous	graying	mature
crotchety		kindly
bilious		
cranky		
muddled		
grouchy		
addlepated		
little old (lady, man)		
stubborn		
gnarled		
grizzled		

Each noun and adjective conveys a slightly different image that can be explored: what does a *cantankerous* old person look like? Act like? Describe a *crone*. Can you think of examples of such a person? How is a *crone* different from a *little old lady*? An *elder*? Telling or writing stories about people described by these terms is a good way to discover the nature of the terms' connotations.

Another way to illustrate how language and attitudes are linked is to give students pictures (from magazines) of old people and ask them to match descriptive adjectives or nouns with the person in the picture and write a story about the person using those words. This activity can be done in several ways: (1) Give each student a *different picture* and an envelope containing a phrase or two (for example, *little old lady/man*, or *wizened elder*). Give some students identical words or pairs of words and give others pairs of words in which one word or phrase is the same (*gnarled old bat* and *gnarled senior*). (2) Give each student an envelope containing the *same picture* and a different word or pair of words. With either procedure be sure that the students keep their pictures and words secret. Ask students to write stories about the person in the picture conveying, in their descriptions, the impression given by the words. Their descriptions might include where the person lives, what the person is thinking about, what the person did that day, what the person wishes for, and so on. In sharing stories and pictures, students will discover similarities among the descriptions/stories by people who received the same words and different pictures. For example, a *grizzled geezer* is likely to be described as a grouch who chases children and dogs regardless of how kindly or grumpy the old man appears in the picture. Students who write about the same picture will discover that the person in the picture is attributed different characteristics depending upon the words the writers received. For example, the *gnarled old bat* is likely to be mean and complaining, while the *wizened ancient* (same picture) is a respected great-grandmother. In these explorations, students may also discover that the negative words fall into categories. Some terms suggest mental defects (*senile, addlepated*), others refer to physical deterioration (*wizened, gnarled*), and some imply unpleasant personalities (*crotchety, cranky*). Few of the images make old age attractive.

Another group of activities illustrates that in thinking about old age and people we tend to limit our vocabularies. We rarely use words such as *lithe, witty, energetic, vivacious, resilient, capricious, flirtatious, scintillating, ambitious, frivolous, theatrical, empathetic, audacious, silly, brave, daring, playful, talented, pretty, original*, or *smart* to describe people over seventy, although there is no reason we couldn't. The words are simply unfamiliar in that context; they more often describe young people. To demonstrate to a class the limitations of our descriptive language, put in a bag many slips of paper, each with a different adjective written on it. The bag should include adjectives that commonly describe old people as well as those that don't. Next, collect a group of close-up pictures of people — referably portraits — from magazines. The collection should include men, women, boys, and girls — people of all ages, and be displayed in front of the class or in a place where students can see them all easily. In class, have each student (or each small group of students) draw an adjective from the bag. Next, ask each student to select a picture to go with their adjective. Finally, have the students write at least two sentences (or more, depending on their ages) describing the person in the picture they chose by using the word they drew, making sure that their description centers on the word. Predictably, students will put youthful adjectives with youthful pictures. In the converse of this activity, students draw pictures from a bag and choose one or more adjectives from a long list on the board or handout to accompany the picture.

All of these activities will elicit some words that are descriptive of the features of old age — the texture, look, smell of skin, hair, hands, the posture, the movement. To explore further the predictable ways we describe the features of old age, list a feature on the blackboard and have students fill in the most commonly heard or read words, phrases, or metaphors to describe it: *skin* will be "creased," "transparent," "furrowed," "wrinkled," "leathery," "papery," "saggy," "thin," or "deeply grooved." *Old hands* are typically "gnarled," "knotty," "frail," "veined"; *eyes*, particularly blue ones, are "faded," "watery," or "dim," and sometimes even "sparkly." Old people *walk* by "shuffling" or "tottering," and their *bodies* are "bent," "decrepit," "fragile," or "shaky." (Pictures may be helpful to stimulate thinking.) But we know that not all old people have the same physical attributes or qualities, let alone these. After students have identified the clichés, they can create original ways to describe these features and write realistic, fresh, and more vivid descriptions of an elder's unique physical features. My grandmother's skin, for example, sometimes smelled of old face powder and sometimes like carnation bath soap. She never once smelled musty, like a damp cellar. Her skin was velvety, not papery, particularly on her neck and earlobes. Old hands can be freckled, velvety, knuckley, strong, ropy, or stiff. Bodies can be robust, sedentary, energetic, arched, uncertain. (Other activities in Chapter 4 illustrate new uses of language.)

Like our descriptive adjectives, the terms of address we use for old people tell about our feelings. For example, we have many words to refer to grandparents:

grandma	*grandpa*
grandmother	*grandfather*
granny	*gramps*

gran	*grampie*
grandmama	*granddad*
	granddaddy

Each of these has a slightly different connotation (note that the prefix *grand* is positive). For me, Granddad is more proper, formal, tall, well-dressed, and better educated than Gramps, who is bent over, wears suspenders, rarely shaves, and is fat. For other students, the connotations may be quite different, depending on their experiences. One way to introduce this discussion in a class is to list each term on the board and have students fill out the semantic differential (see Chapter 2) on each term. Or provide a long list of adjectives and have students associate three adjectives with each term.

Our language has a number of expressions to describe the state of being old: "over the hill," "one foot in the grave," "going downhill," "in the twilight years," "in the autumn of life," "the golden years," "past one's prime." Some are euphemistic, others are metaphorical. After collecting as many of these as they can, students might enjoy making up new metaphors or euphemisms. Inventing positive ones might prove an interesting challenge: "far out to sea," "on the top of the mountain," "at the pinnacle," "on the top rungs of the ladder," and others.

The expressions people use to describe old age, the terms of address, and the way people address elders vary from culture to culture. Students can explore the differences among the words used in other languages and their connotations in those cultures. Of particular interest would be a comparison of terms used in cultures that respect and revere old age with English terms. Some cultures within and outside North America—for example, Native American and Asian cultures—value old age more highly. Elders are sources of wisdom and knowledge, and hold much power. In some societies, grandparents have more influential roles in the grandchildren's upbringing, and even in the government of the family and community. Grandparents are often the teachers of the culture's traditions and have special relationships with their grandchildren. Nez Perce poet Phil George wrote of his grandmother in his poem "Season of Grandmothers": "Ancient language—pantomime hands—/Your own people's creation in story and song./Not one word, not one movement, must you miss."[3] Such attitudes are reflected in the terms of address and words commonly used to describe the old people in any culture. Students can enjoy doing research on cross-cultural terms of address. They can interview friends and people of other cultures in the community, perhaps their own families if any members are non-English speaking and/or from a non-Anglo culture. Once students have collected terms of address and their meanings they can place all the positive terms in one group and the negative terms in another to see the differences among and within cultures.

In addition to exploring language cross-culturally, students can examine the English language historically. How have the terms for old people and old age changed over time? As our society's view of old people changes, so do the terms of reference. In Shakespeare's day an old man might have been called a "graybeard." And in contemporary America one rarely hears an old person referred to as "venerable." Slang words change, too. The slang used by our grandparents and great-grandparents may not be ours. I have not heard "old fuddyduddy" in some years. Popular terms of address seem to change over generations. My son calls his grandfather "Grandpa"; his grandpa called his grandfather "Granddad." Terms of address are traditionally familial and regional; but today, terminology may be influenced by television and other popular media. Students can ask old people what words they used to describe their elders when they were young, and prepare a historical dictionary of terms. They might also investigate the etymologies of current words to determine whether their meanings have changed over time, and whether a word was always pejorative or positive.

Attitudes in Literature, Film, Television, and Advertising

A plaque above my stove bears the inscription, "To love a person means to agree to grow old with him." These words can be rearranged to mean something a bit different: "To love a(n) old person means to agree to grow with him." If children form friendly relationships with elderly people, these relationships can continue to develop as the children grow into adults. The perception children have of elderly people will, of course, affect their desire to have relationships with them.

—Camille Tovey, grade 12

Although language shapes and expresses our views and values, it is not the only cultural source of our attitudes and beliefs. What we read and see — particularly what we read and see as young children — contributes to our conceptions of being old and to the nature of our images of elders.

A stereotype is a depiction that reduces a group of people to a set of simple, standardized characteristics. It may be flattering or unflattering. Several researchers have found that much young people's literature and popular media contain stereotypes of aging. (Two books provide particularly good summaries of the research up to 1980: Catherine Townsend Horner's *The Aging Adult in Children's Books & Nonprint Media*[4]; and Richard O. Ulin's *Teaching and Learning About Aging*.[5]) Several studies of children's and young adult's literature conducted prior to 1980 indicate that old people were frequently portrayed as warm, loving, passive grandparents whose main concern is their grandchildren, and who have little to do but entertain them. They were typically shown as sedentary and engaged in hobbies and activities that are traditionally appropriate to their gender; women bake or sew, men fix things. Old people were notable, too, by their absence. The danger of a stereotype is, of course, that it attributes the same qualities to all people. The reality is that each elder is unique. If we want children to acquire realistic and positive attitudes about aging, we need to help them identify portrayals that are stereotypical, particularly ones that are unflattering. By becoming aware of the stereotypes, young people become more receptive to old people and appreciative of what it is really like to be old.

Take a look at elders from a child's point of view. Here is what a child who watches television and is acquainted with magazines and books (particularly older books) is likely to see: grandmother has gray hair, probably pulled back in a bun. She wears a dress from the early 1940s and "sensible" shoes. Grandfather is bald and wears a bow tie or suspenders. Both wear wire-rimmed glasses. Grandmother is most often found in the kitchen (probably baking something sweet for the grandchildren or a high cholesterol delight for Grandpa) or sitting in a rocker in the living room knitting or sewing. She is overweight. Grandfather also sits in the living room, but he reads and smokes a pipe. Sometimes he is outdoors, sitting or walking, and then he wears an old hat. Unlike Grandma, he is thin or fat, never a healthy medium. Grandparents are short. Their houses are furnished with old-fashioned (usually early American) furniture and knickknacks: antimacassars on the arms and backs of overstuffed chairs; tables and shelves full of figurines, vases, and, most prominently, photographs in frames. Cats sleep in cozy chairs and dogs on hearths. Kitchens are as old-fashioned as their living rooms. They contain no modern appliances (Grandma may even cook on a wood-burning stove). Houses are white and have two stories, chairs or swings on their front porches, and lots of flowers in front. The grandparents are lonely when their grandchildren are not around. Visits from the grandchildren are the highlight of their lives.

The stereotype of the kind, loving, jolly grandparents isn't necessarily a negative one, and may serve positive functions for young people. First, it can reinforce the belief that older people are sources of love, comfort, and support. Second, an image of grandparents whose lives are centered on children can help children and teens feel valued. When peers and parents don't seem to care, Grandma and Grandpa will. So the study of stereotypes should be undertaken with some caution, particularly with younger children. If a stereotypical representation in a book serves a positive purpose for a young reader, the book should not automatically be labeled as damaging or bad. On the other hand, the danger of clichéd images is that they do not reflect the diversity in the population of elders. Young people whose grandparents are nothing like the characters in books may find the discrepancy disturbing and put more energy into wishing their grandparents were like the imaginary ones than into discovering the virtues and worth of the grandparents they have.

> This is a prime example of how many TV commercials today portray the elderly as senile lumps on a log who serve two purposes: to inspire laughter through their loss of physical coordination, and to devote their time to "serious stuff," abandoning all thoughts of having some fun in their retirement years. The saddest part of this situation is that this image has become so accepted, viewers don't even notice anymore.
>
> —Bea Wallins, grade 11

Literature, film, television, and advertising contain other images of elders that are less flattering than the ones described above. One is the "old witch," typified by the witch in "Hansel and Gretel." This elder is ugly, blind, bitter, stingy, and eats children. She is the counterpart of the wise, nurturing, generous grandmother. A similar stereotype exists for the kindly grandfather. He is the mean old man exemplified by Beatrix Potter's Mr. McGregor. This man is grouchy, angry, hates children, play, and mischief, and values his own property and plants above the health and happiness of animals or people. He is essentially bitter, lonely, and frightening. Some children's literature and folktales center on the conversion or conquest of these characters—usually by children, who, in the process, become wiser about life's potential sadness and hardships.

A third image prevalent in literature and the media is that of the old person as child. This image can be either positive or negative. A grandmother who rides a motorcycle (*Kevin's Grandma*)[6] or a grandfather who knows Halloween tricks (*Grandpa Witch and the Magic Doobelator*)[7] can help a child feel understood. These elders are playful and able to share activities with young people in a way parents often do not. Mr. Pignati, the old man in Zindel's *The Pigman*, appreciates and enjoys protagonists John and Lorraine's youthful silliness in a way John and Lorraine's parents do not.[8] But portrayals of old age as a time of second childhood can be negative when they dehumanize elders and rob them of power by creating the impression that most old people long to be young again, and that they are incompetent, helpless babies who need others to think and act for them. Arnold Arluke and Jack Levin, in their article "Another Stereotype: Old Age as a Second Childhood," label this stereotype "infantilization" and point out that it "reduces minority group members to the status of children, ranging from infants to adolescents, who lack moral, intellectual, or physical maturity."[9] Infantilization negates the wisdom and experience that accompany aging, and can lead to paternalistic attitudes, disrespect, and discrimination.[10] One manifestation of this stereotype (which appears more frequently on television than in books) is the "dirty old man/ lusty woman" character, the sexual adolescent. Another is the runaway—the old man or woman who decides to abandon responsibility for the freewheeling, adolescent life, often abetted by a young protagonist. Sometimes one or both people must learn some hard lessons about responsibility; other times, the two celebrate a triumphant victory of the human spirit over social protocol.

Activities for Examining Images in Literature

Students of any age can enjoy examining the images of old age in literature for young people—folk and fairy tales, children's story books and picture books, and adolescent novels. (High school students can enjoy and learn just as much from examining children's literature as can fourth-graders.) Explorations may focus on both the text and illustrations, for both contribute to a reader's responses. Obviously, in picture books the illustrations tell the whole story, whereas books with pictures and text impart meaning from both sources. Illustrations generally reinforce the meaning in the text, although sometimes they supply information that the words do not make explicit. Because pictures and text both play a part in shaping readers' impressions, and because very young children often rely more on the pictures than the words to understand a story, I prefer to have students initially review illustrations and text separately.

   Providing students with a set of questions helps guide students in their examinations of texts and pictures. Questions about illustrations should address, first, *the way the elder characters are depicted physically*. How are they dressed? How do they wear their hair? Do they have any notable physical features, such as large noses, bushy eyebrows, pointed chins, warts, others? Describe the person's posture. Is it straight? Stooped? How do the illustrations show the characters' body types? Are the people fat, thin, tall, short? Are they in good, average, or bad physical conditions? Does a character wear or use any accoutrements such as glasses, canes, walkers, hearing devices? Other questions should focus on *the nature of the action and the setting.* Where is the person shown? If indoors, what is the room like? What is on the walls? Kind of furniture? What things are on the tables and/or shelves? Are the elders shown standing or sitting or engaged in some other action? Are there other people with the elders or are they alone? Who are they and what are they doing? Artistic style will, of course, contribute greatly to peoples' responses to illustrations. Questions can also focus on *the effects of color, medium (watercolor, oil, pen-and-ink, pastel), and technique.* Are the pictures stark or lush? Are they highly detailed or "busy"? Are they realistic or more abstract? Are the brush strokes heavy or fine? What kinds of feelings about the elders does the style convey? Finally, questions can address *the general tone or feeling the picture evokes.* Do the pictures make you feel that the old people are happy or sad? Are they friendly or unfriendly? A handy way for students to record their overall responses is with a checklist similar to the semantic differential described in Chapter 2:

Name of character shown _____
Name of book _____
Page of illustration _____

This picture makes me feel that the character(s) is ...

Active	_____	Inactive
Friendly	_____	Unfriendly
Happy	_____	Sad
Busy	_____	Bored
Smart	_____	Ignorant
Fashionable	_____	Unfashionable
Healthy	_____	Unhealthy
Well-liked	_____	Lonely
Attractive	_____	Unattactive
Safe	_____	Scary

Additional lines of inquiry might include these:

- What would you change about a picture (or set of pictures) to make it better?
- Which pictures do you like best and why?
- Write a letter to the illustrator telling him or her what you like or don't like about the pictures.

- Compare the illustrations of several books. In what ways are the old men alike? The old women? Are any different from the rest? Are any of them people you would especially like to know?
- Which pictures seem the most realistic?
- Which person pictured would you most like to be when you get old?

Similar questions are useful guides for examining the text of books, either those with illustrations or those without. Older students can focus on how an elder character is portrayed in direct description and dialogue, on the nature of a character's role in the story, and on how elders are shown in relation to the setting. To examine description, students can study the language a writer uses to describe a character's physical attributes and personality — the metaphors, adjectives, and adverbs, and their connotations. Is the elder character attractive or unattractive? What physical features stand out? What adverb phrases does the writer use to describe the person's actions or voice? By isolating the descriptive terms, students can readily see whether they are positive or negative and whether they create fresh characters or stereotypes. For example, a grandmother in Ella Cara Deloria's *Waterlily*, a book about a Dakota (Sioux) girl growing up in the 1800s, is described by terms such as "patient," "skillful," and "energetic."[11] Patricia MacLachlan describes old great-uncle Wrisby, in *Arthur, for the Very First Time*, as "uncommonly tall, with a small head much like a graying tennis ball .... perched on top of his body precariously, as delicate as the gold-rimmed glasses that rested on his nose."[12] In each book, the descriptions reveal much. The characters are old, yes, but definitely not the conventional stereotypes. Books for younger children generally tend to be less descriptive and use simpler terms like "old man" or "old woman" to give a general impression. The illustrations provide physical details that the texts omit.

Dialogue also gives us impressions of characters. How does an elder talk? In long sentences or short phrases? In dialect? Does the person have particular idiosyncrasies or habits, like calling someone "child," using certain expressions, or repeating? Does the character's way of talking reveal anything about his or her personality, likes or dislikes, background? What kinds of things does the person tend to talk about? How does the elder respond to other people? Is he or she friendly or unfriendly? Articulate? Educated? This line of investigation may be more appropriate for older students because it requires an ability to analyze dialogue and speech patterns. Although younger children can certainly talk about their reactions to the ways a character talks, the impressions they gain from dialogue often come more from other information, such as verbs or adverbs used to describe the speech ("'Go home,' shouted the old man, angrily.").

While not all books for younger children contain a great deal of dialogue, some that do make interesting material for older students to examine. In the *Seven Little Postmen*, cited earlier, the old woman's speech is highly stereotypical in its usage. The speech of elder characters in other books is not: In *Hi, Mrs. Mallory!* by Ianthe Thomas, the old woman talks in a rural dialect.[13] From her speech alone — not only what she says but how she says it — we know that she is uneducated, caring, strong, and interesting. In *Oma and Bobo*, by Amy Schwartz, the grandmother shows her dislike of the dog and her (surface) sternness by lapsing into German phrases.[14] In Tomie dePaola's *Watch Out for the Chicken Feet in Your Soup*, the Italian grandmother's speech shows her to be loving and exuberant.[15] With a bit of investigation, a teacher can locate a number of children's books that contain interesting elders' dialogue.

Of course the core of any research on the images of elders in literature is the role played by the elder characters in the story. Where is the character located (setting), and what does that tell us about the person? What is the character's relation to other characters? (In *When the Wind Blew*, a story for children ages three to six, an old woman lives alone on a beach. Her sole companions are cats, and when a storm comes and she gets a toothache, she has no help but theirs.[16] If it were not for the cats, her old age would be extremely lonely; the setting intensifies the theme.) What does the character do, either with others or by her/himself? (*Matt's Grandfather* enjoys his walk with Matt, but he also likes to enjoy the world by himself.[17]) Is the character's role in the story believable? Realistic? (Has grandmother ever been waiting at your house with freshly baked cookies when you got home from school?) Too predictable? (You knew from the first page that she would die.) Clichéd? (Aren't *all* nursing homes horrible, sad places?)

A major concern is the importance of the elder character to the main action of the story. Is the character absolutely necessary? What function does the character serve? How does the character change during the story? How does the character cause others to change? In *The Pigman*, Mr. Pignati, the old man, is an important character. If it were not for their friendship with Mr. Pignati, John and Lorraine would not learn some valuable lessons. However, Mr. Pignati himself has very little direct or *intentional* effect on the two teenagers. It is his death (precipitated by John and Lorraine's irresponsibility) that causes their growth. Although an important character, he is, in a way, a prop. On the other hand, the dying grandmother in Hadley Irwin's *What About Grandma?* consciously works to help her daughter and granddaughter better understand each other before she dies.[18] Without her efforts the story would not end with the maturing and reconciling of the two younger women. Her role, therefore, is instrumental to the plot.

Exploring Film, Television, and Advertising

When the adults of today were children, they did not disrespect the elderly and authority as much as today's children. The difference: today many children are left at home for hours on end, entertaining themselves. Many watch T.V. programs, most of which do not encourage good, wholesome thoughts, let alone respect for others.

—Kathy Peterson, grade 12

Advertisers are most interested in the age 18 to 55 audience because it is comprised of the major consumer group. Unfortunately, growing old and being old is not an issue of major concern to this group. Consequently, aging is not seen as having much to offer in comedies aimed to appeal to this audience and, when it is a useful topic in dramatic programs, it is often because it is seen as tragedy.

—Richard H. Davis
"T.V's Boycott of Old Age"[19]

Old people are a minority in film, television, and advertising. They are notable by their absence. Film and television have few significant older characters. Nor do old people appear in the background: the numbers of people over sixty that one would normally find in shopping malls, on streets, or in restaurants are not reflected in the same settings on screen or in magazine advertisements. (Another similarly underrepresented group in the population is the physically disabled—the blind, the wheelchair-bound, and others.) Only when the focus of the story or sales pitch is an older person or people does the elder population increase. In 1984, Richard H. Davis, in an article in *Aging*, reported that according to several studies, "The percentage of elderly characters in prime-time programs ranges from a low of 1.5 percent to a high of 13 percent depending on the year, the time, and the manner of sampling. ... Women are especially disadvantaged. ... Content studies indicate that more than 90 percent of the older people seen on television are males. ... [Elders] are played as more comical, stubborn, eccentric, or foolish than the other characters, and are more likely to be portrayed with disrespect."[20] While the nineties have brought more attention to elders in the media and to showing characters with more vigor and intelligence, the problems Davis described have not gone away.

When young people examine the number and roles of elders in film, television, and advertising today, they will discover not only their absence but a variety of portrayals that range from realistic to grossly stereotypical.

Feature films, whether viewed in a movie theater, on television, or video cassette, have a potentially powerful influence on young peoples' impressions of being old. They are a part of our culture's visual literature and bear the same kind of examination as books. There are a number of approaches a class of individual students can use to explore elders in feature films:

1. Survey the movies currently showing in local theaters. How many of them contain significant older characters? Minor older characters? In those that do, how are the elders portrayed? Are the images positive or negative? Realistic or unrealistic? The guidelines of evaluating the depictions of elders in literature described above can be helpful here.

2. Watch one film selected *randomly* from the "new releases" section of a video rental store. Hose many older characters are in it? How many older people are included in scenes in airports or bus stations? On the streets? In restaurants? In waiting rooms? In banks? In sports arenas? In supermarkets or department stores? Do they tend to appear only in certain locations? Visit similar locations in the community and observe the number of elders. Do the numbers match the numbers in the film?

3. With an older companion, attend a film with significant (or at least secondary) older characters. After watching the film, discuss the nature of the portrayals of the older characters. Are they favorable or unfavorable? Realistic or unrealistic?

4. Watch a selection of older films (some television channels specialize in showing these). Examine the presence, absence, and portrayals of elders in these films. Do they differ from films of today?

5. Select and view several feature films (they may be old, new, or both) that deal specifically with the subject of old age or focus on older protagonists. Which films do you like best and why? What do the portrayals of old age have in common? What statements about being old or about elders do the films seem to make? Are the elders believable? How are the characters unique? Do any exhibit features that are attractive or desirable? Do you recognize any stereotypes?

6. Survey a selection of feature-length animated or puppet films for younger children. How are old characters (people or animals)

represented? How might younger children perceive of elders if all they were to watch were these films?

Probably television has a wider influence than film in shaping our views of our community and culture. As Robert Probst points out, "Watching television is usually a passive activity, often accompanied by other activities such as eating or doing homework. Most families do not talk much about television, and thus its more subtle messages tend to go unexamined. Our failure to analyze makes us susceptible to the indirect messages of the medium."[21] And the indirect messages about being old are generally negative. Like feature films, television often segregates elders from the main action. Elders generally appear only on shows in which they are central or important characters, and infrequently on other programs or in the background. The activities described below are designed to help students analyze the portrayals of elders on television. I have included excerpts from several high school students' essays here and in other parts of this chapter to illustrate what students doing this research may find.

1. Watch a selection of dramatic programs aired during the prime-time viewing hours (7–10 PM). How many elders appear as major, minor, or peripheral characters on each? What are they like? How are they portrayed physically? What do they do? A tally sheet can be helpful.

   Title of show _____ Network _____ Time _____
   Kind of show (circle): drama series, TV movie, comedy
   Elder character _____ major _____ minor _____
       Outstanding qualities _____

       _____
   Elder character _____ major _____ minor _____
       Outstanding qualities _____

       _____
   (Use more lines if a show has many elder characters.)
   Elders shown in crowd scenes? (Note approximately how many and where shown.)

2. Compare the presence, number, and portrayal of elders on different types of prime-time television programs — comedies, dramatic series, soap operas (day and night), game shows, "action" shows such as westerns and detective shows, and others. Which shows have the most older people? Which have the least? If you were watching any one kind of program, what would be your impression of old age?

> I watched three programs of prime time television that had people that appeared to be over the age of 60. The first show I watched had two old men, one rich and black, and the other white and still working. The second show that I watched had a character very similar to the white and still working character in the previous program. The last show I watched had an old female police officer. Although these people were all old, most of them still worked and tried to fit in with the world.
>
> — John Hieb, grade 11

3. Analyze the existence and portrayal of old men and old women on the different networks (including networks for children, public television, and pay/cable and sports networks). Do you find any similarities or differences?

4. Take a look at the ways elders are shown on a variety of programs aimed at children. Watch a sample of Saturday morning and afternoon cartoons, educational programs like *Sesame Street*, after school specials, science shows, and evening specials. What images of old age and old people would children acquire from watching these programs?

> A common reaction to those who are different is to shy away or treat them differently. A television show in which all are treated equally is *Sesame Street*. The fact that some puppets are space creatures or grandmothers doesn't change the way they are treated. A puppet game show host on *Sesame Street* conversed with an elderly woman puppet. The only reference to her age was her name — Granny. The host spoke in the same way with her as he did with other puppets of various ages.
>
> — Camille Tovey

5. Watch a selection of shows from the early days of television and compare them to the same kinds of shows today in terms of their treatment of older people. For example, examine a selection of family comedies from *Ozzie and Harriet* to *Family Ties*. Do the older shows contain more stereotypes or negative portrayals? Do you find similar depictions or characters?

6. Watch some programs that are aimed specifically at an older audience. What ideas and issues are presented on these programs? What concerns do elders seem to have? How do they differ from the concerns of elder characters on television dramas?

While the students found the television elders on network programs portrayed positively, they found images in television and magazine commercials far less flattering. In many ways, television ads make stronger and more lasting impressions on young viewers because of their repetition, brevity, and intense focus. Commercials can be explored in much the same way as the television programs themselves.

1. Watch and analyze a sample of ads during prime-time hours on one (or more) network. Note the product and the number of older men and women who appear either as central or peripheral characters.

   Product _____ Show _____
   older men as central _____ as peripheral _____
   older women as central _____ as peripheral _____

   How are older characters portrayed (positively, negatively, stereotypically, any unique features, etc.)?
   Do the same for ads during the day, ones designed for different audiences. Do you find fewer or more elders? Are they in more or less prominent roles? Are the roles more or less flattering?
   If these commercials were all you saw, what would your impressions be of old people or of old age?

2. After watching a selection of ads on television, come to some conclusions about what products are associated with older characters in ads. Why are the older characters used? How does their presence help sell the products?

3. Examine television ads aimed specifically at older buyers. (The teacher may wish to videotape some ads for class analysis.) Are the images of elders in these ads flattering or unflattering? How so? If you were an older viewer, would you be attracted to the product?

4. Make a list of ads you can remember with significant older characters. What specific features of the ad do you remember? What image of the old person was being projected? If you can, watch the ad again. Analyze, using the guiding questions if they are helpful, the way the older characters are depicted. Are they people you would like to know? Are they stereotypes?

Here is a sample of what other eleventh- and twelfth-graders found:

> Famous elderly people are the only members of the age group who are ever featured in advertisements targeted at everyone. People of all ages brush their teeth and people of all ages advertise toothpaste. However, the only elderly person advertising toothpaste is a famous elderly person. ... From viewing these commercials we get the impression that elderly people can't begin to have fun until their arthritis pain is relieved, their dentures are free from danger of falling out, their leaky bladders are under control, and their hemorrhoids have stopped swelling.
>
> —Amy Bollinger

The only things they [elders] sell are "old people" products, foods, and on occasion, cars. The commercials which elderly people appear in are forcing untrue stereotypes about older people into America's young minds.

How many times have you seen a young beautiful girl on t.v. trying to sell denture cream or antacid?

Older people are not all on the verge of dying. Many are healthy as ever, but t.v. commercials suggest they are ill and they all need their products to make them feel young again.

—Debee Rice

The older generation is presented to us as a group of subhuman creatures who are no longer capable of surviving independently. They must be led along on a leash by the young and cannot perform even the most basic biological tasks without assistance. . . . The seniors presented in commercials are always victims of either physical or mental deterioration.

—Jon Roffler

It seems the old are *only* acceptable if they are bouncy (which most are physically unable to be) and brimming with life. After studying commercials on television, one soon notices a definite lack of elderly people. Sure, it is all right for them to be gardening and shopping at Sears, but wearing makeup and perfume or even sitting with the family eating French fries is out of the question.

—Sian Griffiths

After seeing all these commercials, one almost automatically associates rather demeaning products with the elderly. Because companies use older people to promote their goods, people assume *all* old people use those goods. They harbor the stereotype that everyone over fifty has false teeth, smells like muscle-ache cream, and has irregular bathroom movements.

—Naomi Ferguson

Advertising in magazines is another interesting subject for young people to study. Like their television counterparts, magazine ads are selective in their use of older people. Because ads are designed to sell a particular product, they contain a specific pitch aimed at a particular segment of the market. Some companies intentionally exclude elders from their ads because they want to sell a youthful image. Elders may be used in ads to create a warm, folksy atmosphere, or one of stability and security. (As one teenager put it, "Typically American products are promoted with an American Dream version of a grandparent.") Sometimes they are included for humor. ("We watch a group of starry old dodderers swilling a soft drink and dancing around to rap music. Such behavior is pretty disgusting when performed by people in my own age group, but with senior citizens this is downright deplorable.") Ads of course differ from magazine to magazine, depending on the target audience and product. A teacher might have students compare the number of elders found in ads in magazines for men, for women, teenagers, children, elders, blacks, whites, and so on. Or, students might survey the ads in different kinds of magazines: sports magazines, hunting magazines, fashion magazines, music magazines, tabloids. They may find that while some ads exclude old people, others use them selectively to market certain products, that more elders are in ads in senior's magazines (naturally) and in magazines for women on homemaking (for example, *Good Housekeeping*) than in magazines aimed at teens that feature, say, fashion, or magazines for men about sports. Ads that include elder characters can be analyzed in terms of their visual as well as verbal messages: What does the elder(s) look like? In what setting is he or she placed? What is the person doing? Additionally, the language of ads contains both overt and covert messages. A picture of a grandmotherly old woman holding a steaming apple pie says not only that the pie will taste good but that it will make you feel loved and secure when you eat it. Students should examine pictures and words (their tone, diction, connotations) and their arrangement in order to determine *all* the messages ads convey, not only about the product but about the elders as well.

While many portrayals of elders in literature, film, television, and advertising are patronizing and belittling, others are not, as students will discover. Increasing awareness of our society's past tendency to discriminate against this segment of the population—a phenomenon called "ageism" by sociologists and gerontologists— has made us more sensitive to reductive or derogatory depictions. More children's books published today show a diversity of old people in a positive and frank manner, and some television and films have made recent attempts to present elders realistically. But we still have a way to go before our media reflect the older population adequately. In the next chapter, I discuss some of the ways young people can use experiences with language, literature, and film, as well as experiences with elders themselves, to go beyond the stereotypes, become better acquainted with old age and its realities, and begin to see that elders are an important part of their communities.

Notes

1. Golden Press. *Seven Little Postmen*. Based on the original story by Margaret Wise Brown and Edith Thacher Hurd. Pictures by Tibor Gergely. (Racine, WI: Western Publishing, 1952).

2. Murphey, Milledge, Jane E. Myers, and Phyllis D. Drennan, "Attitudes of Children Toward Older Persons: What They Are, What They Can Be." *The School Counselor* (March, 1982), pp. 281–288.

3. George, Phil. *Kautsas*. (Spaulding, ID: Phil George, 1978).

4. Horner, Catherine Townsend. *The Aging Adult in Children's Books & Nonprint Media*. (Metuchen, NJ: The Scarecrow Press, 1982).

5. Ulin, Richard O. *Teaching and Learning About Aging*. (Washington, DC: National Education Association, 1982).

6. Williams, Barbara. *Kevin's Grandma*. (New York: E.P. Dutton, 1975).

7. Kessler, Ethel, and Leonard Kessler. *Grandpa Witch and the Magic Doobelator*. (New York: Macmillan, 1981).

8. Zindel, Paul. *The Pigman*. (New York: Dell, 1968).

9. Arluke, Arnold, and Jack Levin. "Another Stereotype: Old Age as a Second Childhood." *Aging* (August/September, 1984), p. 7.

10. _____, pp. 7–11.

11. Deloria, Ella Cara. *Waterlily*. (Lincoln: University of Nebraska Press, 1988), p. 7.

12. MacLachlan, Patricia, Illus. by Lloyd Bloom. *Arthur, for the Very First Time*. (New York: Harper & Row/Trophy, 1989).

13. Thomas, Ianthe. Illus. by Ann Toulmin-Rothe. *Hi, Mrs. Mallory!* (New York: Harper & Row, 1979).

14. Schwartz, Amy. *Oma and Bobo*. (New York: Bradbury, 1987).

15. dePaola, Tomie. *Watch Out for the Chicken Feet in Your Soup*. (Englewood Cliffs, NJ: Prentice-Hall, 1974).

16. Brown, Margaret Wise. Illus. by Geoffrey Hayes. *When the Wind Blew*. (New York: Harper & Row, 1977).

17. Lundgren, Max. Illus. by Fibben Hald. *Matt's Grandfather*. Translated by Ann Pyk. (New York: G.P. Putnam's Sons, 1972).

18. Irwin, Hadley. *What About Grandma?* (New York: Margaret K. McElderry Books, 1983).

19. Davis, Richard H. "T.V.'s Boycott of Old Age." *Aging* (August/September, 1984), p. 14.

20. _____, p.15.

21. Probst, Robert. *Response and Analysis—Teaching Literature in Junior and Senior High School* (Portsmouth, NH: Boynton/Cook, 1988), p. 177.

Chapter Four

Getting Acquainted
Discovering Realities

Living Alone Poem

In the night, I turn and look out of the window with my white
    shiny
Face, and I thank the Lord, I'm alive and I'm happy.

In the night, I would read and dream nothing. I'm a Kewpie doll.
I sleep till 7 in the morning.

Once in a while you have a dream (unless you eat too much or are
Not feeling well). I dream about my thirty-two grandchildren.

In the night, living alone, you don't disturb anyone. The nights
Are so peaceful, get good and warm in bed, and I never feel that
    I'm alone.

> —Frances Houghton, Bertha Gibbons,
> and Bertha White, St. Mary's Day-Time
> Care Center for the Elderly,
> Lansing, Michigan[1]

This poem expresses an idea that might surprise some young
people—that being old and living alone can be pleasurable. It is a
happy, warm poem, about good feelings and well-being. It captures
a reality not often shown on television or in advertising.

When young people investigate the sources of their attitudes
toward any segment of a community, they discover that attitudes
are shaped in part by the attitudes of their society. As they examine
the culture's publications—literature, film, television, and advertising—they are likely to find, in addition to a number of myths
and stereotypes, depictions that are realistic: images of people in

various media that resemble people they know; characterizations that are believable and unique, created in part by fresh and original language. These media, then, can be a source of understanding reality. Accurate portrayals can help young people become acquainted with elders (or any segment of the community) from their own and other cultures, now and in earlier times, without having to leave the classroom. By working with language, literature, and the visual media, young people can come to see elders — a group once remote — as familiar. They can learn that not all old people are the same, that each has unique attributes and qualities, and that when one is old, one's life can be rich and rewarding.

Getting Acquainted Through Language, Literature, Film

Language and Writing

As I described in Chapter 3, language and thought are interrelated and help shape our attitudes. While trite descriptions and euphemisms foster stereotypical thinking, novel uses of language can change thought. Activities centering on creative uses of language are a means for helping children think of old people as a diverse group of individuals and of old age as a potentially vigorous time. I described three such activities earlier: inventing positive euphemisms for aging, creating new metaphors to describe the features of old age, and inventing stories by filling in blanks in CLOZE-type paragraphs with unpredictable words. These and other activities help students not only stretch their vocabularies and imaginations but also develop new ways of thinking about old age. Once students identify the terms typically associated with old people and aging — the clichés, the familiar nouns and adjectives, the predictable descriptions of action and physical features — they can experiment with new, more original language, and use that language to create lively descriptions and stories. Here are some additional exercises:

1. Write about the most _____ (daring, absurd, handsome, conceited, clever, sneaky, loving, generous, etc.) old man or woman in the world. The adjectives should be ones not usually associated with old age.

2. Rewrite a magazine, newspaper, or transcription of a television advertisement that features elder characters in a stereotypical manner. The new ad should promote the same product, but present the elder as an individual. Students may want to change settings, dialogue, description.

3. Rewrite clichéd descriptions found in children's or young adult's books. The challenge is to keep the same character but make the descriptive words more interesting.

4. Create interesting older characters for stories: each student writes a bio sheet on a character he or she invents. The bio sheet (Figure 4–1) should include facts about the person's life, significant events, family, profession, likes and dislikes, and descriptions of the person's physical attributes and personality. Then, the teacher copies each fact sheet (to make a sufficient number), and gives each student two that are not his or her own. The student then writes a story, dialogue, or narrative about the

Figure 4–1
Bio Sheet

Bio Sheet

Name:

Height: Weight: Eye color: Corrective lenses?

Hair (amount, color, texture):

Distinguishing physical features:

Birthdate: Birthplace:

Education (years in school, degrees, etc.):

Health:

Personality traits:

Childhood (significant experiences, friends, typical activities, etc.):

Adolescence:

Work history:

Marriage/family:

Major achievements, contributions, high points:

Current favorites:
    foods: entertainment:
    activities with friends:
    solo activities:

---

meeting of these two people. The teacher might provide a list of settings where the people meet to help students get started.

5. Write stories about unique individuals: how (old) Mr. _____ saved the city; how (old) Ms. _____ got rich; why (old) Mr./ Ms. _____ is our favorite (or most embarrassing, or funniest, or cleverest) relative; how Mr./Ms. _____ came to land in jail. The teacher may help students start their stories by giving each a picture. Useful books that contain photographs of elders are Imogen Cunningham's *After Ninety*[2], Maria S. Forrai's *A Look at Old Age*[3], Dorka Raynor's *Grandparents Around the World*[4], Virginia Alvin and Glenn Silverstein's *Aging*[5], and Harriet Langsam Sobol's *Grandpa: A Young Man Grown Old*[6].

The topics for writing need not stress exclusively the positive side of old age. While we want young people to grow up with enriched notions of what old age (including their own) can entail, we also want them to understand that old people come in a range of shapes, sizes, and personalities, just as they do. Some are nice, some are not. Therefore, we want to avoid creating a false impression that all old people are generous, warm, loving, etc. By promoting only a positive view of old age we are perpetuating a stereotype. Writing topics should introduce a range of people, situations, and activities in which elders could realistically engage — situations that perhaps we don't normally associate with people over sixty-five, such as heroism, athleticism, ingenuity — and encourage students to describe elders using more original language so that they become more vivid, real.

Literature

One of my first recollections of old people in literature was Old Father William, the addled man whose knees were being eaten by chickens. Although bizarre, he seemed familiar and comfortable. He was tough, funny, and full of life. Children and teens can get acquainted with older people through literature in a variety of ways. The first way is by reading stories, novels, poetry, and plays about old age or with significant older characters; characters in literature can seem as real as a breathing, living beings — a part of our experience. A number of recent books written for children and young adults contain portraits of elders that are rich and unique: a grandmother is an explorer (*Hurry Home Grandma*, by Arielle North Olson)[7]; a grandfather shops (*Just Grandpa and Me*, by Mercer Mayer)[8]; a smart old woman lives alone in a shack with two dogs (Ianthe Thomas's, *Hi, Mrs. Mallory!*, cited in Chapter 3); a grandfather shows off his song and dance routines (Karen Ackerman's *Song and Dance Man*).[9] Young adult literature also contains a number of engaging characters: a grandfather who is remote and uncommunicative (Mazer's *After the Rain*)[10], a grandmother who is a compulsive thief (*Sweet Bells, Jangled Out of Tune*, by Robin Brancato),[11] a grandmother who welds and sculpts (Betty Levin's *The Trouble With Gramary*)[12]. These and other works can provide a valuable contrast to the more belittling characterizations and stereotypes of old people as passive, sad, and uninteresting that exist in a large number of books for young people. In addition, children's and young adult literature contain portraits that show some of the realities of growing older. Donna Guthrie's *Grandpa Doesn't Know It's Me*, for younger children, shows in a frank, unsentimental, supportive fashion the stages of Alzheimer's disease.[13] For older children, Tolan's *Grandpa—and Me* explores the same topic.[14] In *Ring of Endless Light*[15] and *After the Rain* (cited in Chapter 3), two novels for adolescents (and adults), the grandfathers' physical deteriorations are treated directly and honestly.

Fairy tales, folk tales, and myths contain a range of elders, from the kindly and supportive to the meanest people imaginable. Some old protagonists are resourceful, clever, and strong. Others are vengeful, sinister, and/or the perpetrators of chaos. Myths and folk tales are also valuable sources for exploring cross-cultural images of and attitudes toward aging. In the Japanese folk tale *The Funny Little Woman*, a giggling old woman outsmarts a group of evil spirits who live underground.[16] In some cultures, age means power because old age is a culmination of life. Old people have a storehouse of knowledge and wit—or negatively, of grievances and animosity. Elder characters may use this power to help others solve problems or to create them.

While a great deal of literature on the theme of old age is available, not much is included in anthologies or readers for young people. Literature on the subject is often relegated to units on growing old and dying rather than mainstreamed into the literature program. Teachers may be leery of this literature because they fear that it will not interest young people, that it lacks relevance to adolescents' or children's lives. But the subject can have meaning for young people because every person in the classroom will one day become old. When students approach the literature with their own futures in mind, the stories become quite relevant. A teacher who wants to use poetry, short stories, and plays about old age or containing older characters in their classes can find materials in a variety of places. College literature anthologies that are organized thematically are a good source of stories and poetry for junior and senior high school students; they generally contain the more well-known works. Other useful books include Corrine Streich's *Grandparents' Houses: Poems About Grandparents*[17]; *Autumn Light: Illuminations of Age* (a book of short stories edited by L. M. Schulman)[18]; *When I Am an Old Woman I Shall Wear Purple* (an anthology of short stories and poetry by women about being old and aging)[19]; and *A Wider Giving: Women Writing After a long Silence* (primarily essays).[20]

Because most well-known literature with older characters contains themes other than those related to being old, it is easily integrated into thematic or other classroom units. *Silas Marner* is about greed, duplicity, and loneliness. Pamela Frankau's "The Duchess and the Smugs," a powerful short story about a teenage girl who wishes for a more ordinary life, is not only about the relationship between an adolescent and an old woman but about conformity and maturity. Hemingway's "A Clean, Well-Lighted Place" speaks not only about youth's callousness to old age but to anyone who has ever questioned the meaning of existence. Frost's "Birches" evokes images of the freedom and innocence of childhood; his "The Death of the Hired Man" concerns the other end of life. Tennyson's "Ulysses," a poetic monologue by an old Ulysses frustrated by retirement, is about the importance of adventure and travel to youth—a theme that could be thoroughly understood by teens facing the responsibilities of growing up. Many elder characters in literature confront problems and experience delights faced by teenagers and children: the death of a friend, conflicts with family members, a test of survival, a shared joy. Here are a few well-known works (and a few less well-known) that can be integrated into a literature program for older students. I have not included children's or young adult's literature here; titles of more recent books on the theme of old age or with major older characters are included in separate bibliographies.

Poetry

- Paula Gunn Allen, "Grandmother"
- Matthew Arnold, "Growing Old"
- Catherine Davis, "After a Time"
- Robert Frost, "Nothing Gold Can Stay," "After Apple Picking," and "Birches"
- Edward Hirsch, "In a Polish Home for the Aged (Chicago, 1983)"
- Stanley Kunitz, "The Layers"
- Diana Manning, "For Grandma"

- Edward A. Robinson "Mr. Flood's Party"
- Yvonne Sapia, "Grandmother, A Caribbean Indian, Described by My Father"
- Sappho, "Here Are Fine Gifts, Children"
- Alfred, Lord Tennyson, "Ulysses"
- William Stafford, "Waiting in Line"
- Dylan Thomas, "Fern Hill"
- William Butler Yeats, "Sailing to Byzantium," "A Prayer for Old Age," "Among School Children," "When You Are Old."

Short Stories

- Arna Bontemps, "A Summer Tragedy"
- Willa Cather, "Neighbor Rosicky," "Old Mrs. Harris"
- Pam Durban, "All Set About with Fever Trees"
- William Faulkner, "A Rose for Emily"
- Pamela Frankau, "The Duchess and the Smugs"
- Ernest Hemingway, "A Clean, Well-Lighted Place"
- Shirley Jackson, "The Island"
- Katherine Mansfield, "Miss Brill"
- Katherine Anne Porter, "The Jilting of Granny Weatherall"
- Gail Y. Miyasaki, "Obāchan"
- Tillie Olsen, "Tell Me a Riddle"
- Alice Walker, "To Hell with Dying"
- Eudora Welty, "A Worn Path"

Plays

- Enid Bagnold, *The Chinese Prime Minister*
- Ralph Edmonds, *Old Man Pete*
- Horton Foote, *Death of the Old Man*
- Lorraine Hansberry, *A Raisin in the Sun*
- Stanley Houghton, *The Dear Departed*
- David Henry Hwang, *Family Devotions*
- Joseph Kesselring, *Arsenic and Old Lace*
- Arthur Miller, *Death of a Salesman*
- Paul Osborn, *On Borrowed Time*
- John Patrick, *The Curious Savage*
- William Shakespeare, *King Lear, The Tempest*

- Howard Teichmann, *The Girls in 509*
- Ernest Thompson, *On Golden Pond*
- Thornton Wilder, *Our Town, The Long Christmas Dinner*
- Lorees Yerby, *Save Me a Place at Forest Lawn*

Novels/Autobiography
- Ray Bradbury, selections from *Dandelion Wine*
- Charles Dickens, *A Christmas Carol, David Copperfield, A Tale of Two Cities, Great Expectations*
- George Eliot, *Silas Marner*
- Sarah Orne Jewett, *The Country of the Pointed Firs*
- May Sarton, *Mrs. Stevens Hears the Mermaids Singing*
- Jonathan Swift, *Gulliver's Travels*
- Maya Angelou, selections from *I Know Why the Caged Bird Sings*
- Jessamyn West, selections from *Cress Delahanty*

Another good way for children to become acquainted with elders is through the words of the elders themselves — their stories, novels, essays, memoirs, poems. The community itself can be a wonderful source of literature. Every neighborhood, town, or region contains writers who produce poetry, essays, children's stories, and fiction for local organizations' newsletters or journals. Some writers have formed writing groups that meet regularly to share their writing. But others write only for themselves or their families.

> My preacher sez "You're full [of] evil.
> If 'n you don't want to meet the devil,
> It's got to come out."
> My Dentist sez "Your teeth's a mess.
> I'd better shuck them is my guess.
> They got to come out."
> My Doctor sez "That lung's done gone.
> So's your stomach," and on and on.
> "They got to come out."
> If 'n I'm to listen to those three
> Good God there's nothing left of me.
> Sez I, "You all git out."
> —Ralph M. Zeigler

The man who wrote this poem is not a published poet. But at age seventy-five, he has written over three hundred poems. Writing poems has always been an important part of his life, and he writes whether or not anyone reads them. His poems about being old are sometimes funny, sometimes sad, and always original. Even though they may not be artistically perfect, they enable readers to share his frustrations and delights. We become participants in his experience of aging. His poems about being old reflect a range of feelings. Some are humorous, such as the one above; he may not like being old, but he can make the best of it because he still has his wit and mental strength. In other poems his humor is poignant, such as in this poem, written during a hospital stay:

Night Nurse

She was blessed with a bountiful four foot beam
Her coiffure was tangled and thatched
With breastwork ample for ten to feed
And size 12 feet that matched.

Her mouth was always packed with gum
She chewed it like a cud.
When people asked as they always did
She insisted her name was "Spud."

She never announced her coming,
She merely loomed into view.
That was probably just as well
For her voice scared the hell out of you.

Yet she never complained if a sheet was twice soiled;
She was thorough yet gentle too,
And wasn't afraid to challenge the hospital staff
If she thought it best for you.

Her patients soon longed to see her barge in
When restless retirement hours came,
And all who were blessed with her tender care
Never forgot her name.

                             —Ralph M. Zeigler

I would not hesitate to use these or others of his poems in a classroom. First, they express one man's feelings about being old with clarity and force; the voice is true. Second, the concrete images and narrative style make them easy to read and understand. Third, they qualify as poetry: they use poetic devices (rhyme and rhythm, figurative language) to convey emotions and experience. Finally, they are accessible because they are *not* written by a well-known writer. Students sometimes feel more encouraged to write when they read writing by amateurs—other community members like themselves. For many young people, well-known writers are less than real. Young readers often don't connect the printed word on the page with a human being who eats and sleeps like everyone else. However, when they read literature written by someone's grandfather or mother, the school principal, the person who fixes the television set, or any amateur whose words are not between hard covers on glossy paper, they see the act of writing as a normal human activity, something anyone can do.

Writing done by elders can be located in a number of places, including one's own family. Magazines aimed at older readers often publish stories, articles, or poems written by older lay writers: *Modern Maturity*, a magazine published by the American Association of Retired Persons, publishes fiction as well as nonfiction. *Retirement Living*, another seniors' magazine, publishes personal experiences, how-to articles, travel stories, and other material of interest to people over fifty-five. (*Writer's Market* is a good source of information about these magazines.) Area agencies of organizations on aging, retirement communities, religious organizations, and other community groups also publish seniors' writing. *Senior Citizen News*, from Portland, Oregon, *Elder Affairs*, from Seattle, and *The Senior Voice*, from Anchorage, are three publications in the northwestern United States; other communities have similar publications. In some regions, volunteers have organized writing workshops for elder writers in nursing homes, retirement centers, and daytime care centers. Other senior writers meet regularly on their own to share their work, and several such groups have produced anthologies. Some examples are *Recollections*, published by the Brock House Writers of Vancouver, B.C., Canada[21]; *Everybody's Story*, an anthology of stories, essays, and poems written by elders who participated in the COMPAS Literary Post program in Minnesota[22]; and *NIMROD*: "Old People: A Season of the Mind," a collection of elders' poetry produced as a magazine and radio program by the Arts and Humanities Council of Tulsa, Oklahoma.[23] Other collections that include writing by "amateurs" (as well as writing previously or since published elsewhere) are Kenneth Koch's *I Never Told Anybody: Teaching Poetry Writing in a Nursing Home*,[24] Ronald Blythe's (ed.) *A View in Winter*,[25] Koontz and Tammaro's, (eds.) *The View from the Top of the Mountain: Poems After Sixty*,[26] and Sandra Martz's (ed.) *When I Am an Old Woman I Shall Wear Purple*, cited earlier. Some communities, educational groups, and other organizations have collected audiotapes of interviews with elders, elders' reminiscences, stories, and poetry. This oral literature can be integrated into a classroom literature program.

In addition to helping young people get acquainted with the old, the writing of elders teaches children about the creative power and potential of later life. Creativity does not decline with age, and many artists produce their best work in their later years. Mark Twain wrote "The Man That Corrupted Hadleyburg" after he was sixty. William Carlos Williams, W. H. Auden, William Faulkner, Henry James, Robinson Jeffers, Sophocles, Jonathan Swift, Miguel Cervantes, Herman Melville, Walt Whitman, Henrik Ibsen, Benjamin Franklin, Robert Frost, and many others wrote into their older years. Many contemporary writers were and are prolific after sixty: Stanley Kunitz, Gwendolyn Brooks, William Stafford, Norman McLean, Grace Paley, May Sarton, Eudora Welty, Wallace Stegner, and others. Harriet Doerr wrote her first novel, *Stones for Ibarra*, in her seventies; Dan James (Danny Santiago), published the adolescent novel *Famous All Over Town* at age seventy-three, and William Stafford published his collection of poems, *An Oregon Message*, at seventy-one. Although we as teachers tend not to point out the ages of writers when we ask students to read a poem or story, we might help our students begin to see old age as a potentially productive and even lucrative time of life if we did. (Using art by elder artists in the classroom, as prompts to writing or in bulletin board displays that feature art by one or several artists, can accomplish the same goal.)

Film

When students explore images of elders in film and television, they will uncover many that seem realistic — unique people with concerns that go beyond those associated with their age, that cross generations and are universal. These are the characters who stand out not just as a "great old man" or "wonderful old woman" but as people we feel richer for knowing, people we might like to emulate, people who become part of our experience. Documentary and short dramatic films are as valuable as full-length feature films for helping young people get acquainted with old age. There are many sources of information on films about elders and old age. Francis Pratt's *Teaching About Aging* lists three film guides:

- *Film Forum*. KWIC Training Resources in Aging Project, Center for the Study of Aging and Human Development, Duke University, Box 3003, DUMC, Durham, NC 27710.
- *Films on Aging* (AoA). Stock No. 1762−00071. U.S. Government Printing Office, Washington, D.C. 20402.
- *About Aging: A Catalog of Films*. Margaret E. Neiswender, compiler. Ethel Percy Andrus Gerontology Center, University of Southern California, University Park, Los Angeles, CA 90007.[27]

In addition, an annotated list of films on aging, *Aging: A Filmography*, is available from the Educational Film Library Association,

Inc. (45 John Street, Suite 301, New York, NY 10010). Another excellent source is Catherine Townsend Horner's *The Aging Adult in Children's Books and Nonprint Media*, which includes extensive bibliographies of films, filmstrips, transparencies, and audiotapes and records on the theme of old age and aging up to 1980. The following list of films, compiled by Citizens for Changing Attitudes About Aging, was recommended by *Aging* magazine:

- *Water from Another Time.* Documentary of three elder artists (Kane-Lewis Productions).

- *Because Somebody Cares.* Documentary about the value of friendships between the old and young (New Dimension Films).

- *Luther Metke at 94.* Academy Award nomineee for best short documentary in 1981; the story of a man who builds log cabins (New Dimension Films).

- *Close Harmony.* Documentary about a program that brought together fourth- and fifth-graders and an elderly choral group. Winner of the 1982 Academy Award for Best Documentary Short Film (Learning Corporation of America).

- *Forever Young.* Documentary in which 26 elders illustrate that old age can be a vital and productive time (Learning Corporation of America).

- *Miles of Smiles, Years of Struggle.* Documentary about the history and struggles of the black Pullman porters. Includes narratives by retired porters and a 100-year-old woman (Benchmark Films).[28]

In a special issue of *Media and Methods* (February 1980), Judith Trojan recommended several other film portraits of men and women that "emphatically contradict commonly held misconceptions about the aged." Among the portraits of men, Trojan cites two documentaries: *Best Boy*, Ira Wohl's documentary about his mentally retarded fifty-two-year-old cousin and his aging parents (Entertainment Marketing Corporation); and *Grandpa*, by Stephen L. Forman and Paul Desaulniers, about the life of Forman's 86-year-old grandfather, a Jewish immigrant (Films Incorporated). In addition, Trojan recommends the following short dramatic films: *Home To Stay*, starring Henry Fonda and directed by Delbert Mann, about an old man's oncoming senility and his relationships with his granddaughter and son (Time-Life Multimedia); *Portrait of Grandpa Doc*, starring Melvyn Douglas, about an artist's memories of his grandfather (Phoenix Films, Incorporated); *Death of a Gandy Dancer*, about the effects of an old man's dying and death on his family (Learning Corporation of America); and *The Last Winters*, about an old man's search for his lover, who is temporarily missing (Perspective Films).[29]

Trojan also notes several worthy portraits of older women:

- Three parts of the PBS series, "The Originals: Women in Art" — Nancy Baer's *Alice Neel: Collector of Souls* (Cine 16 Films), Perry Miller Adato's *Georgia O'Keeffe* (Films Incorporated), and Susan Fanshel and Jill Godmilow's *Navelson in Process* (Films Incorporated).

- Jill Godmilow and Judy Collins's *Antonia: A Portrait of the Woman*, about conductor Antonia Brico (Phoenix Films, Inc.).

- Susan Wengraf's *Love It Like A Fool*, about folksinger Malvina Reynolds (New Day Films).

- CBS-TV's *Imogen Cunningham at 93* (Carousel Films).

- The Center for Southern Folklore's *Four Women Artists*, which features a writer (Eudora Welty), quiltmaker (Pecolia Warner), embroiderer (Ethel Mohamed), and painter (Theora Hamblett); three segments of Lucille Rhodes's and Margaret Murphy's *They are Their Own Gifts*, about poet Muriel Rukeyser, painter Alice Neel, and choreographer Anna Sokolow (New Day Films).

- Sandra Greenberg's *Four Women Over Eighty*, which features interviews with four active women (MTI Teleprograms, Inc.).[30]

Of course, there are many, many others, including feature films.

Like the literature, good films with older major characters deal with themes other than aging, and can therefore be integrated easily into many focused units of study. The film version of *On Golden Pond*, for example, can be used with junior or senior high school units on intergenerational communication, parents, rebellion, love, or responsibility. Similarly, *Harold and Maude*, about a friendship and love between an eccentric old woman and introverted young man, might be shown in conjunction with *Of Mice and Men*, or *Flowers for Algernon*. These films need not be relegated to units on old age or death; their characters may be old, but they are also human, and as such, belong in the mainstream of literature and film study.

What Is It Like to Be Old? Exploring the Facts About Aging

When I am 100, I will have a staff. When I am
100 I will have a beard. I would be very old,
but I would still be me, and you would still be you.

— Jackson Ludwig, grade 2

Is it true that all old people sit around and wish they were young? When I am old will I forget everything? What will I think about? How will I spend my time? Most children and even adolescents know very little about the actual processes of aging. They know that people get wrinkled, that they begin to forget (actually, long-term memory can improve with age, although short-term memory may decline), that they aren't as steady on their feet, that their eyes don't work as well. What they often don't realize is that, as Jackson wrote, they will still be themselves. Norma Farber's book *How Does It Feel To Be Old?*,[31] although a children's book, can help all people understand this important principle: that inside every old person is all the person he or she once was — the baby, the child, the adolescent, the young and middle-aged adult. Just as we change throughout our young lives emotionally and physically, so do we change as we age. Exactly how we change is a bit of a mystery to the young. By reading and viewing informative material and by talking to experts in the community, including elders, students can solve the mystery.

Inside the School

Finding the Facts. In addition to watching documentary films and reading literature about old people, students can read nonfiction books, magazine articles and pamphlets, and watch films, filmstrips, and slide programs that describe the aging processes and the effects of those processes on thought, emotion, and personality. Regional and national agencies provide informative material: area agencies on aging, the Administration on Aging, the Gray Panthers, the National Council on the Aging, Retired Senior Volunteer Program (ACTION), the Andrus Gerontological Information Center, and the Clearinghouse for Elementary and Secondary Aging Education are a few. Filmstrips and films on the subject of old age and aging are plentiful and available for rental from educational distributors such as the Learning Corporation of America, Sunburst Films, Films Incorporated, and BFA Educational Films. (A list of information agencies and the addresses of the film distributors mentioned in this chapter are included in the bibliographies).

Another source of information is people in the community who work with elders—doctors, nurses, gerontologists, ministers or rabbis. These people can visit a class individually or as a panel and provide facts about aging and answer questions. The panel format has the advantage of providing information from a variety of perspectives for students whose attention spans are longer. A panel might include a doctor, to talk about the physical realities of aging, a geriatric nurse, to talk about the emotional needs of the very old, and a psychologist, to describe how aging affects mental processes. A series of individual speakers scheduled throughout one or two weeks can serve the same purpose and is sometimes more effective with younger children.

Elders in the Classroom. One of the best ways for young people to learn about old age is from elders themselves—by hearing their views and by simply getting to know them. There are many ways elders can participate in a classroom. They can come more formally as guest speakers or panelists and present their views on aging and to answer questions about what it is like to be old. One strategy described by Francis Pratt in *Teaching About Aging* involves bringing several elders into the classroom for small-group rap sessions. Pratt first had his high school students prepare for the elders' visit by writing down (using the hand they don't usually write with so they could experience a physical disability faced by many elders) the age to which they *expected* to live and the age to which they *wanted* to live and why. When the visitors arrived, each elder met with a group of three students to discuss "their perceptions of each other's generation and about anything else they wanted to explore."[32] Pratt found this activity very successful in breaking down negative attitudes and stereotypes by helping the students become more comfortable with older people.

Even if they are not talking directly about what it is like to be old, elders can be valuable assets in classrooms. They can serve as aides, tutors, readers, and responders to writing. Several school districts throughout the country use older volunteers to help in these ways. Some schools have adopted intergenerational learning programs in which elders join younger learners in projects ranging from creating oral history collections to sharing their responses to books. For example, in 1978, Jerrold Berkson initiated an intergenerational project at Richard S. Sherman North Middle School (Great Neck, New York) in which students read a novel about immigrants, interviewed their grandparents, and wrote autobiographies. In addition, Berkson brought in elders from a local seniors' center who had volunteered to be interviewed by the students and videotaped.[33]

When elders become a part of a classroom they become a familiar part of the learning environment; they no longer seem strange, but instead, are comfortable figures with whom students feel at ease talking and sharing. By reading stories aloud, they help young people become familiar with old voices. They can give talks about books they like, help students select material for individual reading, participate in discussion groups, listen to oral reading, share reactions to the reading, and help create more formal responses (an art project, a skit or puppet show, a written report). Elders can participate in the writing program as well. Senior volunteers can work with young peoples' writing, not as editors or graders but as interested readers who are willing to write down their personal responses to a young writer's ideas. One elder reader may work with each writer, like a penpal, and read and respond regularly to writing the student has chosen. Young writers might share any writing—a story, a written book response, an argumentative essay, a poem. The elder reader should be encouraged to respond in a nonjudgmental, person-to-person fashion by noting similar experiences, reactions to interesting ideas the writer has proposed, questioned the reader would like answered. Or, teachers can pair students with elder readers who also like to write, so that the two may share and respond to each other's writing at regular intervals during the school year. On a daily or weekly basis, elder volunteers can help young people with their regular classroom writing assignments— getting ideas, defining and focusing their topics, revising, polishing final drafts. When elders respond to students' writing, young writers expand their notions of audience. The reactions of "real people" to their ideas help them realize that their thoughts and creations are important to people outside the educational institution.

Outside the Classroom

Obviously one of the best ways to find out about anything in a community is by experiencing it firsthand. Students can learn just as much about being old and the status of old age in their society when they leave the school and see and talk to elders in various settings.

Observations. Careful observation is a prerequisite to good descriptive writing. While youngsters notice old people in a variety of community settings, they may not truly see them. Many of us simply do not notice older people, perhaps because we fear old age and death. It doesn't take a great deal of looking to see that some older people walk with greater hesitancy, have wrinkled skin or sparse hair. On a street or in a shopping mall, where people tend to walk quickly and purposefully, the gait of an elder using a walker is noticeably slow. But exactly what kinds of walkers do elders use and how do they use them? Can a group young people describe the devices and the bodily actions connected with their use? Observation can help open students' eyes to a segment of the population that may have been largely invisible. It also can sharpen their abilities to perceive people generally and improve skills of descriptive writing. Students might begin strengthening their observation powers by closely watching their own relatives or friends, and then strangers in places such as supermarkets, restaurants, and other familiar neighborhood locales. (Of course, students should not be encouraged to spy on people or to stare at them so as to make them uncomfortable. It is easy to observe unobtrusively and informally by simply paying more attention while one is strolling, or by sitting in one place and taking occasional glimpses while pretending to read.) Before students observe, they should be encouraged to think about a few focusing questions: How many elders do you see? What is each doing? Wearing? If observing one person, notice his or her face, hair, skin, movement, posture, dress, unusual features, voice, and other traits. A notebook is useful for recording information and impressions either during or after the period of observation. (Some people find a checklist helpful.) Following the observation, students can turn their notes into written descriptions or narratives.

But shopping areas, public buildings, and streets are not the only places where students can observe elders. Nearly every community has organizations that sponsor seniors' activities. Some restaurants, theaters, or amusement parks have seniors' nights, when elders pay less for admission or dinner. Church groups and residential centers host seniors' picnics and shopping trips. Some civic groups sponsor bingo nights, or other events that draw large groups of older adults. These places afford young people, who often do not see elders in more social or leisurely settings where they are in the majority, an excellent opportunity to observe. For those who think of old age as a dreary and passive time and of all old people as sad and quiet, a visit to any of these events can be most rewarding.

Rarely, too, do young people have the opportunity to see groups of older adults in retirement centers, nursing homes, hospices, convalescent homes, or day-time care centers. For many, these places are scary. Yet when they learn more about the centers, how they work and what goes on there, they are less uncomfortable.

Students who plan to visit such centers individually or as a group should prepare beforehand a list of questions that concern them most: What do old people do during a typical day? What services does the center provide? Are people able to engage in a variety of activities? How do residents feel about the place? Why are people here? Can people leave? Do they have opportunities to learn and do new and interesting things? Can people have pets? Are there social activities? What are the rooms like? What is the food like? What do the residents most complain about? Personnel at such centers are often willing to arrange visits for a class or group and to answer questions.

Writing activities are a natural follow-up to such a visit. Here are some topics that encourage students to reflect on and react to what they have learned at a residential center (some are more appropriate for children, others for junior or senior high school students):

- The most unusual thing I saw.
- What I would like best if I lived here.
- The most interesting machine.
- What I learned about _____ that I didn't know before.
- The most interesting person I met.
- A diary entry from the point of view of a resident.
- A plan for one significant change in anything about the place (the layout, the facilities, the routine, the care, etc.).
- A mystery story or romance that takes place in the center.
- A dialogue between two residents.
- A description of the room you would have if you lived there.
- An argument to convince the state to provide more money for the center.
- A letter to convince someone that the center is a good place to go.
- A song that captures the mood of the center or that tells about its activities—an alma mater or a fight song.
- An advertisement for the center that might appear in a magazine or on television.

Interviews. When my son's second-grade class visited a nursing home on Halloween, the children saw a large room filled with people in chairs; some people were sleeping, others talking quietly, others silent and staring. The children didn't know what to do—

where to stand, what to say to the people they had come to visit. Several children said that they felt sorry for the old people, who seemed so alone in this place. But did the home residents feel this way? What were their lives like? How did they spend their time? What was each person really thinking? None of the children knew how to ask.

Elders themselves are an obvious source of information about what it is like to be old (and a number of other topics, as well!). With a little bit of work, a teacher can locate seniors in the community willing to serve as informants for students' interviews. Students' family members and elder acquaintances make excellent subjects for interviews. No matter what the focus of the questions, a good interview depends on the skills of the interviewer. In an article in the *Detroit Free Press*, writer Carol Stocker described several guidelines for interviewing older people developed by Dr. Eva Kahana and Patricia Pilling of Wayne State University. Although these guidelines are intended for people who wish to conduct more extensive interviews for the purpose of collecting oral history, they can help even the one-time or informal interviewer in search of answers to more immediate, simple questions about old age and aging.

1. Help the person being interviewed feel comfortable by chatting informally before asking questions; perhaps discuss some common interests to help the person feel at ease.

2. Use a tape recorder (with the person's permission), placing it in some unobtrusive spot.

3. Listen to the person's answers carefully and seriously, and respond the same way. Kahana and Pilling note that older people who repeat themselves often do so because they fear they are not being heard or understood.

4. Listen with patience. An elder may take longer to get to the point than a young person would. Try to differentiate between long, prefatory explanations and digressions.

5. Be prepared in advance with specific questions. A questionnaire can be a helpful guide.

6. Be aware that elders may not use years as a time indicator. Significant events make better reference points than dates (the Depression, World War II, etc.).

7. Allow people to express feelings and emotions. Don't worry if a person cries; expressing emotions is a healthy part of reminiscence. (Kahana and Pilling caution against trying to play psychiatrist.)

8. To help a person's memory, ask questions about specific people or events in a person's life. People often reveal a lot about themselves when asked about their siblings, parents, or grandparents.

9. Remember that events may not be entirely factual. In reminiscing, we give dramatic shape to our experiences.

10. Ask questions that you know the person is able to answer. Questions that draw blanks can be embarrassing and should be recast. Ask easy questions that anyone living during that time could answer.

11. Don't push if a person's memory fails. Go on to another question.

12. Respond in nonjudgmental ways. Accept the other person's perspective with tolerance.[34]

To these helpful suggestions I will add a few of my own based on my own experience interviewing elders about their memories of school. Keep questions very concrete. When I asked "When was school like when you were young?" I got responses like "I don't remember much," or "OK." When I made my questions more specific, such as "What books did you read in school?" "What did your elementary school building look like?" and "What games did you play before or after school?" I got much better, more specific information. Some elders have trouble leaving one subject for another. One woman I interviewed kept returning to the subject of her sister no matter what question I asked. A more effective tactic, I discovered, is to tie your questions to the topic the person seems stuck on. When I asked the woman about her memories of her sister at school, she was able to shift gears for a short time. Be prepared for fascinating information to come up unexpectedly. I found that my best responses did not always match my questions but were extremely interesting. When asked about favorite school games, one person told a story of a school fire that killed several children because the school doors opened inward so the children became trapped. "And that is why," she said, "school doors always have to open outward." Keep an open mind, and let the interview take interesting turns.

Interviewers should be aware of cultural differences in speech and responding styles. They should know what behavior is respectful in the elder's culture and how people are taught to answer strangers' questions. In some cultures (and families and regions), it is considered rude or presumptuous to talk at length about one's life. An awareness of these cultural styles will help ensure a good interview with someone from another culture. (More tips on interviewing are in Chapter 7.)

My home was right next door to the school, and when I was three years old, I ran away and went to school. I used to sit on the teacher's lap and he gave me a big bunch of keys. If a student was going to sleep or something, he'd throw that bunch of keys at them. He never hit anyone, but he made a big noise. I used to laugh.

—Wealthy Hillier[35]

I lived in a big city. We had nine grades in our school: a separate room for each grade. St. Martins was a brick building up on a hill, and it was a Catholic school, with a nun in each room. I remember my teacher, Sister Mary Genevieve; she was very kind. Every Friday we were taught sewing, crocheting, knitting and any fancy work. The boys learned manual training—like building and that. Every child had a wooden desk, not the kind that open up, just flat. We used slates to write on. If you were using your left hand to write with you got your fingers spanked. They used a yardstick.

We didn't wear uniforms, but real calico dresses with aprons on them. We had to keep our dresses clean for the whole week.

—Elizabeth Morrissey[36]

When we used to go to school, they had prayer in school. They don't have it today. . . . There was more discipline. You got a licking on the hand with a big, heavy ruler. If we told about getting a licking at school, we got one at home. Everybody knew about it because everyone went and told your folks, too. Sometimes if you misbehaved you'd be set in front of the class with a book on your head for a half hour. The parents would uphold the teachers so there was nothing for you to do but behave.

We always had declaration for the flag. We always had a morning exercise. The teacher would read a story to us for ten or fifteen minutes following the prayer and the salute to the flag. Sometimes we would recite or we would sing from our songbook, *Knapsack*—songs like "Twenty Froggies Went to School," "Tramp, Tramp, Tramp," "One Little, Two Little, Three Little Indians," "Rally Round the Flag Boys," "My Old Kentucky Home," "John Brown's Body," "The Bear Went Over the Mountain," and "Good Night, Ladies."

The book that we had in each grade was always the same. There was usually the Baldwin's readers straight on through school. There was one for each grade. Now they change the books every year. When there's large families and they change the book so much and so often, you can't hand that book down to one younger than yourself. They had less people in the classes so you could learn better, too.

—Bessie Waldo, Carol Collins,
Thelma Norris, Florence Cleveland[37]

Additional helpful hints on how to conduct interviews and collect oral history are included in *Reaching Out: School-based Community Service Programs* by the National Crime Prevention Council,[38] the ERIC publication *You and Aunt Arie: A Guide to Cultural Journalism Based on "Foxfire" and Its Descendants* by Pamela Wood,[39] *Oral History in the Classroom*, published by Social Studies School Service,[40] and Van Hastings Garner's *Oral History: A New Experience in Learning*, published by Pflaum/Standard.[41] Peter Stillman's *Families Writing* has some excellent suggestions for interviewing someone in your family.[42]

Other community members familiar with age and aging are also good candidates for interviews when they cannot speak to a class. Questions for interviews might include physical facts about aging: What happens to the body? What is osteoporosis? A stroke? Hardening of the arteries? Why do most old people wear glasses? Why do people lose their hair? How does/can aging affect mental processes, such as short- and long-term memory, personality, or emotions? What is senility? Alzheimer's disease? Does aging affect sexuality? What aspects of aging are hereditary? How does aging affect communication abilities, such as speaking and hearing? How do people's interests change with aging? Does aging affect creativity or the ability to learn?

A pre-test to determine how much students know about aging is a good starting point for developing a list of interview or research questions. Interviewers should gear their questions to the expertise of the person being interviewed and arrange them in a meaningful sequence (for example, moving from a definition of Alzheimer's and it's physiological effects to the effects on the patient's family, and finally, to the prospects for future cures). Sometimes opening the interview with a statement about the interviewer's goal ("I'm here to find out about what happens to a body as it gets old") is an effective way to initiate talk.

Some people prefer to talk freely and at length on the larger subject rather than answer a number of more detailed questions. But the interviewer should have all his or her questions written down as a reminder, in case the person does not touch on all the information. The length of an interview is important. Students should not wear out their welcome, even if all their questions have not been answered; better that they schedule another interview later. To record information during the interview, students can use tape recorders (and should practice using them ahead of time) or take notes. (I don't recommend note-taking when interviewing very old people or with people who may feel ill at ease during an interview because it interferes with your ability to listen carefully and use eye contact to put people at ease. Listening carefully is a cultivated skill—one that can and should be practiced before any interview takes place. Also, some people tend to speak very quickly, and the note-taking can be too difficult.)

As I said before, writing is a way to remember, shape, and solidify experience. Immediately after an interview the interviewer should write in a journal or dictate into a tape recorder his or her first reactions. These first impressions are important and may easily fade from memory if not noted soon after the interview session. Later, the interviewer may play back any tapes or look at notes taken during the interview (if the interview was a lengthy or complex one), and organize the information. The material gained from an interview can be organized in several ways. Younger students can make lists of what they learned about the subject that they did not know before, beginning with the most important facts and ending with the least important. They can present their information in question and answer form listing answers beneath each question. Students should be encouraged to write information in their own words and use quotations sparingly and selectively. Another method appropriate for children is to summarize what they learned in a letter to a friend. Older students are able to report their findings more formally as reports or articles, brochures, and more extensive narratives. (Chapter 6, on publishing, includes numerous ideas for presenting information gleaned from interviews.)

By this stage in their investigation, students should be well informed about their subject. They won't be experts, but they should know much more than when they embarked upon their explorations. Their expectations, attitudes, and views may have changed; they should feel comfortable with their topic. Now, they are ready to take their research even farther.

Notes

1. Houghton, Frances, Bertha Gibbons, and Bertha White, "Living Alone Poem." *The Life-Writing Review*, Number 1 (1978). Michigan State University Department of English, p. 1.

2. Cunningham, Imogen. *After Ninety.* (Seattle: University of Washington Press, 1977).

3. Forrai, Maria S. *A Look at Old Age.* (Minneapolis: Lerner, 1976).

4. Raynor, Dorka. *Grandparents Around the World.* (Chicago: Albert Whitman, 1977).

5. Alvin, Virginia, and Glenn Silverstein. *Aging.* (New York: Watts, 1979).

6. Sobol, Harriet Langsam. *Grandpa: A Young Man Grown Old*. (New York: Coward, McCann and Geohegan, 1980).

7. Olson, Arielle North. Illustrated by Lydia Dabcovich. *Hurry Home Grandma*. (New York: Dutton, 1984).

8. Mayer, Mercer. *Just Grandpa and Me*. (New York: Golden Press, 1985).

9. Ackerman, Karen. Illustrated by Stephen Gammell. *Song and Dance Man*. (New York: Knopf, 1988).

10. Mazer, Norma Fox. *After the Rain*. (New York: Morrow, 1987).

11. Brancato, Robin. *Sweet Bells, Jangled Out of Tune*. (New York: Scholastic, 1982).

12. Levin, Betty. *The Trouble with Gramary*. (New York: Greenwillow Books, 1988).

13. Guthrie, Donna. Illustrated by Katy Keck Arnsteen. *Grandpa Doesn't Know It's Me*. (New York: Human Sciences Press, 1986).

14. Tolan, Stephanie. *Grandpa — and Me*. (New York: Charles Scribner's Sons, 1978).

15. L'Engle, Madeleine. *Ring of Endless Light*. (New York: Dell, 1986).

16. Mosel, Arlene. Illustrated by Blair Lent. *The Funny Little Woman*. (New York: E. P. Dutton, 1972).

17. Streich, Corrine, comp. Illustrated by Lilian Hoban. *Grandparents' Houses: Poems About Grandparents*. (New York: Greenwillow, 1984).

18. Schulman, L. M., ed. *Autumn Light: Illuminations of Age*. (New York: Thomas Y. Crowell, 1978).

19. Martz, Sandra, ed. *When I Am an Old Woman I Shall Wear Purple*. (Manhattan Beach, CA: Papier-Mache Press, 1987).

20. Zeidenstein, Sondra, ed. *A Wider Giving: Women Writing After a Long Silence*. (Goshen, CT: Chicory Blue Press, 1988).

21. *Recollections*, published by the Brock House Writers of Vancouver, B.C., Canada, is available from Dr. Syd Butler, The University of British Columbia, Faculty of Education, 2125 Main Mall, Vancouver, B.C., Canada V6T 1Z5.

22. *Everybody's Story* is available from COMPAS, 308 Landmark Center, 75 W. 5th St., St. Paul, MN 55102.

23. *NIMROD*: "Old People: A Season of the Mind," Vol. 20, No. 2 (Spring/Summer, 1976), is available from NIMROD, Arts and Humanities Council of Tulsa, 2210 South Main, Tulsa, OK 74114–1190.

24. Koch, Kenneth. *I Never Told Anybody: Teaching Poetry Writing in a Nursing Home*. (New York: Vintage Books, 1978).

25. Blythe, Ronald, ed. *A View in Winter* (New York: Penguin, 1980).

26. Koontz, Tom, and Thom Tammaro, eds. *The View from the Top of the Mountain: Poems After Sixty*. (Daleville, IN: The Barnwood Press Co-operative, 1981).

27. Pratt, Francis. *Teaching About Aging.* (Boulder, CO: ERIC Clearinghouse for Social Studies/Social Science Education and Social Science Education Consortium, Inc., 1977), p. 62.

28. *Aging* (August/September, 1984).

29. Trojan, Judith. "Film Portraits of Aging Men." *Media and Methods* (February, 1980), pp. 20−21, 42−44.

30. _____, p. 43.

31. Farber, Norma. Illustrated by Trina Schart Hyman. *How Does It Feel to Be Old?* (New York: Dutton, 1979).

32. Pratt, p. 3.

33. Berkson, Jerrold, and Shirley A. Griggs. "An Intergenerational Program at a Middle School." *The School Counselor* (November 1986), pp. 140−142.

34. Stocker, Carol. "The Elderly Are Living History Books," *Detroit Free Press.* (May 31, 1977) pp. 1C, 4C.

35. Scott, Lynn, ed. *The Memory Album.* (East Lansing, MI: Michigan State University Department of English, 1979), p. 10.

36. Scott, p. 11.

37. Zahorchak, Kaye, and Francine Danis, eds. *The Memory Book.* (East Lansing, MI: Michigan State University Department of English, 1978), pp. 52−53.

38. *Reaching Out: School-based Community Service Programs* by the National Crime Prevention Council, 733 15th Street, NW, Suite 540, Washington, D.C. 10005.

39. Wood, Pamela. *You and Aunt Arie: A Guide to Cultural Journalism Based on "Foxfire" and Its Descendants* (Washington, DC: Institutional Development and Economic Affairs Service, 1975). Available from ERIC: ED 120 090.

40. *Oral History in the Classroom.* Social Studies School Service, 10,000 Culver Blvd., Culver City, CA 90230.

41. Garner, Van Hastings. *Oral History: A New Experience in Learning.* Pflaum/Standard, 38 W. 5th St., Dayton, OH 45402.

42. Stillman, Peter. *Families Writing.* (Cincinnati, OH: Writer's Digest Books, 1989).

Chapter Five

Digging Deeper
Projects to Challenge Assumptions

100 Years Old — This Is Your Life

If I were a hundred years old, I would have 11 grand-children and 13 great ones. I would go to the park once a day and feed the pigeons. I would not be crabby, and I would be generous. I would read a lot and own a ranch with 25 horses and 35 colts. I wouldn't act old, and I would act young. I would only have 10 wrinkles. I would live in California where Disneyland is and go there once a day, and after that I would go surfing.

—Marjory Whitaker, grade 2

As children learn about a part of their community they may discover that things are not as they should be. Their earlier notions of a group of people, a place, or an event may turn out to be full of inaccuracies and misconceptions. They may learn that much popular knowledge is myth and has little bearing on the subject at all. When they make these discoveries, students often want to take action, to correct what they see as discrepancies between the realities and the myths. For examples: A class learns that victims of cerebral palsy can think and feel as others do although many people treat them as if they were retarded; they decide to do what they can to change community awareness. A group of students learn that gyppo logging (free-lance logging by individuals who own their operation), once a viable profession in their area, is becoming obsolete; they decide to preserve the lore and traditions of that profession so that its history will not be lost. Another group of students studying a local fire department becomes interested in the department's history and its change from a volunteer to a professional unit; they set out to investigate the causes of the change. Learning should create the desire to learn; discovering the existence of social problems should lead to a search for solutions. At this phase of their community study, students want to dig deeper. They are ready to narrow their concerns and undertake larger projects, on their own, in groups, or as a class. This is the time when teachers should have a number of suggestions at hand, when young people's enthusiasm is high, so that when students are ready to embark on additional research and more ambitious activities, they are ready with the names of people to interview, material to read, speakers to invite, and films to watch.

The projects that students take on will depend on what they are studying and what they have learned. A class studying old age and aging could, as a result of their earlier research, identify several topics or focal issues, each of which could be explored using a variety of language arts activities. Here are five such topics:

1. Young people are not sympathetic to the physical and emotional problems of old age.

2. Contrary to the myths about old age, many elders live and have lived rich, productive, and interesting lives.

3. Creativity and the ability to learn don't decline with old age, as is popularly believed.

4. Some aspects of the community don't take into consideration the needs of elders.

5. Our culture contains too many negative stereotypes of old people.

Each of these five discoveries, individually or together, can give rise to a range of projects and activities centered on reading, writing, listening, and speaking that will engage students with old people more deeply, either in the classroom or by working with elders outside the classroom. Many of the projects will lead to the kinds of class or individual publications (in a variety of forms) described in the next chapter.

Discovery 1: Young people are not sympathetic to the physical and emotional problems of old age.

Nor are we empathetic as a culture. When I walk through a crowded store in a hurry and see an elder moving with a walker, one slow step at a time, I am grateful for my relative youth and good health. My first impulse is to feel sorry for the person and wonder how in the world I will be able to endure moving so slowly when I am very old (even though I know I will probably be in less of a hurry). A college student wrote in response to "The old man . . ." the following thoughts that I think express the feelings of many younger people: "The old man who drove his olive-green Plymouth Valiant drove me nuts as he plodded along at 30 M.P.H. in a 45 M.P.H. zone. I nearly ripped my hair out as I contemplated the possibilities, which were now dwindling, of getting to work on time. Yet as I looked at the back of his head, with a straw cowboy hat, I could picture my fiancee's patient old father."

There are many ways students can be helped to understand the physical realities of old age — understand beyond simply knowing what they are. Simulations, in which class members use the accoutrements of old age and put themselves in situations that are common among the aging, can increase sympathy and empathy. Here are several simulations, most of which can be done right in the classroom:

1. Bring to class several kinds of walking aids. Allow people to practice using each. For an extended project, a student can use the walker all day, even during recess and lunch.

2. Bring in a wheelchair. Have students try to get around the class, the school, the school grounds in order to feel the difficulties of simple things like getting over curbs, door sills, around corners, through narrow doors, up and down slopes.

3. Ask the students to write and draw with the hand they are not accustomed to writing with for a day, to more fully understand what it is like to have arthritis. They should attempt to complete all their regular assignments this way throughout the day; no writing, drawing, or any "handed" activity should be done with the stronger hand. This simulation can be extended as homework so that the student experiences the problems of awkwardness in daily routines such as brushing teeth, combing hair, eating, making a bed, playing video games.

4. To help students experience diminished hearing, speak very quietly. Francis Pratt suggests tape recording the instructions for an important assignment at a very low volume so that they are hard to hear.[1] Children's stories or other material can be recorded and played in the same fashion.

5. Cataracts or glaucoma affect many elders. Young people can sense how those conditions affect vision by wearing glasses with non-prescription lenses that have been smeared with cleansing cream or other ointment. Pratt also suggests duplicating the instructions for an assignment at a very light copier setting.[2] (I don't recommend any of these activities be carried out for an

extended period of time or in nonsupervised settings; they could cause eyestrain or other injury.)

After a simulation, students should record their experiences in writing and talk about them. What was the experience like? Describe your experience using a list of images or metaphors. What was the most difficult task encountered? What was the most frustrating thing about it? Students who elect to do simulations for a long period of time should be encouraged to keep journals (perhaps written with the weak hand) and record reactions several times during the day. And, they can do longer writing activities: an extended narrative of the experience, an essay about the physical condition, a story about a person who has the physical impairment, a play, or a poem.

My great-grandfather, in a letter to his family about being old, wrote that a person is old when he "knows more names on tombstones than in the phone book." One of the emotional/psychological problems that can accompany aging is depression and low self-esteem caused by the loss of friends, diminished physical abilities, and the absence of one's familiar work.[3] Young people who are active all day and have many friends cannot easily sympathize with the feelings some elders have. But they can profit from imagining some of these conditions translated to their immediate circumstances and writing about them. Imagine going through a day without participating in *any* activity that requires exertion: no running, no bike riding, no swinging, no shooting baskets, no driving, no climbing. Students of any age can keep records of every action in a given day that requires active movement; later, they can write about a make-believe day in which they do nothing but watch. (Some students might volunteer to try curtailing all physically strenuous activity for a day to see what it is like.) Similarly, they can imagine what it would be like to be suddenly cut off from a close friend. Although they cannot simulate the death of a spouse or close companion, students can think about the importance of their friends and what their lives would be like if their best friend was to move away unexpectedly. They can keep track of the number of hours they spend during any week with a particular friend talking, playing, or working, and describe the difference in their lives that friend's absence would make.

Writing activities can encourage empathy as well as help students see their old ages as potentially productive. Projective writing encourages students to imagine their lives in the future and to see the world from the perspective of an elder character. Here are some topics:

- Imagine that you are 80. Where do you live? What do you do?

Who are your friends? How is your health? What do you look like, physically? What do you think about? How do you entertain yourself? Write a detailed description of one day in your life, or a complete personal profile of yourself at 80.

- Design and describe a house you would like to live in when you are 80. Consider your physical condition and needs, as well as your interests. Describe what kind of furniture you will have, what the exterior will look like, what pictures and decorations will be on the wall, etc. Here is the kind of house a twelfth-grader wants:

> At eighty I will want a house that is small and comfortably designed. The carpeting should be dark and comfortable to step on, the walls a soft color that will be easy on my eyes, light blues, soft tan or browns, calm white that does not stand out but makes the house seem mellow. No staircases in a house for the old. My house will be only one level and everything should be easy to get to.
>
> — Shelly Jay

- Design and describe some clothes that you might wear when you are 80. Be realistic about how you will look. (Lots of tiny buttons and hard-to-reach zippers are out.)
- Plan and describe a trip that you will take when you are 70. Consider your physical condition as well as your interests when you plan your itinerary.
- Imagine that you are 90 looking back on your life. What events in your life take on the most significance? Write an autobiography from your elder perspective. (You will have to invent your life from now until then.)
- Describe in detail at least four projects (not vacations or trips) you would like to undertake after you retire. These should be ambitious projects that involve learning things you don't know now. Make up a plan for how you will accomplish them — steps you need to take, a work schedule, etc. Explain why you want to do these.
- Write a portrait of yourself as a grandmother or grandfather. What kind of relationship will you have with your grandchildren?
- Visit a graveyard and read the headstones. Select someone who interests you. Imagine who the person was, what kind of life he or she had (you might get some clues about family from surrounding graves). Imagine that you are that person, and write about your life. What were its high points? Low points? Achievements? What kind of old age did the person have?

- Select an elder character in literature or film who interests you, who you like and admire. From his or her perspective, do any of the activities described above: plan a trip, a project, describe your house, keep a diary. Imagine the character as young. What was he/she like?

- Write a series of diary entries (at least a week's worth) as if you were 80. (Write with the wrong hand if you want.)

Diary of Rachel Lambacher
by Rachel Lambacher, grade 8

August 17, 2056

Today was my birthday. I turned 80. I guess I'm on my last stretch of life. I feel a little bit scared knowing that I'm not going to be around too much longer, but I understand things don't live forever.

Mark was put in the hospital today. He had a heart attack. The doctors say it's going to be hard to keep him alive. Mark and I have been married for 58 years. I feel scared for Mark too! I will always love him.

My son is coming up tomorrow to see Mark. The whole family is pulling for him. I just hope he gets better, even if its just for a little while.

August 18, 2056

My son got here today at 2:30. We went to see his father. Of course he's upset, but he's handling it pretty well. We are both going through a lot of heartache.

The doctors say Mark isn't getting any better. There is about a 10% chance that he will pull through. I'm praying for that 10% chance.

August 19, 2056

Today at 10:47 am, my husband died. I cried a lot. The doctors did everything they could and I appreciate that. They were very good to me and Mark.

We called the family and told them of the tragedy. His funeral will be held 3 days from now. That's our anniversary. I wanted it then, it would be a special day.

August 20, 2056

My son Jonathan is going to stay with me for a couple more days till the funeral.

Everybody has given me a lot of support, it has helped me a great deal. Tom and Mary from next door, baked me a cake for Mark's death. That was very nice of them.

August 21, 2056

I started preparing for the funeral now. I'm inviting the family up and friends too.

A lot of people loved Mark, he was easy to get along with and he could always make people laugh. He had a very unique communication with people. He was very special.

He's going to be buried in the cemetery on Mountain Ridge Park, tomorrow at 2:00. I'm excited seeing the family, but not really this way.

August 22, 2056

The funeral went pretty well today. I cried a lot and the family and friends did today too. It was a good feeling seeing how loved Mark was. Everyone will miss him.

When I got home, there was a surprise family reunion at my house. We talked about old times and the future and I had loads of fun. It felt good to be with my family again.

August 23, 2056

I made sure today that when it's my turn to leave, that my grave is right next to Mark's, that way we can be together forever.

The house seems so empty without Mark. I'm already very lonely.

The family went home today. I miss them too.

I don't know what to do with my life now. Jonathon wants me to go to an old folks home. I will not. I'm still ok, just lonely. It does seem hard to move around these days, but not bad enough when I need to go to a place where they treat you like babies. I am not a baby as you can see.

Gee, I wonder what I'm going to do tomorrow. Maybe me and May will go out to lunch tomorrow. That would be nice.

While we can never know exactly what it is like to be old until we are old, we can be more sensitive to our older population — their diverse interests, needs, concerns. Young people who can enjoy or even understand being old in their imaginations have less to fear from aging. By increasing their awareness and sensitivity, they become more tolerant not only of elders but of themselves.

Autobiography

Well, as I look back on my life I feel that I have fulfilled many of my dreams, and I feel very satisfied. I even have accomplished many things I had never even thought of!

When I was about 2 years old my parents got divorced. My grandmother told of what I used to say to her while I was going through all of it. I guess it was a pretty traumatic experience for me then, but as I grew up I was happy and accepted it as a fact. Besides, because of it I ended up with a pretty terrific stepfather, Stan, and a stepbrother, Tran.

I had a pretty rough time in elementary school. I wasn't really sure where I fit in, but overall it was all right. When I went to Jr. High I felt much better. Unlike a lot of people it was a great change for my life! My mom was a counselor, and Stan worked giving speeches all over Idaho for the Martin Peace Institute. Both of them were great at supporting me. We always got along pretty wonderfully! My dad was a great guy but I never felt like I knew him very well until I visited him after college.

When I was in 8th grade my sister moved away to college. Afterwards I realized how much I appreciated her and really missed her. ...

—Julie Richman, grade 8

Discovery 2: Contrary to the myths about old age, many elders live and have lived rich, productive, and interesting lives.

One of the wonderful results of Foxfire and other similar projects is that they have focused attention on the fact that a community's elder population is a rich resource. The knowledge and skills of elder artisans can be preserved for future generations if we take the time to collect and record their stories. Every community has elders who are experts at something—quilting, lace-making, boat-building—and who know the community's history. Their crafts and their tales are a part of our culture's past, and we should treasure them. A host of projects for students, particularly older students, center on highlighting the special lore and interesting lives of the community's senior residents.

Biographies and Autobiographies

I've already written up my life. I decided when I retired that I would write up my life. I took it to where my daughters could take over and write it. I typed it up and it's about that thick.

—Marjory Waterman,
Burcham Hills Retirement Center,
East Lansing, Michigan.[4]

Students can become biographers and work with interested elders on recording and writing life histories. The purpose of this project is to record for the elder (and perhaps his or her family) important personal events and significant memories. No more than two students should work with one elder so that the elder and young person can become acquainted and feel comfortable with each other (too many students can be overpowering). If the student already knows the elder, better yet; grandparents and great grandparents make wonderful subjects for biographies. To create a good biography or to help an elder write his or her autobiography, the student should spend time with the elder getting acquainted. He or she should visit the elder in the elder's residence, talk, conduct interviews, and define the scope of the work. (This project may be done in more or less depth, with a biography or autobiography coming out of several interviews, or out of several months of visits.) Initial interviews should center on the biography project itself—what the elder would like to record, what the student is interested in learning. Once the scope and framework of the project is defined, the student can structure successive interviews focused on particular events or topics. A number of books can help biographers get ideas for interview topics and strategies: Peter Stillman's *Families Writings*,[5] Frank P. Thomas's *How to Write the Story of Your Life*,[6] and William Fletcher's *Recording Your Family History*[7] are three. Interviews may be supplemented with other activities that can yield important biographical information: looking at a photo album together, talking about the pictures and objects in a person's residence, looking at books or magazines that were published when the person was young, listening to the person's favorite music. A student doing an extensive biography may even want to participate in some activities with the elder—attend a concert, church, play, film, go on a picnic, etc. Seeing how a person spends time can help the biographer become more sensitive to his or her subject. (In the next chapter, I describe several specific kinds of biographies young people can write.)

> I originated in Mt. Pleasant, Iowa in 1901. Then, we went to Kansas. We had a farm there. There are all sorts of things about that to write down. I remember we had to run to the outhouse, when the snow was clear up over our heads, and we used a Sears and Roebuck catalogue for toilet paper. Once we had quite a storm. It snowed for five days, and we couldn't get out for a week. I got up one morning and wanted to go to the toilet, and a calf was sitting on it. I tried to push it off, but it wouldn't get off!
>
> My father worked for the railroad, and they put him in Denver, so the whole family moved there. My father made a train, and he had horses that pulled the train to get it started, then they put the horses on the train.
>
> I remember my father used to play for the old country dances. He'd sit in the pantry and play the old fiddle. He played classical music too.
>
> Quite awhile ago, I hitchhiked through to Michigan from Denver. I don't like to hitchhike, it's too tiresome.
>
> —Olive Dodds[8]

Oral History

The Model T sold for about $250, and then they jumped to about $300. One day Ford would make Model Ts and the next day he'd

make a different car. I was down there and able to see them being
built. When he upped the wages from $3.50 to $5.00 a day, he
upped the price of each car $200. He had about 200 men working
for him at that time with a day shift and night shift.

—Walter Hale[9]

The purpose of biography is to record events significant to the
subject; the focus of oral history is on the events themselves and
the culture surrounding them. In oral history projects, students
interview one or more elders in order to retrieve and record information about a time period, a particular craft or skill, an historical
event, an institution. Types of oral histories vary:

1. Interview several elders about a significant historical event in
   the community or nation: a natural disaster (earthquake, drought,
   fire, blizzard), the construction of an important building or
   road, a war or the day a war ended, the closing or opening of an
   important factory or town industry, etc.

2. Collect from elders in the community recollections about important life events, celebrations, or inventions: school days,
   coming to America, getting married, getting along with sisters
   and brothers, the Fourth of July, shopping, religious holidays,
   funerals, courtship customs, going camping, toys, the introduction of television or automobiles, traveling on trains.

3. Interview elders about crafts, skills, or hobbies that they know
   or do well. The interviews might focus on anything from how
   to turn an oil drum into a rhythm instrument, to a doll collection.

4. Interview someone (or several people) in the community who
   knows the community's history better than anyone in order
   to prepare a biography of the area. The interviewer should
   begin with a set of topics, such as (if the community is recent)
   the first settlers, early buildings, the first industries, education,
   churches, most colorful characters, important stages in growth.
   Although their emphasis is on history and not so much on
   the elders personally, oral history projects strengthen students'
   awareness of elders' lives as interesting and productive.

As with any interview, collecting oral history or biographical
information requires that the students learn in advance of their
interviews how to use a tape recorder, and possibly a video camera
and still camera. Students who don't know how to use their equipment can miss or botch valuable opportunities. Interviews cannot
always be rescheduled, and people don't always tell the same stories
twice. While photographs make excellent supplements to written
material, students should be aware that some people feel uncom-

fortable being photographed and, as with the tape recorder, they should obtain permission before shooting pictures. A natural culmination of these projects is the publication of how-to books, history and memory books described in the next chapter. (Several books helpful for students wishing to collect oral history are mentioned in Chapter 4.)

Life Review, Life-Writing, and Storytelling

We all enjoy telling stories about ourselves. As we remember events in our past, we reshape and renew our lives. The process of sharing those memories with interested listeners helps to give our pasts meaning and value.

We're Never Too Old to Remember

I remember the first airplane I saw. I called my father
    to come out and look. It was circling the Capitol.
I remember the first phonograph we heard. We gathered
    for hours listening to it.
I remember the first Ford Car. It was black with red
    wooden spokes. A man drove to Luther from Detroit
    so we could see it.
I remember the first radio, in the early 20s. It was a crystal set.
You had to have earphones and only one person at a time could
    listen. I heard them announcing Station WKAR.
I remember the first ferris wheel, sometime before 1910. It
was a small one, and it was cranked by hand. It was fun for
    us, but the poor man!
I remember the first airship I saw. It was at the County Fair in
    Charlotte.
I remember the first time I saw ice cream cones being made. They
were like waffles wrapped into a cone. You had to wait till they
were cold till you filled them with ice cream. I didn't
    buy one, but I thought I could make one.
I remember a song we sang, "Don't Forget to Remember."
I remember a saying, "If you don't remember the past, you can't
    judge the future."

          —by Carol Collins, Frances Sevy, Bessie Waldo,
          Thelma Norris and Florence Cleveland[10]

Life review, as identified and defined by Robert N. Butler, is a natural, functional phenomenon of aging. It is a process in which the aging person, or any person facing the end of life, reconsiders and re-evaluates past experiences. Life review may occur during dreams, in silent recollection, or in out-loud reminiscence. According to Butler, the tendency of an elder to reflect on unresolved conflicts, troublesome relationships, or key experiences repeatedly is not, as many believe, a sign of senility. Rather, it serves a healthy, positive purpose by allowing the person to come to terms with his or her life and to reintegrate the past with the present. It enables people to think about the remainder of their lives in fresh ways and can lead to renewed feelings of self-worth, friendships, and closer kinship with family and/or community.[11]

In 1978, Dr. Linda Wagner and I, with the help of students and staff in the Michigan State University English Department and funds from the Michigan Councils for the Humanities and Arts, began a project of writing workshops for elders based on Butler's theory that reminiscence about one's past was functional and therapeutic. Dr. Wagner called the project "Life-Writing," although the participants, most of whom were very old, did little actual writing. Instead, each group of elder volunteers met weekly for storytelling, reminiscence, and to share memories about common subjects. Each workshop was run by a leader whose job it was to introduce topics, encourage responses, tape record sessions, transcribe people's stories, and select passages for inclusion in our project newsletter, *The Life-Writing Review*. The elders who participated loved the project, although at first some were reluctant to speak. As groups became comfortable, they tried other kinds of oral composing— stories and poetry. The project yielded a great deal of writing (some appears in this book) and tape recordings of regional history, which we donated to the university's Voice Library. High school students who are interested and willing to contribute the time and effort could initiate a similar project.

The hardest part of a life-writing project is getting it going. Many elders don't feel as though their lives are interesting to anyone else. When trying to drum up business for our workshops, we heard again and again, "I don't have any good stories to tell." (Our culture's devaluation of our elders has contributed to this attitude.) Yet we discovered that these same people had fascinating stories. Because writing and storytelling are not immediately attractive to many people, we relied heavily on the assistance of nursing home and care center staff to help us form our groups.

Once a group is established (groups should not be too large— eight is a good number) and introductions have been made (people should introduce themselves and wear name tags so everyone gets to know everyone else quickly) the leader's job is to collect and bring in a number of story starters, interesting topics to get people talking. The ideas suggested by Kenneth Koch in *I Never Told Anybody: Teaching Poetry in a Nursing Home* (cited in Chapter 4) work well, as do readings from published autobiographies and old photographs. The leader should maintain an informal atmosphere, let the talk wander. While the purpose is to share recollections, the leader should not stifle open discussion. If a session is on the Depression and the talk strays to marriage customs, fine. Keeping the sessions congenial and comfortable is more important than sticking to a topic. A good group leader will be directive but non-obtrusive, and always friendly and receptive, willing to share examples and illustrations from his or her own life. It is very important that the leader be patient and not patronize the elder group members. Also, individual attention spans can vary widely. Young people who have not worked or had extensive contact with older people should be aware that a participant may pay no attention or even fall asleep, and not take this personally. Leaders should also speak clearly for participants who have trouble hearing.

We all know what a thrill it can be to see our writing published. Printing all or parts of people's stories is an important part of a life-writing workshop. In our workshops the participants looked forward each month to seeing some of their narrative in print. Transcribing, deciding what to print and how to print it is another task of the leader. By listening to the audio tapes, the leader (alone or with a group of other workshop leaders) can collect sufficient material — at least a sentence or two from each person — to transcribe on two or three typed pages (double-spaced in very large type, for easy reading) in the form of paragraphs or poems. The leader should be sure to read the writing aloud when the group meets next; the stories will be certain to trigger new thoughts, narratives. Life-writing groups that meet regularly generally discover common interests that make excellent topics for other group publications: memory books, cook-books, how-to books, and others described in the next chapter.

Biographies, oral histories, and life-review workshops are long-term projects that require a great deal of preparation, enthusiasm, commitment, and some skill. Before embarking on any of these projects, students should be well acquainted with the processes of aging and old people. They should have read books, watched films, met and talked to many elders. These projects will reinforce what they have already come to learn, that elders are not only interesting but highly individual.

Famous elders

By doing a bit of research, students can discover the accomplishments of older people — either around the world or in their own communities. Occasionally, newspapers, magazines (particularly magazines focused on concerns of elders), and television feature the work of an aged artist, musician, writer, athlete, or politician. Students can collect information for a who's who of famous older public figures — a directory featuring brief biographies and descriptions of their accomplishments, awards, showings, etc.. Or, students might investigate the accomplishments of elders in their own communities by talking to community leaders, ministers and rabbis, nursing home staffs, people in charge of activities for community elders, doctors, and even friends. From this research, students can compile biographies, profile articles for a school or local newspaper, or a community who's who. Another activity that can be fun for classes of all ages is to investigate the accomplishments of people's own grandparents and ancestors. In this activity, each student talks to as many people in the family as possible about his or her grandparents, great-grandparents, or other older relatives. They ask the family members about any adventures, awards, interesting projects, productions, or other things the elder family members have done in their old age. If possible, they interviews the elders, too. Students should be encouraged to consider small personal accomplishments as significant: a grandmother's trip, a grandfather's homemade root beer, a great-aunt's hand-knit sweater, the chair a step-grandparent built, a picture Great-grandmother painted.

In a variation of this activity, each student chooses one well-known elder to become an expert on and investigate that individual's life and works — particularly later works. Legislators, artists, actors, musicians, writers, filmmakers, athletes, doctors, scientists, and others whose contributions continued well into later life make excellent subjects.

Discovery 3: Creativity and intelligence do not decline with old age, as is popularly believed.

In addition to showing students that elders can and do live interesting, active lives, these activities underscore the fact that artistic skills do not decline as one ages. In fact, some people's creative power increases. Likewise, intelligence is not necessarily affected by aging. While studies have shown that age does tend to diminish short-term memory and the ability to learn and retain new information, intellectual ability, if kept active, will not decrease.[12] In the last several years, a number of travel/study programs for seniors, like Elderhostel, have become highly popular. But many older people do not have the physical ability, the money, or the opportunity to participate, or to otherwise keep their minds active. People whose eyesight is very poor, whose speaking ability has been impaired by a stroke, who are bedridden, or whose education has been limited are unable or less able to take advantage of educational programs.

Some elders live in environments that provide little stimulation despite the efforts of care centers to provide opportunities for mental as well as physical exercise. Here are some projects for older students that will draw on elders' creative and intellectual abilities.

Editing

Every community has elders who, like Ralph M. Zeigler, like to write. For some, writing is a physically difficult task. A young person might assist an older person who wants to write a book of poems, a novel, a cookbook, a book of family history, or, like Marjory Waterman, an autobiography. I am always encouraging my students to undertake a project such as this with their grandparents because it gives the young person valuable insights into the family and its history, helps the young and old person become better acquainted, and can give the older person a sense of accomplishment and pride in his or her life. An elder who is physically able to write might welcome the assistance of a copy editor. A student with good editorial skills can help with spelling, punctuation, usage. Elders unable to write can be aided by a student with a tape recorder who tapes sessions of oral writing and transcribes written copy. Students with access to computers and desktop publishing software can help elders lay out their material and publish it in attractive formats.

Collaborative Writing

Students know that it is so sometimes more fun to write with a friend. Why not with an older friend? Pairing young and old to create an original book or other writing can satisfy the creative urges of both. Creations can be about anything the two want it to be, depending on the age of the student: a realistic story, a book of jokes, a folk tale or made-up fairy tale, an animal story, a fable, a mystery, a script for a puppet show, a letter to an editor, a parody of a well-known author, a rap—the list is endless. (The biography "My Grandfather," in Chapter 6, was written collaboratively by a boy and his grandfather.)

Writing Workshops

Some communities have groups of writers who meet regularly to share their work. A student can enjoy participating in such as group (and sharing his or her writing, of course). If none exists, a student might like to set up and lead one. Kenneth Koch's project of writing workshops in a New York City nursing home (*I Never*

Told Anybody) shows how fruitful these workshops can be. Most of Koch's students, like ours in the life-writing project, were very old and physically unable to write. Many were relatively uneducated and not accustomed to reading and writing as regular leisure activities. Yet Koch was able to help them write oral poetry by suggesting particular forms ("start every line with _____," or another kind of repetition) and topics (a lie, quietness, colors). His students particularly enjoyed collaborative poetry, where each person adds a line. Other good ideas for writing workshops can be found in a number of books about the teaching of writing. Three good sources are Kirby and Liner's *Inside Out: Developmental Strategies for Teaching Writing*, Jacqueline Jackson's *Turn Not Pale, Beloved Snail*, and Peter Stillman's *Writing Your Way*. From Jackson: Write about a time you did something bad or mean on purpose—pranks or tricks you played on people. Write a poem in which each line begins with "Misery is _____." Describe favorite tastes and smells.[13] From Kirby and Liner: Compare a place or thing "then" and "now" (church, school, cooking); this can be done as a poem, with alternate lines beginning "Then, . . ." and "Now, ..." Close your eyes and imagine yourself in a setting described by the leader (a street, a place in the country, etc.), and concentrate on the sights, sounds, smells, and touches. Then write about the place. (I found that asking people to think about a place that is most familiar to them, a place they love, a place they have been to many times, evokes powerful memories and results in some highly imagistic writing.) Write "color prose poems," poems or prose about a color and the feelings it evokes. Write extended answers to "strange questions," such as "Which is sweeter—rain or July?" "Which is crisper—winter or celery?"[14] From Stillman: Write about specific memories, such as a time you were thoughtless or cruel, a friend you no longer have and wish you did, something that once scared you and no longer does, your grandparents. Write morals to go with fables or fables of your own to illustrate a moral. Write about a time when someone tried to teach you a lesson and it didn't work. Write down stories someone in your family told. Write about something that you do or used to do that gives you special satisfaction, like building a fire or baking bread.[15] (His book *Families Writing* contains a wonderful section on writing family stories.)

These ideas can work well with older people because they are concrete and stress memory. They are effective with people who are physically able to write as well as with people who must compose orally. They are not too complex and require little expertise with the mechanical or organizational aspects of the writing process. Topics that don't work are those that are vague or too unstructured, such as "write an essay about a significant event in your life." Also, participants in writing workshops may not be familiar with techniques or terminology of creative writing. In all likelihood, terms like *metaphor* or *characterization* will have little meaning. Writing to them may mean studying grammar or writing formal essays. The best activities are those that require only experience and imagination and a willingness to share them.

The leader should allow the group to determine the direction the group takes. In one group, members may wish to share writing they have done or are currently working on (and the leader should share his or her writing, too). In another, the participants may, like the life-writing groups, wish to publish an anthology or other kind of book. Also as in life-writing groups, the leader's role will depend on the nature of the group. Some groups need more direction, others will run themselves, in which case the leader becomes more of an administrator, making sure materials and refreshments are available, transcribing and photocopying if necessary, and helping with editing and publishing.

> **Poem for Louise**
> **(to wish her a speedy recovery from eye**
> **surgery)**
>
> Louise and I have been together
> ever since the beginning.
> I take her to the table and bring her back.
> I miss her face.
>
> I miss her every morning when she climbs the bus.
>
> I can't help thinking about her—always
> on my mind.
>
> I miss her visor at the table.
>
> I miss her friendly smile and cheery good morning.
> When she talks you can hear her perfectly.
> She's the only voice I can hear.
>
> Your friends all miss you.
>
> We'll kiss you hello as long as we can kiss you goodbye.
>
> > love from your life-writing group.
> >
> > > —the Lansing, Michigan, Daytime Center
> > > for the Elderly[16]

Reading and Reading Groups

Students who are good oral readers might enjoy reading to an elder whose eyesight is poor. The staff of a nursing, convalescent, or retirement home can suggest people who would welcome this service.

Also, some communities have book groups that meet regularly for discussion of a particular work. These programs exist in libraries, seniors' community centers, and residential centers. Junior and senior high school students who enjoy reading might ask to visit such a group and participate, or look into establishing a group where there is need and interest. Leading a reading group involves, in addition to reading the work the group has selected, preparing a list of questions to get the discussion started and some information about the book or author—a bit of biography, historical context, interesting criticism. What a group wants to talk about will depend, naturally, on the group itself—the interests, backgrounds, and experiences of the members. A leader will want to take these into consideration when creating questions; however, discussions often take their own course once they begin.

When preparing questions for discussion, a student leader should remember that the readers are intelligent and interested people and avoid overly simple questions such as "Who was the main character?" Most participants are not literary critics nor are they interested in learning critical theory. Thus the kinds of questions in literature anthologies are generally inappropriate for an adult book group. The best questions are provocative, do not have right or wrong answers, and concern issues in or even controversy surrounding the book. Questions for which there are many, possibly opposing, points of view work very well ("Should the book have ended as it did?" "Was this scene believable?"), as do questions that ask the readers to relate the book to their experiences ("Have any of you ever had a similar experience?" "Could this actually have happened during this time?").

In most book groups the participants determine the reading list. Sometimes the groups choose best-sellers, works from a particular time period, works by one author, a genre such as detective fiction or science fiction, or simply a sampling of each. A teacher and students might interest a group of community elders in forming a reading/discussion group centered on books of interest to children or adolescents: realistic young adult fiction, fairy tales, literature by and about an ethnic group, American literature, children's fiction about families, even a group of novels the high school class is reading. Unlike the book groups that have one or at most two student leaders or participants, this kind of group may include equal numbers of young people and elders. For each meeting, which might take place at a seniors' center or in the school classroom, one student and one elder together can be responsible for discussion topics.

On a smaller scale is a reading pals (like pen pals) program, in which one young and one old person share books they have read. The two may read the same books and meet regularly, in or out of the class, and talk over their reactions; or, every week or month, the two can meet to exchange favorite works and talk about them later. The two might also prepare written responses to share.

Drama Groups

People who enjoy acting or simply viewing drama continue to do so when they are old. But some elders who love drama often have little opportunity if they are housebound or immobile, or limited to the facilities and recreational activities of a residential center. These people, as well as other elders, might welcome the chance to perform, help with productions, or simply view and talk about plays or films with others. Students with dramatic inclinations and experience might find elders in the community who would enjoy putting on a play, producing a puppet show for children, or simply meeting occasionally to do improvisations, pantomime, skits, and other dramatic activities. A group might enjoy getting together regularly to attend (or view on videotape) and later discuss a local theatrical performance. Students can help produce a talent show or theme party in a residential center or nursing home, lead play-reading and discussion groups similar to the book groups described earlier, initiate a screen- or drama-writing workshop, help a group of elders make a videotape, or lead a series of discussions on television programs and issues surrounding television (with "images of aging on television" as the first topic). The number of dramatic projects is unlimited and depends only on the interests of the elder community.

Discovery 4: Some aspects of the community don't take into consideration the needs of elders.

Interviews with people in the community and visits to stores, shopping centers, parks, libraries, and other places may awaken students to an ignorance of or insensitivity to very old residents and patrons. Do curbs at intersections in downtown shopping areas have wheelchair ramps? Are stores equipped with ramps? Are the doorways to public places wide enough? Do public buildings, such as the courthouse, motor vehicle licensing bureau, the library, state and federal offices, have elevators? Are the buttons low enough for people in wheelchairs to reach? Do shopping areas provide a sufficient number of bathrooms, benches and chairs? Are advertisements and notices in windows written in large, clear print? Do the "walk" signs on street lights provide sufficient time for people who must cross slowly? Do city parks provide paths smooth enough for people who use walkers? Do community groups that sponsor events such as picnics, fireworks, parades, or fund-raising dances make an effort to solicit seniors' participation or arrange transportation for elders? Upon discovering deficiencies in their communities, action-minded students of any age can initiate one or several projects to increase public awareness. These projects are by no means limited to high school students; children in younger grades often feel the greatest impulse to rectify social inequities.

The first step in any campaign for community change is to test one's assumptions. Is the problem, in fact, a real one? Would more elders attend an event or patronize a particular shopping area if the accessibility and facilities were improved? Do elders themselves identify certain public places as inadequate? Students will want to conduct new or additional interviews, and perhaps accompany elders on errands or visits to public places. Once students establish that a true need does exist, they can explore the feasibility of change. What is the cost of change? Would the addition of a paved walkway be prohibitively expensive? Are there simple, economical ways to provide services? City officials, store owners, building contractors, and others can provide answers. Once this research is completed, students are ready to plan their campaign — to find out who is empowered to make changes and decide how to best persuade them. In a project to raise community awareness, students become detectives and strategists, conducting interviews, reading, listening, and taking notes. They can even enlist the aid of seniors' advocacy groups, city planners, and merchants themselves.

The most direct form of action is letter writing: letters to the editor of the local newspaper; letters to organizations, store or restaurant owners, members of the city council, city or state agencies, legislators. This kind of project is an excellent opportunity for introducing students to concepts of audience and purpose in writing. Some letters will be more informal and personal, others will require tighter organization and formal usage. Letters will range in tone from neutral and informative to impassioned and argumentative. Younger students will be able to learn about the form, style, and content of formal letters, and older writers may learn or strengthen skills of writing persuasively, writing effective proposals, using logic, and supporting ideas with facts and illustrations.

Another effective form of action is public speaking. Students in elementary as well as secondary grades can request to speak to meetings of a city council, rotary club, a board of directors, and various commissions to present their research and proposals (practiced, of course, in front of the class, other classes, or the school). They can illustrate their speeches with slides, homemade videotapes, or photographs, and use other graphic material to support their points. The teacher might also encourage the class to bring their campaign to the local newspaper, radio, and television.

Discovery 5: The younger community has inaccurate ideas about old age because of the prevalence of negative images and stereotypes in our culture.

What can we do to change our culture's attitudes and the images presented in the media? One challenging activity for a group of students or a class is to initiate change within a school first. Here are a number of possible projects:

1. Take a look at the number and images of elders portrayed in school-adopted textbooks: readers, science books, history books, and others. If elders are absent or the images are unsatisfactory, make a presentation, in writing and/or in person, to the teachers and administrators, school board, and parent groups. Include in the presentation an analysis of the nature of the stereotyping and offer some supplementary information that teachers and classes should know. Write to the textbook companies explaining the problem.

2. For the school library or hall, create a series of displays featuring the accomplishments of elders.

3. Approach the student council and administrators about initiating school projects that might feature or include elders: inviting elders to serve as teachers' aides; setting aside one day for speakers and programs on elders (the program might include panel discussions, rap sessions, presentations of facts about aging, the showing of a documentary film, and other activities that would interest a range of grade levels).

4. Find books in the library that include positive and realistic images of elders. Review these books for the school newspaper; perhaps feature them in a library display case.

5. Compile and prepare an annotated bibliography of all the books for children of all ages with interesting, nonstereotypical older characters that are in the school or local library. Make the bibliographies available for teachers, parents, librarians.

6. Select books with positive images for a younger grade level and volunteer to read these books aloud in that class. Prepare a discussion to go with the reading.

7. Encourage the school library to subscribe to at least one magazine for and about elders, such as *Modern Maturity* or *Aging.* Write a list of suggestions for using the magazines in a variety of classes.

8. Find out about the old-age achievements of famous people in history. Not all historical greats were young when they were the most influential; many became more productive and powerful as they matured (Albert Einstein, Georgia O'Keeffe, and Eleanor Roosevelt to name a few). Write up the information and distribute it to social studies teachers or elementary teachers of other grades levels.

Students can focus their energy, too, on the media. They can write letters of complaint to the producers of television programs that ignore or stereotype elders or portray them derogatorily. They can write to network executives suggesting specific changes they would like to see on existing programs, the kinds of new programs they would like, and why. They can question the presence or absence of elders on certain kinds of programming; for example, why there are so few contestants over sixty on particular quiz shows, or whether a certain talk show plans to feature issues of concern to old people. Conversely, portrayals that are particularly insightful and original deserve letters of praise and support. Too often we take for granted the television shows we like, yet viewer support can help keep a show on the air. Similarly, advertisers who depict elders negatively in television commercials and magazines can be targets for letters (and even boycotts) as can the sponsored programs, networks, and magazines.

By writing letters to authors, publishers, and illustrators, students can express their feelings about the images of elders in books. Local libraries are usually interested in knowing what books their clientele like and why. They might be happy to work with a group of children or adolescents to prepare a special evening program featuring readings from selected books with interesting, nonstereotypical images of elders. Local celebrities can be asked to serve as readers to draw more public attention to the event. And older students can write children's books that feature interesting older characters, bind them, and donate them to the community library.

To help the business community become better informed, students can enlist the support of local merchants and seniors' groups and create displays for stores and malls. The displays might include photographs and lists of accomplishments of local elders or feature the achievements of one or more well-known older people. Students can talk to local newspaper editors about including news about elders as a regular feature. If students find that local businesses use television or newspaper advertising that portrays elders stereotypically, they can conduct speaking and letter-writing campaigns to have the ads changed.

Most of these and other activities in this chapter focus on changing what students identify as problems — in the school, in the community, and in the culture. The five topics I have presented here are by no means the only ones students will discover, nor are the projects I suggest the only ways students can explore them. The most obvious and probably frequent problem a student will encounter is lack of knowledge. When we learn a few facts about a subject, we often realize how much more there is to learn. Thus another focus for an extended project at this stage of community study may simply be to find out more — to change not the community but one's own understanding. Students may wish to examine in greater depth one aspect of aging itself (physical, emotional, political, social), the history and function of a particular supportive service or agency, an elders' political organization or movement (Gray Panthers, RSVP), professional opportunities for elders, and the status of elders in another culture or time. Regardless of its nature, a project should enrich the child who undertakes it. And when children share what they have learned, they enrich others as well.

> Becoming old is really hard for some people. Some would rather be dead like the known author Hemingway who couldn't see himself as being old and committed suicide.
>
> Being old slows your pace in life tremendously, and you wouldn't be able to do things you used to do. Everyone expects that from life. When someone retires, they enjoy more of life. Others won't retire because they were always used to being busy at work.
>
> You hear more and more stories about "traveling gypsies" who take money from older people for doing services which aren't done properly. They feel very insecure of themselves and visitors because they can't do anything to protect themselves or their property. Some think of just killing themselves.
>
> One of the "nightmares" of some older people is being placed in a nursing home and being in a bed most of the time. I can see why they don't want to go because of the vision of 365 days a year being watched and taken care of. They want more freedom than being isolated in their bedroom and seeing other people walking down the hall with a frown. It makes them feel older and incapable of things.
>
> Some senior citizens hide behind curtains because they're afraid to be considered old or slow by younger people or can't walk as fast as you used to. Older people should be proud about

their age and that they are still moving. I think children need to be considerate of older people. And be patient with them. Because 50 years from now they'll be in their shoes, and how you act to them will make a difference on their opinions on living.

—Mike Chin, grade 8

Drawing by R. Harley Kern, grade 8

Notes

1. Pratt, Francis E. *Teaching About Aging.* (Boulder, CO: Social Science Education Consortium, Inc., 1977), pp. 36–37.

2. ———, p. 37.

3. Young, Margaret. "We're All Growing Older." *Forecast for the Home Economist* 32 (April, 1978), pp. 21–23.

4. Waterman, Marjory. *The Life-Writing Review,* Number 4 (November, 1979). Michigan State University Department of English, p. 2.

5. Stillman, Peter R. *Families Writing* (Cincinnati, OH: Writer's Digest Books, 1989).

6. Thomas, Frank P. *How to Write the Story of Your Life.* (Cincinnati, OH: Writer's Digest Books, 1984).

7. Fletcher, William. *Recording Your Family History.* (Berkeley, CA: Ten Speed Press, 1989).

8. Scott, Lynn, ed. *The Memory Album.* (East Lansing, MI: Michigan State University Department of English, 1979), p. 26.

9. Hale, Walter. *The Life-Writing Review,* Number 2 (March 10, 1978). Michigan State University Department of English, p. 3.

10. Collins, Carol, Frances Sevy, Bessie Waldo, Thelma Norris, and Florence Cleveland. *The Life-Writing Review,* Number 3 (May 10, 1978). Michigan State University Department of English, p. 1.

11. Butler, Robert N. "The Life Review: An Interpretation of Reminiscence in the Aged." *Psychiatry* 26, Number 1 (February, 1963), p. 65.

12. Young, p. 22.

13. Jackson, Jacqueline. *Turn Not Pale, Beloved Snail* (Boston: Little, Brown, 1974), pp. 38, 131.

14. Kirby, Dan, and Tom Liner. *Inside Out: Developmental Strategies for Teaching Writing* (Portsmouth, NH: Boynton/Cook, 1981), pp. 39, 41, 85, 86.

15. Stillman, Peter. *Writing Your Way* (Portsmouth, NH: Boynton/Cook, 1984), pp. 40, 44–45, 47, 63.

16. *The Life-Writing Review,* Number 2 (March 10, 1978). Michigan State University Department of English, p. 2.

Chapter Six

Publishing

Growing Old

The years are getting near the end,
I'm getting old they say.
A little lower now I bend
As I go on my way.

A little slower, now I walk
For I am not so spry.
A little faster I may talk,
A little oftener sigh.

A little deafer I have grown —
My eyes a little dim.
Can't think of names of those I've known.
I've lost all of my vim.

But there are compensations, too —
That make my life worthwhile.
Of folks, I have a diff'rent view.
It's easier to smile.

— Olive Mosher[1]

 If I were one hundred years old, I would have 100 wrinkles on my face, with glasses and ears that stick straight out. I would have clothes from California Team. I would have short, ratty hair with curls on the bottom. I would have hands with lines in them, too.

My shoes would be pink with black spots on them. I still remember my boyfriend's name. I still remember my best friend's name.

I have 100 granddaughters — 50 boys and 50 girls. I am too old to ski. I'm just right to cook, and I'm too young to play outside. I like to sit around the house. I

108

can not drive.
Now I'm 105 years old.

— Sherri Winn, grade 2

What children learn about their community becomes richer when it is shared. Whether the sharing is in the form of informal talk or a public presentation, it helps young investigators internalize their new knowledge so that it becomes part of their experiences. In addition, sharing provides new opportunities for using and learning language arts. During their explorations of community suggested in this book, students will and should share in various ways: plan research and talk about the results, write to each other and to people in the community, show what they have found. Publishing is a more complex and formal kind of sharing that enables students to share their knowledge with each other, the school, other schools, and the community, and to preserve for themselves and others what they have learned. It is a way to strengthen skills of composing, speaking, organizing, editing — of language — to participate more fully in the community outside the classroom.

Students can publish in different ways at different stages of their community study. They can make books or displays, produce drama, a newspaper, a film. Publishing generally, though not necessarily, occurs toward or at the end of the process of discovery, when students have collected material and see a need to communicate it to a wider audience. A publication may be incidental to another project, such as a newsletter produced during a writing workshop, or a project in itself, such as an original play.

This chapter is a grocery list of the publications that individuals or groups of students might do when they explore the subject of aging or any other subject in the community. Some might be the culmination of a unit, while others could occur throughout or be incorporated into other projects described in earlier chapters. I have organized the publications according to their general type — books, periodicals, visual presentations, and productions. Some require very little preparation or expense; others are more costly.

Books

Class books can be published on a limited or nonexistent budget. They can be very simple, with handwritten pages and a front and back cover of construction paper, held together with simple metal fasteners (the covers hold up better if they are protected with laminating material). Or, the text can be typed on a typewriter or a word processor and the pages stitched together and glued into cloth-bound cardboard covers, or bound at a copying service with spiral plastic or heat. For much more money, a book can be run on a laser printer or offset press and bound at a bindery. Because books usually have several recipients (the writer, the subject, the school library, the teacher, and perhaps others) they will have to be duplicated. Students should keep in mind that ink and type copy better than pencil, and that color photographs and drawings often copy poorly. (There are many books on the market that explain techniques for classroom or home book making, so I will not go into much detail here.)

Nonfiction Books

Biographies. One form of biography is a *chronology*, in which significant events in the person's life are described roughly in the order that they occurred. Chapters of an elder's biography can focus on life stages — childhood, adolescence, early adulthood, and so on — and include important dates and factual information as well as descriptions of events that are meaningful to the person. However, the organization of a biography depends mainly on the kind of information the biographer has collected — the focus of interviews, the topics of conversation between the students and the elder. The trick for the writer is to keep the chronology from being dull, to help the reader see and know the person.

My Grandfather

My Grandfather was born Ogden Theodore Bowman in Grangeville, Idaho on May 26, 1916. He was adopted in 1926 by Peter O. Fountain.

Everyday Events

When he saw Senator Borah it was like seeing the Jolly Green Giant himself. When an airplane flew over our cabin on the 4th of July celebration, we could see the pilot sitting out in front in his open air seat.

Fun and Games

At home we made bows and arrows out of syringa and played Cowboys and Indians and horseback. We rode bareback. Early toys were "Log Cabin" syrup cans and iron hoops from wagon hubs. We rolled them with a "T" stick. We played games at school like "pump-pump, pull away" and "run sheep run". Everyone played baseball. We played marble games like "Cincinnati Fats" and "bull ring".

Schooling

He attended the first three grades at Slickpoo Mission, near Lapwai. Before daylight one day, the pioneer priest Father Cataldo (over 90 years old) gave one of his final services.

The legendary World Champion cowboy, Jackson Sundown, was buried at that time, in the Mission's Indian cemetary. He also was a "giant" in his time. It was rumored that he was Chief Joseph's nephew. The year he was 10 there was a dormitory fire from a kerosene lamp that killed 5 of his playmates. He went to fourth and fifth grades at Eagle Creek on the Salmon River. There were 7 pupils in the fourth grade and 5 pupils in the fifth grade. The teacher boarded with the ranchers. His house was a nearest to the school. The teachers read current books to the class. He read "King Arthur" and daydreamed that he as a noble knight of the Round Table rescuing damsels and "righting wrongs". He drew pictures instead of doing his arithmatic. He remembers when Lindberg flew over the ocean and a visit by the Queen of Romania to the Lewis Clark Hotel in Lewiston. From 6th to 12th grade he "batched" and "boarded" at Lewiston. He took vacations up the Snake River by boat or by horseback when the river was frozen, sometimes 40 miles up the river. He graduated from the University of Idaho in 1942.

Flying

He recalls sitting above the bluffs in the spring sunshine, watching the eagle soar in the updrafts from the canyon below. It was a full days ride over the Divide from our ranch on the Salmon to Cave Gulch on the Snake. Now he flys it in 10 minutes. He started a flying service in Moscow in 1945 — Moscow Sky Ranch. Now it is Fountain Flying Service under Craig, Steve, Ron, Tim and Doug Gadwa. This is a story about my Dad that my Grandpa told me.

When Steven was about 9 we had a little Shetland mare. She was spoiled, headstrong, independent and unbroken. She was a pet and the boys all enjoyed fashioning harness and a pony cart to train her. One day Steven asked his mother "Mom, why do I keep falling off of Sandy? I ride her a little way then I fall off." Grandma consulted Grandpa who was raised among wild horses on a cattle

ranch. We watched Steven and Sandy out on the taxi strip. Steven
mounted bareback in true Indian style, but from the left side like a
cowboy. But Sandy did not behave like a good cow pony. She took
a few steps then bogged her head between her front legs and went
into a vicious violent bucking act and Steven bit the dust, wondering
why he couldn't stay aboard. Without a saddle spurs or "surcingle"
with hand holds, not even World Champion cowboy Jackson
Sundown could stay on a slippery, round-backed, twisting and
pitching Shetland. So Grandpa made a "surcingle" and Steve
stayed on top mostly after that, and Sandy behaved until she
stampeded with Tim (age 4) in the dark across busy Highway 95
traffic. So Sandy was transported to run loose and unclaimed in
the Salmon River hills.

> —Benny Fountain
> (grade 3) in collaboration
> with his grandfather

Another format is the *multi-genre biography*. As explained by
Tom Romano, a multi-genre research report includes writing in a
variety of forms, nonfictional and literary, so that the entire work
captures the essence of the subject, such as Michael Ondaatje's
biography of Billy the Kid.[2] A student or class doing a biography in
this style would write poetry, fiction, essay, narration, even journalistic segments to convey the major events of the subject's life. For
example, the biographer might describe the subject's courtship of
his or her spouse by writing an imaginary (but believable) series of
love letters, and convey the death of the spouse by writing a fiction-
alized newspaper account of the funeral. Imaginary interior monologues, diary entries, short stories, editorials, character sketches,
descriptive essays, even advertisements could be included in a
biography, so long as they contributed to the portrait of the person.
The multi-genre biography is similar to one done in the style of
new journalism, in which the journalist writes in the first person,
keeping him or herself clearly present and not invisible, as would
be more likely in a chronology. A new journalistic biography tells
the story not only of the person but of the writer's relationship with
that person—how they met, the writer's reactions to the person's
stories, and so forth. "When I first met Mr. Jones, he was shy and
did not say much" might be the opening of a biography in this
style, which has advantages for students who tend to depersonalize
their prose.

Chronological or more creative biographies need not be about
elders if a class is studying another aspect of a community. Students
might write biographies of handicapped persons they know, people
in particular professions, or even of places. A farm, a factory, or
a hospital, for example, make excellent biographical subjects.

(Younger students might enjoy writing place biographies from the point of view of the place — "'The Story of My Life,' by the Dairy Farm").

A third kind of biography is a *collection of letters*. Occasionally, people have in their possession the letters of a deceased spouse, a close friend, a grandparent, or other person. The letters can be arranged chronologically and bound to make a biography of the author. The biographer may need to add footnotes, introductory remarks ("In 1943, Grandmother visited her cousins on the Oregon coast. She was pregnant with my father at the time, her first child, and wrote this letter to her mother"), and other narrative throughout to clarify facts or events and add context.

Memory books. As the name implies, memory books are collections of memories by elders (or others). The book itself is usually an outgrowth of a workshop or series of meetings in which people reminisce and compose stories, although it can be made up of an individual's recollections (as a kind of autobiography). A book may focus on a particular time, event, place, or persons: brothers and sisters, grandparents, school, the Depression, the March on Washington, camping, coming to America, presidents, a town park. Or a book may consist of memories about a group of subjects that serve as chapter headings: childhood, travel, where we came from. Several life-writing groups in the Michigan State University Life-Writing Project published memory books with topical chapters. "Entertainment," "People Who are Gone Now," "Old Ways and Progress," "School Days," "Crimes and Punishments," "Living with Nature," "Holiday Memories," "Romance," and "Women at Work" were the chapters of one. These books also included brief biographies of the contributors and their pictures. Editors might also add statements about the background of the book itself — the group that produced it, the students who edited it, the kinds of memories it contains. If the editors are ambitious, they can index the topics. An index is helpful if the memories include material of historical interest and if the book is going to be donated to a library.

Memory books are an excellent way to record and preserve the traditions or lore of people in particular occupations or other community groups. A good friend whose grandfather ran a lumber mill in the Sierras spent every spring in the logging camp while her father cut the logging roads. Her and her sister's stories of the people and life in the camp, including the one-room schoolhouse she and the loggers' children attended, would make a fascinating book, particularly since the camp closed many years ago. Community landmarks make excellent subjects for memory books — a well-known, popular restaurant or market, a public square, a prominent sculpture or other work of art, even a colorful street corner (Hollywood and Vine?)—that include people's narratives of significant historical moments in the place, stories about interesting events that occurred, or any other memories people of all ages might have.

Grandparent Books. Younger children especially enjoy making books about their grandparents (or surrogate grandparents). These can be simple books in which a child records important biographical facts and his or her own recollections about one or more grandparents. The book can include a family tree, a description of the grandparent (with photo or drawing), earliest memories of the grandparent, a list of the grandparent's favorites—foods, books, hobbies, leisure activities, places to visit, etc.—a favorite story the grandparent told, a recollection about a special time with the grandparent, a poem written about the grandparent. A variation is a grandparents book, published by an entire class, that contains biographical sketches of the grandparents of each class member, including likes and dislikes, where they were born and raised, and other interesting biographical facts.

Famous Elders Books. These are similar to grandparents books but about particular elders, usually (though not necessarily) well-known, and their accomplishments. The books may feature one person, with each class member contributing a section, or several people.

Histories. Histories are similar to memory books. The purpose of such a book is to shed light on the history of a place, a group of people, an event, or an artifact, such as the automobile. They are generally based on a series of interviews—with elders, if appropriate. They may take the form of a collection of reminiscences or stories about the topic, or a factual report illustrated with quotations from the elder informants. Also like memory books, history books can include descriptions of how the material was collected, brief biographies if appropriate, and illustrations—diagrams, maps, photographs.

The Depression Years

Used to be everytime you'd get off a streetcar, someone would want a dime for a cup of coffee. Some of those people who lived on skid row would go into a restaurant and take a cup of water and put ketchup, mustard, salt, and pepper in it to make soup. They were broke.

If you were not married, a woman couldn't rent an apartment.

During that time, I joined the Young Woman's Club. I lived there until I got married, and I had to put all my things in storage.

I know Ford paid $6 a day for people, but he wouldn't hire a married woman. I couldn't get in there because I was married, even though I didn't have children, and that was about the best paying job there was around.

—Clara Drehmer

The thirties remind me of Tom Mix, Hoot Gibson and the WPA. At that time I was living on my farm five miles east of Mason. My father and I farmed the land. We grew corn, beans, oats, hay and sugar beets. We got $6 a ton for sugar beets.

—Gordon Bravender

I lived in South Boston during the depression. I remember my husband would take the sled and the big bushel basket to the wharf to get coal for the stove. It was hard to get coal then. That was before we had furnaces or steam heat. We had stoves in the living room and kitchen too. My husband happened to have a job all through. He was a tool and die maker.

—Dora Snow

from *The Memory Album*[3]

How-to-Books. These focus on one or more crafts, hobbies, or skills that elders (or others) in the community possess. Many of the Foxfire projects resulted in books of this nature, whose value and purpose is the preservation for future generations of information that is not widely available and that might otherwise be lost. Topics for how-tos might include: how to make candles, build an outhouse, pickle asparagus, make corncob dolls, drive a buggy, smoke meat, make a poultice, fish with a spear, or use medicinal herbs. A book can be about one or several topics. Here are some examples of collections that would be appropriate to the study of old age: Favorite Recipes (of the residents of a retirement or nursing home, elders in a town or neighborhood, or members of an elders' social or educational group); Things I Learned from My Grandfather/Grandmother; Home Remedies; Homemade Toys from the Past; Handy Hints for Homemakers; Camping in the Old Days; Making Hats; Fishing Tips; Games for an Empty Lot; Predicting the Weather. In other projects on a community, how-tos can enlighten readers on different aspects of a profession or industry (the process of making asphalt, canning fish, shoeing horses, assembling an automobile, and so on).

One Batch of Soap

5 lb. fat	1/3 cup ammonia
1 can lye	2 tbs. sugar

1 qt. cold water   1/4 cup washing soda
2 Tbs. Borax   (dissolve in hot water)

Mix lye, water, ammonia and Borax in dissolved soda. Mix well. Pour in warm fat and stir until consistency is thick cream. Be sure the fat has been cleared. This is done by using a potato. Cut it up and cook it in the grease until the settlings have gone to the bottom of the kettle. Strain fat.

> Members of the Life-Writing group of
> the Lansing, Michigan, Daytime Center for
> the Elderly[4]

Autobiographies. In helping an elder (or any member of the community) put together an autobiography, a student becomes an editor, responsible for giving the autobiography a meaningful shape and for ensuring that the information is presented in the most interesting fashion possible. Some elders who are writing autobiographies for their families require editors only to transcribe and polish. But others might welcome an editor's suggestions on format and content. And there are, of course, a number of ways to tell life stories:

- *Letters*: While some people save the letters they receive, others are in possession of their own letters. It isn't unusual for an elder to have his or her own letters that were once written to and saved by a deceased or living spouse. My great-grandfather typed most of his letters, even those to friends, and made and kept carbon copies. Collections of these letters either *en toto* or excerpted, can make excellent autobiographies.

- *Self-portrait collections* make good projects for a class. One variation is a book of autobiographical sketches by grandparents or elders in the community. They are different from memory books or history books in that their focus is autobiography, not history or recollections focusing on other people or places. The material for such a collection may be gathered by students with tape recorders or contributed in writing by the elders themselves. To make the portraits in the book interesting, students should encourage the autobiographers to include unique facts about themselves — unusual accomplishments or achievements, special talents, and so on.

- *Reminiscences* are essentially memory books, but by individuals. They include narratives of special occasions, people, and events in one's life for the purpose of sharing that life with family, friends, and others. The meaning of the events to the individual is more important than their possible historical or cultural significance. In a good reminiscence, the narrator's personality is present in his or her voice. If a student is helping an elder write such a book, he or she will want to ensure that the writer's style and voice remain as intact as possible.

Fact books. These are summaries of important facts about a subject. One way for students to learn about and disseminate information about the process of aging (or any subject in the community) is by preparing pamphlets or fact books. A series of pamphlets, each on a different subject relating to old age and aging, produced by one or more students, make good displays for a bulletin board in the school or community center. They are easy to read because they are short and clearly focused, and are relatively easy and inexpensive to lay out and duplicate. A student with the right software or even access to a copier can arrange the information attractively in a small space so that it can be printed on two sides of a legal-sized sheet and folded. Or students can make pamphlets out of notebook paper stapled or stitched together, like a small book. These larger volumes may be about individual topics or contain chapters devoted to several topics (Alzheimer's, senility, presbyopia, stroke, aging and memory, etc.). A provocative approach is to phrase the topics as questions, such as "Will I remember my teen years when I get old?" "Why does grandfather forget who I am?" (Questions may also serve as the titles of individual pamphlets.) Questions are especially attention-getting, whereas topic statements by comparison can seem dull and irrelevant (compare "Old Age and Exercise" with "Will You Run the Marathon at 70?").

Fact books by young people can make valuable contributions to a school or community library. They are one of the strongest methods for changing community attitudes. Student-written books and pamphlets about mental or physical handicaps, how a sewage treatment plant works, the types of architecture on a downtown street, or what to expect in a hospital stay can seem more meaningful and persuasive than professional publications to young readers.

Letters to community members. Letters to editors, merchants, and community organizations concerning a civic issue that are written by class members can be collected, organized, and, along with the letters received in response, bound as a book. This kind of book provides a record of a class project and is a source of information about the community itself, including names and addresses of influential organizations and people, in addition to an example of argumentative and persuasive writing. In these capacities it is useful to other classes wishing to embark on similar projects.

Literature

Nearly any community project will provide ample opportunity for young people to write in a variety of literary forms — stories, poems, tales, plays.

Anthologies. This is the ubiquitous collection, the king of classroom publications. Students involved in elders' reminiscence groups or writing workshops might compile an *anthology of elders' writing*: poetry or stories written individually or collaboratively. A book can be focused, like memory books, or contain writing on several topics (colors, seasons, etc.). Other topics for anthologies are elders' favorite ghost stories, fairy tales retold, fables or other stories with morals, superstitions, legends and myths, and bedtime stories.

Older students can help elders like Ralph Zeigler who write poetry, fiction, song lyrics, drama, or other literature compile their own anthologies. The student editors can help writers choose the works to include, put the selections in a meaningful sequence, proofread copy, perhaps illustrate, and add introductory remarks, dedications, and any other pertinent comments. These books make wonderful family gifts.

Anthologies of student's writing offer students the opportunity to publish many kinds of books about old age or any other subject they are studying. *If I Were One Hundred Years Old*, a collection of second-graders' stories and art that I have quoted from in this book, was published very inexpensively by Tina Woods, a teacher at Russell Elementary in Moscow, Idaho. After the class wrote their stories, parent volunteers typed them and the children drew illustrations on separate pages. Then Ms. Woods pasted the pictures and the typed stories on legal-sized paper, duplicated them on a photocopier, and folded and stapled the pages into books. The cost was probably no more than 40 cents each. Topics for similar class books include: The Smartest Old Person in Town; Favorite Stories My Grandmother/Grandfather Told; If My Grandmother/Grandfather Were Magic; My Strangest Old Ancestor; My Mother/Father at 100; When I Am Old and President of The World; When I Fell Asleep for 60 Years; A Hair-Raising Adventure with My Great-Grandmother/ father; When My Grandmother/father Was My Age; My Favorite T.V., Film, or Music Personality Reaches 90 (a popular topic for junior high school students).

Students can make up stories about actual elders or create characters of their own. They can project themselves into the future or into someone else's past; imaginary diaries of the students at age 80, the descriptions of houses students will live in at 80 and other projective writing activities described in Chapter 5 can be anthologized. Poetry, monologues and dialogues, drama, song lyrics, and even commercials also make good material for anthologies. Here are some additional anthologies a class can produce: books of advertisements that portray elders positively; collections of stories or outlines for television comedies or dramas that feature older people realistically; collections of fables or folk tales about old men or women; famous fairy tales revised to make the old characters more interesting. Or instead of a class book, each student can make an anthology of his or her writing—poems about a local river, animal fables to teach respect for people with handicaps, stories about railroad workers, songs about the sounds of a city, and many others.

"My House at 80" by Debbie Anderson, grade 8

Single works. Sometimes students are inspired to write full-length short stories, short plays, or even television scripts. These, along with the anthologies and fact books, may be bound and contributed to a school or class library. Another fruitful venture is the making of books—about non-stereotypical older characters, for example— for young children. Students in junior and senior high school can write and illustrate original stories for toddlers, pre-schoolers, or kindergartners and donate the books to the community library or to a child care center. Sturdy bindings and laminated pages help the books last longer.

Art books. These are bound books of photographs or drawings, usually with some accompanying text, by either elders or young people. Books of photographs may include original or reproduced pictures, although only more expensive photocopying will satisfactorily reproduce black-and-white photographs. Collections can take the form of photo albums with specific themes: "My Grandparents," "The Residents of _____ Retirement Home," "The High School's 50th Class Reunion," or a photo-biography of one person's life. A good album tells a story, like a photo-essay, and requires minimal narrative explanation beyond an introduction and some occasional labels. While they do not require a great deal of writing, they nonetheless demand composing ability. Students should select photos carefully and organize them in purposeful ways to give readers a deeper understanding of the theme (the joy of the reunion, the warmth of the grandparents, the busy atmosphere of the retirement home). Class members can design and/or arrange collections of original drawings in much the same way, so that the book tells a story from beginning to end ("Our Visit to the Care Center," "Our Picnic with the Seniors' Group") and conveys a theme. A number of community topics lend themselves to art books — sketches and/or photographs of buildings, people, or places, accompanied by stories, poetry, or narrative, are as educational as they are creative.

A student may have the occasion to collect the drawings or photographs of an older person and help him or her arrange them into a book or album. In fact, when young people begin asking around, they may discover many older people who would welcome a helper to put pictures into albums or paste them on pages that can be stapled or stitched together. While many people want their photos in chronological order, others are amenable to a more thematic or dramatic organization that a student could help achieve. And elders in a community who draw, paint, photograph, or sketch as a hobby might appreciate a young person's assistance selecting pictures for a display (perhaps for the school library or classroom) or for a gift book for someone in the family.

Periodicals

Magazines, newspapers, and newsletters can play a role in a number of community projects, including a study of elders. Here are some activities students can do:

1. Help elders in a residence home publish a monthly newsletter for residents. The students do most of the writing and layout, or share the task with elder writers/journalists and other community members. The main purpose of the newsletter is to provide information and entertainment. Each newsletter might include announcements of upcoming events, an interview with a featured elder, a column of residents' news (who has a new pet, who took a trip, golf scores, who spoke to a civic group, etc.), a short article by a local physician about health-related topics of concern to older people, a poem, story, essay, or sketch by a resident, and some brief comments from the home administrator.

2. Students who participate in a writing or reminiscence group might start a literary magazine with the participants' stories, poetry, art, and recollections. The magazine might be distributed bi-monthly to the group members and to other interested people through a local seniors' center. A class might even interest the center or local agency on aging to fund the magazine's publication.

the LIFE-WRITING REVIEW

Published by the Michigan State University Department of English
under a grant from the Michigan Council for the Humanities

NUMBER 4   NOVEMBER, 1979

WELCOME TO THE FOURTH EDITION OF THE LIFE-WRITING REVIEW. THANKS TO A GRANT FROM THE MICHIGAN COUNCIL FOR THE HUMANITIES, THE LIFE-WRITING PROJECT OF THE MICHIGAN STATE UNIVERSITY DEPARTMENT OF ENGLISH IS BACK IN BUSINESS FOR THE 1979-1980 YEAR. AS SOME OF YOU WHO PARTICIPATED IN THE EARLIER PROJECT KNOW, THIS PROJECT BRINGS TOGETHER UNIVERSITY GRADUATE STUDENTS AND SENIOR CITIZENS TO TALK AND WRITE RECOLLECTIONS, PERSONAL HISTORIES, POEMS, AND STORIES. THIS YEAR WE HAVE A NEW STAFF AND NEW WRITING WORKSHOPS; FROM SOME OF THE WRITING THE GROUPS ARE DOING SO FAR, IT LOOKS LIKE AN EXCITING YEAR.

IN THIS ISSUE, THE PARTICIPANTS IN WORKSHOPS AT BURCHAM HILLS AND ST. MARY'S DAY-TIME CENTER INTRODUCE THEMSELVES AND SHARE SOME WRITING. IN FUTURE ISSUES WE WILL PUBLISH MORE WRITING FOR YOU PLEASURE.

WE ARE GLAD TO BE BACK, AND HOPE YOU ENJOY YOUR NEWSLETTER.

-THE LIFE-WRITING STAFF
CANDIDA GILLIS AND LINDA WAGNER
DIRECTORS

3. Meet with a group of elders in a residence center to publish an in-house, weekly newspaper. The newspaper might be printed at the expense of the center and contain news about center staff and residents, editorials, letters to the editor, sports news, reviews of books and films, a medical column, a travel column, and obituaries.

4. Students who have interviewed elders about life in their city 50 years ago might put their information together in the form of a newspaper that could have been published in the city in the 1930s. The paper might include lead news articles about two or three national events, a feature story about the accomplishments of a prominent resident, a column about local goings-on, letters to the editor about new inventions and city growth, an editorial about a current political event, a gossip column, a sports article, and a cartoon page. All the information could come from interviews with people who lived in the city during that time. (This project would be appropriate for the study of something historical in a community — a battleground, fort, old shipyard, railroad, significant building, or monument. For example, one of the most historical areas near my town is the Lewis and Clark Trail. Students could create a mythical newspaper of the expedition as it camped along the Clearwater River. Or, if a city has a building with historical importance — a famous person's residence, the first city hall, a place where major events occurred — classes could create a newspaper focused on that building, the people who lived or worked there and the activities within it.

5. With the assistance of a local agency on aging, a group of students and elders in the community might publish a quarterly journal for area seniors. The journal could contain articles of interest to older readers contributed by professionals in the community — doctors, social workers, ministers, builders, educators. Articles might feature information about social security and medicare, income taxes, leisure activities, local history, the role of elders in society and the community, and each issue could feature a biography. Students would be responsible for soliciting contributions, selling advertising space, arranging the layout, editing, and some writing.

Visual and Audio Media

Art books are one form of publication in a visual medium; yet many more types of visual and audio compositions can be useful in community study, including slides, displays, videotapes, audiotapes, and storyboards.

Displays. Displays are arrangements of informative material usually mounted on a poster board or on three boards joined together so the display can stand freely. (A cardboard box with the top and bottom cut away works very well and is inexpensive. The purpose of a display is to explain and illustrate a concept or series of facts, or to tell a story. The display should feature photographs or drawings, with perhaps some text (or an accompanying audiotape), laid out in a format that is attractive, interesting, and easy to follow. (Displays of nothing but written material are generally pretty dull.) Displays on aging might include a photo-biography of an elder in the community, a photo-story about a day with a grandparent, a photo-essay about an elder's craft or hobby, or an illustration of how aging affects a part of the body.

Storyboards. These are poster boards divided into smaller squares, each of which contains, in sequence, a sketch of a key scene for a short film. The board itself tells a story, very much like a cartoon. The sketches show approximately what the viewer would see: the same distance from the subject, the arrangement of people and props in a scene, the shadows and light, the angle. Dialogue for the scenes is sometimes written below each frame. Storyboards are a means of illustrating (publishing) original television commercials, political advertisements, short (one-minute) dramas or informative messages—without the expense of actual filming. Storyboards that students might make during a unit on old age and aging include a political-type ad asking voters to vote for a proposition that would increase medicare benefits for seniors; a political ad for an elder candidate that stresses age as an advantage; an advertisement for a residential center or nursing home; an automobile ad designed to appeal to elder buyers that does not stereotype; a series of 30-second informative pieces on American elders that might appear on television during station breaks; a short film sequence that would

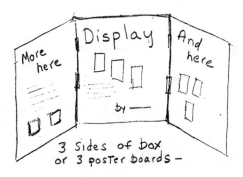

accompany a song about being old or old people (perhaps for a music video); a health message advocating a healthy practice for older people ("Collar cholesterol!").

Films and videotapes. These days video cameras are more accessible than 8 mm movie cameras. Some schools have video cameras available for class use, and an increasing number of parents own them. Students who have the time, money, and ambition can make any number of videotapes: dramas, comedies, advertisements, documentaries, biographies. Storyboard ideas, plus other, longer films, lend themselves to videotape. Here are several on the theme of old age:

- A documentary about an accomplished elder in the community featuring segments of interviews; footage of the person's work; scenes of the person engaged in daily activities, reminiscing, reading from letters or journals; etc.
- A documentary about one aspect of aging itself—the physical or emotional problems, an economic issue, a social concern—that attempts to dispel the myths.
- A documentary about a residential center.
- A short documentary showing community services for elders that could be shown to community groups.
- An original drama centering on conflicts of older characters or about the relationships of old and young people.
- A dramatization of a children's book or folk tale about elders, with student actors or older actors.
- A tape of several interviews with elders documenting common concerns in the community.
- A tape of reminiscences on a particular subject or theme.
- A half-hour situation comedy about life in a residence center, written and acted by the people who live there.
- A filmed, original quiz show featuring young contestants and questions about the facts of aging.

I do not recommend filmmaking on a large scale unless the students and teacher know what they are getting into. First, the process is incredibly time consuming. Second, videotape (except 8 mm) is hard to edit, thus the action must be shot in sequence and with few errors. Third, students are perfectionists when it comes to film. They are used to seeing glossy, high-budget productions, which their films will not be, and are likely to be disappointed with the results of their work. But I would not discourage those who feel comfortable with the medium and want to try it.

Slide shows and slide-tape shows. For students who are handy
with a camera, slide shows are an appropriate medium for presenting,
in a highly dramatic fashion, almost any subject in the community
that has a strong visual component. A show may consist of a series
of slides by themselves or accompanied by taped or live music or
narration. The accompaniment can underscore the slides, provide
context or even contrast. To make a slide-tape show about old
people's recollections of school, a friend and I took pictures of very
modern school buildings, classrooms, and playgrounds and juxta-
posed them with a recording of old voices reminiscing about school
days. The purpose of the presentation was to show the contrast
between old and new, and how different, physically, are the schools
of today. The show was moderately successful, despite poor sound
quality on the tapes and a number of dim or blurry pictures. Some
tips from our experience: To record voices, use a tape recorder and
tape especially designed for voice. To record older speakers, make
sure the volume is up and that the microphone is positioned pro-
perly. Do a test before asking your key questions. Let the tape
recorder run, even when the speaker pauses for a lengthy time.
Tapes can be edited easily by recording sections onto another
recorder. Know your camera, and shoot several rolls of test slides
first. A good slide-tape show has a meaningful balance between the
visual image and the audio; one should not drown out the other or
distract the viewers. Be sure to have the right number of slides. Too
many may overstate the point or get boring. Too few will do the
opposite. Don't go too fast. Slides shown in rapid fire are too hard
to follow. Do not include slides that are out of focus or too dark,
even if they seem good; although you can identify them easily,
viewers who haven't seen them before can't. For this reason it is
important to take many more pictures than you think you need, and
for key subjects take several at different exposures. And practice;
coordinating the audio with the slides is trickier than it looks.

Audiotapes. By themselves, audiotapes are a form of publication
and an excellent way to preserve and make important information
accessible. Tapes of interviews, reminiscences, and panel discussions can be edited to make a tape library. Such a library on
aging might include these tapes:

- facts about aging;
- elders' recollections of a time period, event, or place;
- a group of experts talking about a political or social issue of

concern to elders;

- elders reading their favorite stories or reading children's books with elder characters;
- elders reading from their own writing;
- oral autobiographies — one elder reminisces and tells about his or her life;
- radio programs (complete with commercials) written and produced by students, including drama, documentary, comedy, news, and information.

Every medium mentioned in this section — storyboards, slide-tape shows, videotapes, audiotapes — can enhance other community projects. A group of my high school students several years ago produced an orientation film for new junior high school students. Another group made a film of the trash in and around the school grounds to help other students become more aware of the need to keep their environments clean. The visual media are dramatic and can be highly persuasive; students who wish to promote community awareness or present information powerfully should consider these modes of publication.

Theatrical Productions

Many of the activities suggested for videotape can be produced as live drama (and perhaps videotaped by the teacher or a parent volunteer). To be considered a publication, the drama should be polished, practiced, and performed (an impromptu skit or role-playing session would not count here) and should have a written script.

Oral readings. In an oral reading, students practice and give dramatic readings — perhaps of an elder's writing, a work of literature about old age or aging, parts of their own writing about old age or aging (or any subject they are studying). The students can perform their readings for a young audience, an audience of elders, or a mixed group. A class can sponsor an evening of readings at a local library, community center, or seniors' residential center, and/or organize a program for another class, the school, or another school. The teacher will want to work with the student on skills delivery — use of voice, gesture, pacing, and so on.

Storytelling. Some junior and senior high school students love to read dramatically to little children. At that age they are capable of learning the skills of storytelling — how to use repetition, encourage audience participation, use gestures, voice, and face—and would enjoy reading aloud children's books, fairy tales, and folk tales about old people to groups of children in child care centers or primary classrooms. Students can also use their storytelling skills to entertain groups of elders in nursing homes, hospices, or other care centers.

Reader's theater. In a reader's theater, students create an oral drama out of other writing. They may select key segments of a novel, scenes from a group of short stories, a set of poems, or any combination, and add original material to blend the readings together. Usually the students take parts and do their reading standing together (perhaps stepping forward when reading), holding their scripts. Reader's theater (live or on videotape) is a wonderfully flexible medium, enabling students to create any number of theatrical readings based on their own or other people's writing: elders' reminiscences of a time, place, or event; short stories, poems, and parts of novels about being old; writing by one well-known elder writer. Any aspect of being old or aging can be the subject of a reader's theater: the lessons of experience, the joys of being old, grandparents, friendships in old age, approaching death. The literature students have read and the writing they have done will suggest themes and topics.

In a variation of reader's theater, readers perform original dramatic monologues that illustrate one particular event or tell about a person's life. In this kind of reader's theater, students are actors, pretending to be the elder at certain times in his or her life. For example, a group of students writes a set of monologues about a famous (or not so famous) elder's life, with each monologue featuring a key event—birth, marriage, first job, the war years, etc.— using interviews, articles, or published biographies as sources of material. In the performance, each student reads the monologue he or she wrote.

Any kind of reader's theater can be enhanced with costumes or props. Also, performances are more effective when students know their parts well enough so they can look at the audience and only occasionally at their scripts.

Reader's theater is an engaging way to present literature or writing about other community populations besides elders: the homeless, immigrants, migrant workers, the handicapped, and members of a minority culture are groups about which students will find published fiction, essay, and autobiography suitable for use in reader's theater scripts. For example, there is an increasing amount of children's and young adult literature about a variety of physical and mental handicaps and about recent immigrant groups.

With a little digging through the bibliographies in local libraries (*Booklist* is an excellent source for children's and adolescent literature), teachers will be able to help students uncover the materials they need. A useful anthology for high school students that contains a great deal of contemporary minority literature is *New Worlds of Literature*.[5] Although a college-level text, it contains much poetry, short stories, and drama that will appeal to high school students. The text is organized thematically ("Family Devotions," "Heritage," "Tribe," and more) and therefore easy to skim.

Puppet shows. Puppet shows on any aspect of a community can be performed by and for people of any age—children, teens, adults. Children's stories, short stories, folk tales, fairy tales, and fables with older characters are good subjects for puppet shows about old age, as are original plays written by children and/or elders. Elders' reminiscences can provide excellent material for puppet plays. Children can make several kinds of puppets: marionettes, hand puppets, stick puppets, finger puppets, or shadow puppets (cardboard figures on a stick, cut out so that their distinguishing features are visible in silhouette). These puppets can be constructed simply, from socks or paper bags, or more elaborately, from papier mâché, cloth, plastic, or wood. A sheet suspended from a wooden stick resting on two chairs or nailed across a doorway makes an inexpensive stage for hand puppets. Children, teens, and elders or other members of a community can together plan and perform a show for an elementary school, community group, or for a local seniors' center. A group of older children might make puppets of elder characters, much like the "Kids on the Block" puppets of children with handicaps, and perform a series of shows in several schools.

Play performances. In Chapter 4, I mentioned a number of plays about old age or that contain major elder characters. These can be performed inexpensively in class, or for larger audiences depending on the cost of production rights. Of course, students may write their own plays, too. If a class produces a play, everyone should be involved—in costuming, make-up, directing, and all other tasks.

Other productions. Several kinds of shows appropriate to a study of elders don't fit into any of the above categories but are worth mentioning:

- *Talent shows* may be produced by elders at a residence center or in a community and performed for the residents or public.

- *This Is My Town* is a show that features a collection of performances based on a town's history. It can include monologues of elders' recollections, original skits, songs, and dances. Students and elders might cooperate in the production. Similar productions may be centered on an historical community event (the railroad comes to town), an important person (a founder, a local celebrity), a building (the Chrysler Building in New York, the Sears Tower in Chicago), a prominent geographical feature of the area (a lake, river, ocean, or mountain), or a major town industry (an auto factory, a chemical plant, a paper mill).

- *The Good Old Days* is a variety show, much like "My Town," but with less of a regional focus. Elders of many ages recreate, through skits, songs, and even demonstrations, what life was like when they were young. The show may contain segments focused on themes such as "high school," "kid stuff," "going to work," "the family trip," or might simply reflect the talent and interests of the participants. Teens, middle-aged adults, and elders can create a show that compares the "good old days" of all three age groups.

Notes

1. Mosher, Olive. "Growing Old." *The Life Writing Review*, Number 3 (May 10, 1978). Michigan State University Department of English, p. 12.

2. Romano, Tom. "The Multi-Genre Research Report," a presentation at the Third Annual Conference on the Teacher as Researcher, sponsored by Miami University of Ohio in October, 1988.

3. Scott, Lynn, ed. *The Memory Album.* (East Lansing, MI: Michigan State University Department of English. 1979), pp. 17–20.

4. *The Life-Writing Review*, Number 3 (May 10, 1978). Michigan State University Department of English, p. 10.

5. Beaty, Jerome, and J. Paul Hunter, eds. *New Worlds of Literature.* (New York: W.W. Norton, 1989).

Chapter Seven

The Community as Classroom

"At the Vet" by Jackson Ludwig

Bringing children and the community together in or out of the classroom rewards both. To illustrate the multiple ways of integrating the community and class using language arts activities, I have focused almost exclusively on old people—people who are very much a part of any community yet who are rarely a part of the world of children and school. But the world outside the classroom is a limitless resource of diverse people, purposeful activity, and the innumerable artifacts of a culture—cars, buildings, bridges, art. Our students grow out of and into this world. They are its products as well as its architects. And these are the goals of integrating community and classroom: to help students live harmoniously within their environments by knowing them better; to help students see themselves as capable of shaping and changing their worlds; and to enable them to understand language as a powerful means of interacting with all aspects of one's community. The program of activities described in this book — beginning with exploring attitudes and their sources, then learning facts about a subject, and finally publishing in a variety of ways during and at the end of the research — is applicable to nearly any aspect of a community a teacher and class choose to study.

Discovering Attitudes

What do we know, think, or feel about people with physical or mental handicaps? About the lumber industry? About dentists? About morticians? Many of us carry stereotypical or otherwise inaccurate notions about people and things in our world. I was terrified of the dentist as a child, and even with today's array of high-speed equipment and anaesthetics, I dread my regular visits. I have other vague, undefined assumptions: that police officers are kind and fatherly, that factory workers drink beer and have beefy hands, and that professors are thin, pale, and clumsy. Attitudes can be deeply ingrained and not always conscious; sometimes the attitudes are counterproductive, keeping us fearful or prejudiced. Changing our attitudes requires, first, that we know what they are. All the activities described in Chapter 2 can be used to help children identify their feelings about a variety of subjects.

Using Prompts to Elicit Writing or Talking

Instead of writing, drawing, or telling stories in response to "The old man ...," "The old woman ...," or "When I am one hundred years old ...," students can react to prompts that fit other subjects. If students are investigating a hospital, for example, the teacher might ask them to write stories beginning with "The hospital ...," "The doctors ...," "In the emergency room. ..." People studying law enforcement might write (younger students can draw) about police officers, crime, or the sheriff. Before starting a study of a community's roads and highways, students might write descriptions of or begin stories with "A freeway ...," "The asphalt ...," "The street. ..." Freewriting about a subject itself, if the subject is a specific community place such as a building, landmark, or geographical feature, is an effective way for older students to discover what they know about the place and what they associate with it. Good prompts should elicit initial responses to the substance of what they will investigate. They should focus writers on the heart of a topic and on its most visible, familiar features, and be concrete enough to evoke images and/or call forth experiences, stereotypes, misconceptions.

Pictures also make excellent prompts for helping young people discover and articulate their attitudes toward community places. Magazine pictures may be hard to come by, particularly if the subject of study is unique to a community, such as a local industry. In that case, a camera can be a teacher's best friend. But pictures tell their own stories, so teachers should shoot with caution; a photo of a factory that features garbage in the foreground may bias the students' reactions. On the other hand, a photographer can shoot a subject from a number of angles and capture it more thoroughly, thus giving students more to write about. Instead of writing about Jones's Pharmaceuticals, students can respond to pictures of the factory's inside, outside, and backyard. Instead of talking about "the hospital," children can react to pictures of the waiting room, the maternity ward, an examining room in emergency, the X-ray machine. A variety of photographs enables students to discover that they may have contradictory feelings about a subject — that attitudes are often complex. If a class is studying a group of people in the community the teacher can use pictures of individuals, like the pictures of the old people, and encourage the class to speculate about these people as individuals; for example, imagine the hobbies, interests, families, and personalities of police officers or doctors in pictures, or of people wearing hard hats in construction scenes. Pictures of objects associated with the subject are equally good to write about — a badge, a nightstick, hats, a tool belt, and so on.

Shortcuts

The methods requiring quick and short responses described in Chapter 2 — lists, free-association exercises, scales, and surveys — also can be adapted to other topics. For example, write down, as quickly as possible without stopping, the first thing that comes to your mind with each of these words:

car	*motor*
automobile	*fuel injection*
horsepower	*union*
assembly line	*machinist*
chassis	*V-8*
layoff	*cylinder*
foreman	*strike*

Probably, most of us will have similar responses. Some of your responses probably define or identify the concept, others might be far afield. (Does *fuel injection* call to mind a hypodermic needle? Isn't *V-8* a juice?) My responses to *car* are negative (trouble, stall, gas guzzler, noise), but those who love cars will have positive associations (power, smooth, quick-starting). How we respond tells us not only what we feel but also how much we know.

People learn what they know and don't know about a subject by making lists. List as many reasons as you can for why automobiles are good or bad. How many words can you think of to describe soldiers? Name all the kinds of work that you think go into constructing a building. How many farm machines can you identify? Make a list of 10 words to describe law enforcement officers. What do you like and not like about buses? List as many words as you can that describe the courthouse. True-false tests that include common misconceptions about a subject are useful, too: police officers wear guns, cowboys are bow-legged, librarians hate talking, doctors enjoy giving shots, loggers don't care about forest animals, blind people can't read.

Semantic differentials, like Smith's "My Views" shown in Chapter 2, are another excellent way to bring out the range of attitudes people have about a subject, particularly subjects that students know very little about but have definite attitudes toward. Although Smith's pairs of words were developed to assess attitudes about old people they are applicable to other people in a community: the physically or mentally handicapped, the homeless, doctors, lawyers, veterinarians. Certain pairs, such as *forward-looking/ backward-looking* may not have as much relevance to, say, physicians; those can be substituted by others that are more appropriate (*nervous/calm* for example). For the study of an institution, building, or other similar subject (factory, industry, hospital, or profession), other pairs are more useful:

- *large/small*
- *helpful/not helpful*
- *constructive/destructive*
- *beautiful/ugly*
- *generous/stingy*
- *popular/unpopular*
- *supportive/unsupportive*
- *cooperative/uncooperative*
- *structured/chaotic*
- *permanent/temporary*

- *harmonious/discordant*
- *hot/cold*
- *clean/dirty*
- *colorful/drab*
- *rough/smooth*
- *dangerous/harmless*

The directions, of course, will change: "When I think about *mail carriers* I think of people who are ..." or "When I think about *the pulp mill* I think about a place that is. ..."

Stories with blanks are also adaptable to other topics. Here is one about a person in a wheelchair:

> The __(adjective)__ girl pushed her wheelchair __(adverb)__ over to the __(noun)__ . She was feeling __(adverb)__ because the __(noun)__ had __(verb phrase)__ . Tomorrow, the __(noun)__ would __(verb)__ the __(noun)__ , and she would __(verb)__ again.

(A predictable response: "The *unhappy* girl pushed her wheelchair *slowly* over to the *window*. She was feeling *sad* because the *cure* had *not worked*. Tomorrow, the *doctor* would *try* the *new medicine*, and she would *hope* again." The girl in the chair is sad, lonely, melancholy, hopeful, depressed, passive. A less predictable response: "The *cheerful* girl pushed her wheelchair *quickly* over to the *door*. She was feeling *excited* because the *guests* had *arrived*. Tomorrow, the *family* would bring the *presents*, and she would *celebrate* again." Here, she is happy, active, popular.

Stories with less structure are more appropriate for the study of a place or institution. Try your hand at these:

> The police station was _____. A _____ police officer stood by a desk, _____. Another officer _____ up to the desk holding a _____. Next to the wall, three _____ sat, looking _____. One of the _____ had a _____ and was _____. The door opened, and several _____ _____ in. Soon, the room was _____ with _____.

> When I walked into the hospital, I first saw _____. The _____ was _____ and the _____ were _____. I was _____ and felt _____. Then, the _____, and I _____. The _____ doctor said "_____." The _____ nurse said "_____." Everyone seemed _____. They _____.

More open stories require little knowledge of a place or what goes on there and leave students free to create any atmosphere, characters, and conflicts they wish. They bring out whatever fantasies, positive or negative, students have, and are often easier to work with than the more structured stories.

Cartoon fill-ins work for any topic as well. On pictures of places, instead of filling in balloons, students can write captions beneath the pictures or fill in empty signs on walls or billboards next to buildings pictured.

Creative Dramatics

One of my most memorable experiences in the first grade was when our class turned the room into a city. Each of us chose a part of the community to be: a banker, a store keeper, a street cleaner, a milk delivery person, and so on. We made cars, trucks, and buses with hammer, nails, and wood. (Mine was an ice-cream truck.) We out-lined streets with masking tape and stacked blocks for buildings. First we played make-believe with our characters and props, and then we learned what a city is—who lives in it and what makes it run. In any classroom, a community can come to life with a few props and a lot of imagination. Fire fighters' hats, coats, a garden hose, a ladder, and a toy hatchet can turn a first-grade classroom into a fire station or burning building. With borrowed props such as a wheelchair, a white cane, and crutches, seventh-graders can im-provise skits that involve people with physical handicaps. Students can perform impromptu scenes in hospitals with borrowed scrub suits, nurses' hats, stethoscopes, gauze, and all the paraphernalia in a child's doctor kit. They can turn puppets into police officers, construction workers, or sailors. Improvisation and other dramatic activities have a hundred and one uses. Even an activity as simple as having students create a pantomime about an assembly line helps them find out what they know and feel.

The Sources of Our Attitudes

Young people often have negative attitudes about or stereotyped images of a number of things in their environment. For example, hospitals or police stations may seem threatening to youngsters until they learn more about them. Likewise, people in the community who appear different or act differently, people in authority, and people with whom we associate pain, death, or extreme power can make students uncomfortable: a judge in a robe, a fire fighter in full gear, a surgeon, a person with an artificial limb, a person with cerebral palsy, a person who speaks another language. Feeling threatened by or afraid of these people does not, generally, come from experience but from lack of it. Similarly, children can feel positively about some aspects of a community, such as a park, a restaurant, a store, nurses, or ministers, without having had much experience with them. These may be places and people that are portrayed favorably on television and in books and films. These biases can render children vulnerable. They may lead them to blindly trust some people and to want to visit places and spend money on products uncritically. (Every parent knows this kind of bias: "Take me to ____!" "We have to eat at _____!" "Buy me a _____!") A beginning step in conquering fear and in developing critical judgment is discovering one's biases and prejudices; the second step is to figure out their source.

Our culture's language, literature, and media contain and re-inforce a number of stereotypes of our neighborhoods. Children's literature is full of them. Of the books I loved as a young child, several contributed to my early attitudes toward stores, police officers, business people, and the community generally: In *Let's Go Shopping*, by Lenora Combes, the children and their mother are met by consistently friendly sales clerks, and the stores are never crowded. Most people in the city are white, all the adults in the park are kind and friendly to children, and all the children play cooperatively.[1] In *Tommy's Wonderful Rides*, by Helen Palmer, the town mayor is a plump, white-haired man in a suit, the train conductor wears glasses and a moustache, and ambulance attendants try to force pills down a child's throat.[2] In *The Magic Bus*, by Maurice Dolbier, the bus driver is kind, smart, and loves children, while the bus company official is bald, square-headed, rude, and unfeeling. The company president is lazy, stupid, and weak.[3] In *The Little Fat Policeman*, by Margaret Wise Brown, the police officer is a jolly, short, balding, and chubby man for whom all drivers cheerfully stop.[4] These impressions of people and places in the community remain in my mind despite the realities brought by age and experience. Children's literature is a powerful shaper of attitudes.

It is a simple task to locate and analyze portrayals of just about anything in the community in children's literature. And it is an activity that even high school students find interesting. Places are particularly easy to find because even books about other subjects contain illustrations that include streets, houses, parks, stores, offices, and office buildings, museums, hospitals, bus or airplane terminals, farms and countrysides. Questions and checklists concerning the content of illustrations and text, like the ones described in Chapter 3, help students analyze the way a subject is depicted. For literature that contains more text, students can look at the descriptions of people and places, at the way characters talk, and the roles the characters and even places play in stories. The questions can be modified to suit the focus of study. For example, a class studying city parks might examine books with questions such as these: What does the park look like? Is it safe or dangerous? Who is in the park? Are the people in the park happy or sad? Friendly? Busy? Is the park a crowded or lonely place? Do the kind of people shown represent the kind of people in our community (young, old, of mixed races and nationalities, handicapped, etc.)? What do people do in the park? Does the park contain benches, drinking fountains, pathways, playground equipment, vendors? If a class is investigating banks, the students might look at images of bankers (Are they all bald and plump?), tellers (Are they all bespectacled females?), and the bank's physical properties (Is it made out of big, concrete blocks or is the design more modern? Does it have a vault or an old-fashioned safe?). Children's books contain a variety of community people as well, whether they are the main characters or peripheral: store owners, merchants, taxi drivers, bus drivers, police officers, doctors, librarians, teachers, post office workers, garbage collectors, and others. Some illustrations and stories contain stereotypes. (Are all store clerks bald, mustached, and do they wear wire-rimmed glasses and white aprons? Are all postal delivery people friendly men? Do teachers always wear glasses?) Others simply ignore some community members altogether. (How may professionals, shoppers, or travelers are handicapped? Old? Asian or Latin? Unless the book is about these minorities, they rarely appear.) Because children's books feature people in different professions and show people doing a variety of things in a variety of work and play settings, they are a rich resource for students exploring a community's architecture, occupations, places, or people.

Movies, television, and advertising also shape attitudes in strong and significant ways. For some children, the world on television is the real world or the way the world should be. Images that are false, stereotypical, or even absent may contribute to students' preconceptions or misconceptions about their communities. Old people are not the only group underrepresented or misrepresented on television or in film. The handicapped, the homeless, and people from other cultures are frequently invisible in crowd scenes and street scenes. City streets typically contain no panhandlers, bag ladies, drunks sleeping in doorways, or homeless families in cardboard shelters. There are no blind people with canes in shopping centers or children with leg braces on the playground. Where in the airport are the people in wheelchairs? Where, everywhere, are the men in turbans or robes or the women in saris? On television, these people do not appear in the background, as they would in a large city in real life, unless their presence is necessary to create an effect. A viewer rarely sees a disabled person on a quiz show, or even in a drama, unless the disability is somehow featured.

Film and television can also show locations unrealistically, much like the illustrations in some children's literature: parks are clean and filled with happy children, parents pushing strollers, healthy joggers, and dog walkers. The perfect suburban middle-class house is a two-story Colonial with a lawn in front; beaches are free of paper cups and broken glass; lakes are unpolluted. Children who have had little direct experience with the scenes they see can easily assume that all such places are like these. And because many television programs are filmed near Los Angeles, Southern California's locales can come to represent those in the world at large. (How many children think that the Minnesota prairies of the 1800s or the jungles of Vietnam have brown hills with scrub oaks and black walnuts, or that high-priced neighborhoods everywhere have palm trees?) Children's impressions of people, professions, and things may similarly be skewed: highway patrol cars travel at incredibly high speeds; paramedics are handsome, muscular young men who love children; librarians read all the time and never laugh; old men love to flirt with young nurses; foreign tourists are befuddled, childlike, and not very intelligent; fathers are bumbling; scientists have wild, white hair. The activities described in Chapter 3 for analyzing images in these media can help students understand their misconceptions.

The language people use on television, in books, and in the real world helps shape children's attitudes toward many elements in their community. The English language contains a number of euphemisms and/or slang references for people, places, and things. For example, law enforcement officers may be called *pigs, cops, fuzz, blues, the law, police, officers, bears,* or *smokeys.* Doctors are *sawbones, men in white coats, medics, pill pushers, physicians.* Lawyers are *attorneys, legal eagles, ambulance chasers.* People who are mentally retarded might be called *morons, idiots, slow, simple*, *simple-minded*, *dim-witted*, or (as one education text wrote) *minimally gifted*. Some terms are respectful, others are not. They reflect the attitudes, biases, and prejudices of people in various regions, time periods, and cultures. The activities suggested in Chapter 3 for exploring the connotations and uses of language can help students understand the role of language in shaping attitudes. Some explorations of language will not be appropriate for the study of all aspects of a community, obviously. A factory or local industry, a community building or institution will probably not have a host of slang terms associated with it. However, local businesses often rely on specialized language, a language of the trade that includes technical terms and jargon. These unique words and phrases are an important subject to study: what do they mean, where did they come from, who uses them, and so on.

Getting Acquainted

The purpose of getting to know something in the community, in addition to simply learning more about it, is to change the way one thinks about it — to acquire attitudes based on truths, not ignorance. Only when we have accurate information are we free from the kind of fear and prejudice that can limit our relationships with people and restrict our opportunities in life. Not all deaf people are alike. Retarded people can learn. Dentists can be compassionate. Not all business executives are mercenary. Some used car dealers are not out to cheat you. The more students learn about their communities, the more comfortable they are in them, the less likely they are to behave in destructive ways, and the more able they will be to participate actively. Acquiring realistic attitudes depends on gathering facts and looking at portrayals of the subject that are honest and unbiased. It depends, too, on firsthand experiences, in and outside of the classroom.

Through Language

By using language more creatively students can change the ways they perceive people, places, or things in their worlds: thinking up fresh, original descriptive words and phrases, making unpredictable stories out of CLOZE-type paragraphs, writing stories that portray a person or place in nonstereotypical ways. If the class is studying a group of people, the students can write or tell stories about the "most (*athletic, ambitious, beautiful, comic, energetic, creative, witty*) fire fighter/migrant worker/doctor/shop keeper I ever met," and fill in the blank with a description that identifies the person as unique and human. All people who belong to a group because of their profession are not the same, and people who are physically similar are emotionally and mentally unique. Personalities vary, as do likes and dislikes. These activities, though they may initially seem strange, can help students differentiate among individuals in a group by encouraging them to create characters with unique traits. Students can write non-clichéd descriptions of locations that point out details that are not commonly described: things in a park besides the grass and trees and playground; rooms in a hospital other than waiting rooms, operating rooms, and patients' rooms; machines in a television studio other than cameras and lights. By focusing on the less usual details, students stretch their perceptions. Students can also make places the settings for original stories. "It was a normal day at the bank. ..." "When the detective entered the courthouse, she was struck by. ..." And younger children can write stories from the point of view of a place: "The corner market was not happy today. ..." "The hospital knew something was different. ..." "The subway station could not have been more pleased. ..." This off-beat assignment can help children think about the atmosphere of a place in addition to its physical structure and typically associated activities. If taken seriously, it can give children's imaginations a real workout.

Through Literature and the Media

Realistic images of the community do exist in literature and the mass media. Recent children's books include informative and non-stereotypical, nonsexist, and nonracist depictions of diverse people in a variety of occupations and community locales. Some books for younger children are designed specifically to acquaint children with hospitals, fire stations, schools, police stations, buses, airplanes, museums, and other places children may visit and feel uncomfortable with. Others tell children about being an archaeologist, a baseball player, a cook, or a farmer. The illustrations and texts of many contemporary books represent people and places more accurately than some written 30 years ago. Young adult fiction today contains a wider range of characters and settings. Subjects that were rarely treated in adolescent literature before the 1950s — coping with disabilities, growing up in a poor, rough neighborhood, having no home, struggling with substance abuse, abusive parents, gangs, and other family and peer conflicts — proliferate in contemporary adolescent and children's books. Bibliographies of young adults' and children's literature on certain issues and topics are printed regularly by the American Library Association's *Booklist* magazine, *The Horn Book* magazine, the National Council of Teachers of English's *English Journal*, *Language Arts*, *The ALAN Review*, and other periodicals. The NCTE publications *Books for You*, *Your Reading*, and *Adventuring with Books*, listed in the "Resources for Teachers" bibliography, contain annotated lists of fiction and nonfiction for junior high, senior high, and elementary students (respectively), organized according to topic. The sections on family relations or problems include books on subjects such as growing up handicapped, mental illness, breaking the law, and others that might be useful in community study.

Television frequently broadcasts documentaries and dramas that portray a variety of subjects realistically. Programs on public and sometimes network television feature well-known people in various professions — artists, musicians, actors, doctors, athletes. While some shows glamorize professions, others depict them with candor. Documentaries, filmstrips, video and audiotapes, and records about many subjects in the community are available for every grade level from a number of distributors and educational libraries. Students can watch a carpenter build a house, an artist paint a picture, an orchestra perfect a symphony, or workers assemble an automobile. They can see what the day in the life of a doctor is like, what dairy farmers do, or how pretzels are made. I cannot think of a subject in the community that is not accurately depicted somewhere in film or on tape. Even local industries often have public relations, orientation, or training films that they might be willing to loan a class.

Government agencies are another source of films and written information — pamphlets, research reports, and other documents — on many community subjects, from environmental issues to consumer protection laws. Students can also find facts in nonfiction books, magazine articles, and publications by local or area agencies, and by industries themselves. Local chambers of commerce, city halls, and historical societies are three other places where students can find material.

Through Class Visits

Direct contact with the subject, inside or outside of the classroom, is crucial to an understanding of that subject. Other community groups besides elders can enrich the classroom in the same ways that are described in Chapter 4. The most obvious way is by visiting the class and answering students' questions. What kinds of work does a butcher do? What is it like to be blind? Do you like farming?

What do you have to do to drive a cab? How do you take care of the trees? What were your initial reactions when you arrived in America? Enlisting volunteers to visit class regularly and serve as classroom aides is a good way to acquaint students with members of different cultural groups or people with physical handicaps, or with any people students might feel uncomfortable with, such as law enforcement officers or judges. Class visitors can also serve as writing or reading partners and/or collaborators in projects like the production of a play or anthology of class-written literature. When students listen to community visitors read stories or other literature, share their writing with them, or exchange reactions to a book they have read, they tend to forget people's differences. A police officer is the woman who comes on Friday and helps us pick out library books. The man in the wheelchair is helping us write a play. The deaf woman helps us polish our writing for displays. The dentist knows all about Hemingway. The woman from Central America listens to us read aloud and talks with us about our books. In time, the visitors become individuals, no longer identifiable only by a physical feature, occupational lable, style of dress, or skin color. Now they are familiar and comfortable, both in school and out.

Places, too, can be brought into the class through film or a display of photographs or objects associated with the place. More ambitious classes can construct community settings in the classroom. By taping paper trees, bushes, and benches to the walls, an elementary class studying city parks will feel right at home. With paint and creativity, a classroom wall can become a hospital corridor, a subway station, or a row of tellers' windows in a bank. Students can rearrange their desks to simulate office cubicles, waiting rooms, or seats and benches on a bus. An area of the floor about four feet out from one or two walls can be covered with paper and turned

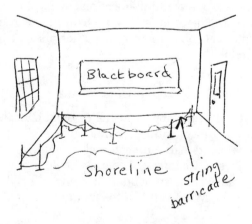

into a shoreline. Students can paint the paper and put on it things they see and find along lake, river, or ocean shore near their town or city—wood, trash, even sand. (A barricade of string keeps the creation from being disturbed.) Students can make models of factories, parks, streets, buildings, an airport, or a city freeway system.

Through Observing and Interviewing

Students can learn even more outside the class on field trips. Obviously, students investigating a local industry should take a tour; a class studying farming should visit a farm. An historical street or ethnic district won't become familiar until the class goes there and observes carefully its architecture and people. To get to know a subway, one must take a ride. If field trips are to be successful, students need to develop sharp eyes for observing places. They need to learn to see detail, to look from different angles, to see the whole as well as parts. And they need to see with all their senses. Several exercises can sharpen young people's observational skills. One is to have students look at photographs of everyday objects taken at unusual angles or very close up (National Geographic's *World* magazine publishes these photos). Another is to have students practice observing in the school first. Walks around familiar school locations during which students are told to memorize everything they see (and list them when they return to the class) and/or notice something they have never seen before are helpful preparation.

A favorite activity that I have used with college writers (and that would be suitable for high school students) asks students to take pencils and notebooks and select a location in the class, in the hallway, or out of doors. They are then to sit in their places, get comfortable, and imagine a 10-inch by 10-inch window on the ground, wall, tree, or wherever they are looking, and stare at the window for five minutes without looking away. They may think of anything they want, but they must not talk and should stare for the full five minutes. At the end of the five minutes they are to write without stopping and as fast as they can for eight minutes, putting down *whatever* is on their minds. When the eight minutes have elapsed, they are to return to class, where they have another 10 to 15 minutes to produce some writing to share—a poem, narrative, stream-of-consciousness, whatever. The writing that this exercise produces is often highly descriptive and personal at the same time. By being forced to limit their vision to a small part of a larger surface the writers notice many and new details. They also become conscious of how much what they see is influenced by what is on their minds and vice versa, and how description can be enhanced by a clear point of view. A middle school English teacher told me of a similar activity she has found successful with seventh-graders. She assigns each student a two-foot by two-foot square of earth on the school grounds that is theirs for the duration of the class. At regular intervals in the fall, winter, and spring she takes the students out to observe their plots and record detailed observations in journals, which they later turn into descriptive writing. Jackson's book *Turn Not Pale, Beloved Snail*, mentioned in Chapter 5, includes other good activities for sharpening perceptions.

When observing a building or other community locale, students should compile lists of things to look for that will help them direct and focus their observations. If the teacher has visited the locale ahead of time with the project in mind, he or she can help students come up with good questions. Without some guidelines, students may find a site an overwhelming confusion of sights and sounds. Going over a map with the class beforehand, if appropriate, can also help students use their time in the field more efficiently. Instead of worrying about where they are or whether they are in the right place, they can concentrate on what they came to see.

Often, more than one visit is necessary to get to know a place. An ideal procedure is to make a first visit with a map and/or a few guiding questions to enable students to get the feel of the place and note first impressions. After sharing their responses in class later, students will have a clearer sense of what they would like to focus on during the next visit. A third or even fourth visit can produce deeper insights and additional responses.

When students observe people, they should heed the suggestions made in Chapter 4: be unobtrusive, do not stare, and notice as much as possible in a few, short glances. Use a set of questions as a guide, and later when alone, record the details and answer the questions. Students should be aware too, as they should be when conducting interviews, that staring, or even looking directly at people, has different meanings in different cultures. Whereas in one culture looking in a person's eyes is a sign of forthrightness, in another culture it might be considered aggressive or even insulting. Children should also try to remain objective when observing people who are different from them and who are engaged in unfamiliar activities. Actions may have very different meanings for the participants than for the observers. For example, some people smile out of politeness or nervousness, not because they are happy. A few lessons in how to conduct good ethnographic research will help students learn to keep judgments out of their observations and to interpret what they see carefully.

By talking to individuals or by meeting with groups to talk or share stories, students can learn details about the community that could not be discovered as easily from reading or even watching. When interviewing any community member, students should heed many of the suggestions in Chapter 4 for interviewing old people: learn to use the tape recorder, have questions planned in advance, listen carefully and be alert for information not anticipated, put people at ease, be aware of cultural differences, and so on. Students wishing to interview people whose native language is not their own and/or whom they might not understand easily should also prepare carefully. They should anticipate that they may have difficulty understanding a dialect and guard against the tendency to repeat questions when they don't understand answers. Prior to the interview, they should become as familiar as possible with the regular features of the dialect — syntax, usage, pronunciation patterns — and listen to other speakers of similar dialects or pronunciations. Any dialect becomes clear when one has heard it for a time. If a student has no chance to become familiar with the person's speech, he or she should tape record the interview and attempt to decode the responses at a later date, perhaps with the teacher's or classmates' help. Better not to understand completely than annoy a speaker by asking him or her to repeat. If the person being interviewed does not comprehend spoken English well, the student should phrase questions in simple, unambiguous language. (The questions, however, need not be simple; students are sometimes apt to assume that because a person's English fluency is limited the person is unable to speak about complex issues.) Better yet, enlist interpreters or have the questions translated before the interview.

Students should be sensitive to the interviewee in other ways: Sit at the person's level (people in wheelchairs, beds, or people who are very short will not be comfortable if you tower over them). If speaking to a person whose hearing is impaired, speak distinctly and always face the person; people who rely on lip movements cannot read lips if the interviewer's head is turned away. Refrain from asking leading questions or questions loaded with value judgments, such as "Wasn't the sanitation awful in your village back home?" or "Aren't you grateful to be in America?" If a person is handicapped and has expressed willingness to do an interview about the handicap, one may assume that the person will speak honestly. In that case, the student should avoid vague phrases or euphemisms ("How long have you had your 'condition'?"). However, they should also avoid excessive bluntness or derogatory slang and be aware of the other person's feelings. If students interview judges, public officials, members of religious orders, or others with titles, they should know the rules of etiquette and appropriate terms of address—whether the person is Mr. Jones or Senator Jones, Ms. Jones or Reverend Jones, Mr. Smith or Judge Smith. These guidelines apply to any kind of interview, whether it be a formal question and answer session with one person or an informal meeting with a group to record recollections. A good rule for students is to check their questions carefully and go over them in advance with a teacher. These preparations will help ensure successful and rewarding interviews.

Projects and Publishing

The kinds of assumptions students are likely to find challenged by their reading, listening, field trips, and interviews depend mainly on the topics they are studying. The projects described in Chapter 5 are appropriate for a study of elders and the issues surrounding that topic; some, of course, are not suitable for other community studies. The discovery that creativity does not decline with age is unique to the study of aging, and the activities designed around it, such as writing workshops, would be out of place in studies of other parts of a community. But there are certain issues or problems that are shared by many aspects of a community. Three problems in particular are (1) the absence in a community of sympathy or empathy, (2) community ignorance, biases and prejudices, and (3) stereotyping or neglect of a community's people or places in literature and media. Studies of any number of community groups, professions, or locales might result in projects centered on these issues.

Absence of Sympathy, Empathy

Students studying the homeless, an ethnic minority, a professional group, or the handicapped may see a need to develop greater sensitivity in themselves and others. For example, although getting to know physically handicapped people is essential in building tolerance and understanding, sharing some of their experiences can build an even deeper appreciation for the obstacles handicapped people face. Simulations and projective writing can intensify young people's awareness. In the Girl Scouts of America, one of the things young girls do to earn badges for handicapped awareness is simulate physical handicaps: work wheelchairs, write with fingers taped together, walk with crutches, spend time blindfolded, and other activities designed to increase empathy. Another activity is to assign each student a handicapped partner, who, if the person is able, accompanies the child through all his or her regular routines at school (and even home, if possible) for a day. The extended contact and sharing of daily routines helps young people understand the other person's perspectives. Although not strictly a simulation, this activity can strengthen students' understanding of others in the community. If a student spends time with a police officer on the job, a factory worker, a doctor, a chemist, an artist, a young person from another culture, he or she is apt to become more sympathetic to the person's daily life — the work, frustrations, and rewards — and to see that person not as a member of a group, but as an individual.

Additional simulations help young people understand the experiences and situations of other community members. If a class is studying neighborhood immigrants who speak little English, the teacher can help the students feel the frustration of not understanding a language by communicating with the class for two days in a code (a real or invented language the students do not understand) that includes only a few English words. All assignments and directions should be given in the code, on handouts or on the board (or spoken, if the code is a real language). For example: "Bllc ulfumnb, e,zxx. My yzud is Ux. Gillis." (This code has a pattern, but you'll need a keyboard to figure it out.) By the end of the first day, students will have deciphered some of the words and will be helping each other learn and use the new language. On the second day, tell the students that all their work must be in the new language. And give a test on the material in the previous day's assignments.

To sensitize students to the plight to homeless people, place them in small groups to become families and give each family the task of planning a shelter for themselves right in the neighborhood of the school. Where would they sleep? What about water? Protection from cold or dogs? How would they cook or read without electricity? What about sanitation? In conjunction with the assignment, schedule walks around the neighborhood and have students meet in their groups several times during the week to plan. At the end of the week, each group describes its plans and the class talks about the advantages and drawbacks of each.

Role-playing, in which students take the roles of community members and act out or improvise situations, is another effective way to increase sympathy and help young people understand the conflicts and concerns of people in various professions or other groups. Students can pretend they are a city council defending their decision to increase taxes to pay for street maintenance; they can become a group of doctors deciding whether to perform controversial surgery. They can become factory managers faced with decreasing demand and layoffs, architects trying to preserve an historic building, or miners arguing for higher wages and safer working conditions. Courtroom trials, union bargaining sessions, school board meetings, and many other events can be enacted in the classroom. Role-playing is often more successful if the teacher invents roles for each student in advance and allows students to prepare their characters. By doing this, the teacher can ensure that certain conflicts will arise. For example, the roles at a city council meeting debating higher taxes for road improvement might include a citizen who doesn't own a car and resents being taxed for roads for teenagers to race on, another who's gone through two sets of shock absorbers in one year, a council representative who is up for re-election and wants to be popular with voters, and a representative who sees road improvement as a means of decreasing the city's unemployment problem.

All simulations and role-playing activities should be accompanied by or followed up with writing so that students can reflect on their roles and the conflicts that emerged in the sessions. In addition, greater understanding can be promoted by more extensive projective writing from other people's perspectives:

- Describe what would be the most difficult for you, personally, if you had no home.

- Imagine that you suddenly moved to a country where you didn't speak the language and where everyone dressed and acted differently. What would you find hardest? Write a series of letters to a friend back home about your new life.

- Write a week of diary entries from the point of view of an emergency room doctor.

- Create an imaginary pen pal who is handicapped. Write a series of letters between the two of you.

- If you suddenly became deaf (or blind, or disabled in another way), how would your future be different?

- Pretend you are an old person with a physical disability looking back at your life. What are you the most proud of?

- Describe your daily life and routines from the perspective of someone from an entirely different culture who has not experienced life as you know it—whose foods, customs, standard of living, housing, and recreation are entirely different.

- Imagine that you have a physical handicap. Describe your handicap as if it were a gift: What can you do that others can't?

The language arts of writing, literature, and drama have value for others in the community besides elders. Reminiscence and storytelling groups, creative writing workshops, book study groups, and drama workshops can be enjoyed by any number of community citizens and are a wonderful way for students and community groups to get acquainted. With the help of professionals and experts in the community, a class might sponsor and help run a writing workshop for handicappers who cannot physically write or a reading group for people who are visually impaired, or work with a wheelchair-bound group to produce a well-known play for a community theater. They might meet with the officers of the local police precinct to collect reminiscences of the station house, help a fishing club write a book of handy hints, or conduct storytelling workshops for mildly retarded children. Language arts are for everyone, and when shared across generations and among diverse peoples, are a means of deepening community awareness, tolerance, and knowledge.

Community Ignorance, Biases, Prejudices

In every community are people and even places about which little is widely known. As a result of ignorance, some young people (and adults) have prejudicial or uncaring attitudes — attitudes that may be harmful to the community as a whole. For example, a young AIDS victim is shunned by classmates; a family of recently arrived Southeast Asians finds that everyone, including school and civic officials, assumes they are poor and unskilled; the oldest hotel downtown is scheduled for demolition, even though it is the last building of a particular architectural style remaining in the city; residents of a neighborhood fight to keep a mental hospital from being constructed nearby because they are afraid of "crazies running around." After students uncover the facts, they may use any of the methods described in Chapter 5 to educate their fellow schoolmates and community. Here are some possible projects:

- Interview experts about the facts (on AIDS, multiple sclerosis, mental illness, the actual duties of law enforcement officers, and so on), prepare fact sheets, and distribute them to classes.
- Collect oral histories of a place from those who lived and/or worked in the place (a factory, business, farm, industry). Present a biography of the place in the form of a display or audiotape for the school, community center, library, or other public place.
- Write letters to newspapers for the purpose of giving significant information and proposals for new community policies, such as accessibility for handicappers, regulations for public parks, or preserving an old building.

- Plan a series of guest speakers for the class or school; invite members of the community group you are studying—people associated with a profession or industry, or experts on a town location or landmark—to give an informative panel discussion.
- Arrange to speak to a number of civic groups about the problem and the solutions you have devised.
- Plan a presentation for local radio or television.
- Arrange and lead tours of a place for other classes.
- Create an informative dramatic presentation for groups of younger children.
- Become familiar with legislation affecting your subject, and write congressional representatives arguing a position.
- Arrange for other students to join in a project to help members of a group or place. Students might be readers for the blind, help a non-English speaking child learn the language, or participate in a shoreline cleanup.
- Locate some literature—folklore, poetry, stories, reminiscences—by writers (well-known and unknown) who belong to the group being studied (handicapped writers, ethnic writers) and encourage teachers of all grade levels to include this literature in their classes.
- Attend (if invited, of course) and participate in activities of a community group—a celebration, an educational event. If you are studying an industry or business, attend some of the official functions.
- Initiate a pen pal program between students outside your class and members of a community group.
- Do research on accomplished people in a group you are studying. The people may be known nationally or locally, or characters from folklore, fiction, films, comics, or songs. Write a who's who and distribute it.

The exact nature of these projects will depend on students' ages and specific topics. To promote handicapper awareness, high school students might contact local merchants with a list of ways they can attract more handicapped buyers to their stores, provide school principals with a list of handicapped volunteers willing to visit classes, or put on a puppet show for pre-schoolers. To promote greater sensitivity to and interest in an immigrant ethnic group, a junior high school class might help the school administration plan a week in which display cabinets and activities feature the history and accomplishments of people in that culture. Or they could write fact sheets for students, locate poetry and stories by writers of that culture for English classes, and prepare brief biographies of the culture's important political figures and maps of the home country for social studies classes. (Activities to promote school awareness are frequently done for major cultural groups in the United States, such as African-Americans; but many communities have residents of lesser-known cultures: the Hmong, Basques, and others.) To encourage greater appreciation of community architecture, members of a fifth-grade class could write a series of profiles of local buildings (with photographs) for the school or local paper, and create displays featuring certain buildings for local merchants' windows. Projects can be adjusted to students' ages by modifying the difficulty level of the writing activities and the amount and complexity of interviewing, reading, and other research. Children in the second grade can talk to community groups, perform dramatically for other classes, and write letters to editors, but in less formal, sophisticated ways than high school students.

Neglect or Stereotyping in Literature and Media

Earlier I noted that many segments of our communities are misrepresented or neglected in literature, film, television, and advertising. Farmers are shown as hayseeds, loggers are burly and bearded, highway patrol officers are mean, lean, and wear sunglasses. Street scenes are frequently devoid of handicappers and do not reflect a community's ethnic populations. Stereotyping is, of course, best combatted by education and familiarity. Any activity that helps young people find realistic images will help diminish the power of negative or stereotypical portrayals on television and in books. In addition, most of the activities suggested in this "Projects and Publishing" section can be used to correct stereotypes of others besides elders. Students can engage in letter-writing campaigns to publishers, authors, television personnel, and sponsors who portray a group or place in demeaning or stereotypical ways, or who systematically exclude a group. They can seek out literature and film portrayals that are accurate and individualistic, and share those materials with students in other classes and grades. They can create original stories with illustrations for children, rewrite commercials, design new television shows. They can make their own books and give them to a class or library. They can locate books and films for children and young adults that contain positive and/or realistic images and prepare bibliographies of these for teachers and librarians. They can give talks to students' and parents' groups in which they contrast the stereotypes with realistic depictions. They can make book displays for the school or library and write reviews for the school and local paper. In all these projects, students use language arts for the very real purpose of changing people's attitudes, whether by informing, persuading, or entertaining.

Besides community ignorance, stereotyping in the media, and absence of sympathy or empathy, other unique issues can arise from student's research into the community. A class may discover that people tend to underestimate the sophistication, strength, or abilities of some people in the community because they do not speak English, because they are blind, or because they have no permanent residence. They may find that a local industry enjoys popular community support not because it has contributed to the growth of the community but because it has conducted a strong campaign of local advertising. Students can uncover more specific unresolved conflicts, such as between industrialists and environmentalists, land developers and park enthusiasts, growers and pickers, immigrant job-seekers and long-time area workers, tuna fishers and Greenpeace. These problems suggest additional research and projects: interviewing representatives from all sides of an issue, sponsoring debates, analyzing written and visual propaganda, and studying the literature and language of controversy.

Publishing

All the materials students produce in these projects are classifiably publications if they are done with care and in forms that can be preserved or duplicated. Through publishing, young people can help each other and the community correct inaccurate notions of people and places, acquiring new insights into their neighborhoods and world in the process. In learning about a community, young people become teachers; and the pen and the voice are powerful tools. With some variations the publications described in Chapter 6 will fit nearly any topic. In the nonfiction category, children can produce biographies of individuals in a community group or profession, or of buildings or locales. Memory books compiled from people's recollections might feature the history of a manufacturing plant or a hospital told in the stories of the people who worked there over the years, immigrants' stories of coming to America, long-time residents' reminiscences about the changes made in a building or other landmark, lawyers' recollections of their most interesting clients, or interesting stories of fire fighters. Memory books can illustrate history, shed light on an occupation, bring out people's most human qualities. Books about one or several people's accomplishments can bring recognition to individuals or groups, and how-to books like the Foxfire series can help preserve customs and skills that might otherwise be lost. Similarly, anthologies of fiction and poetry by students, by others in the community, or by both in collaboration are a good way to record and remember a project as well as to make writers feel rewarded and encouraged. (Literature about any community subject can be anthologized: poems about a park, stories about the subway, fiction with handicapped characters or that takes place in a grocery store.) And art books make excellent informative displays for a library.

Community research might lead students to create or help with the production of a periodical: a literary magazine for a hospice; a newsletter that reports community events of interest to handicapped readers; a fictitious newspaper from the past about a significant community event; a newsletter-type fact sheet for hospital patients; a newsletter for a housing project. Or it might yield a number of audiovisual or theatrical productions: a slide-tape show about farm life; a videotaped tour of the garment district; a photo-essay of historic houses; a reader's theater about factory work; a storyboard for a commercial to sell the city a new transit system. The productions and publications possible when classes explore the community are as endless as the collective imaginations of teachers, students, and community residents.

Notes

1. Combes, Lenora. *Let's Go Shopping.* (New York: Simon and Schuster, 1948).

2. Palmer, Helen. Illus. by J. P. Miller. *Tommy's Wonderful Rides.* (New York: Simon and Schuster, 1948).

3. Dolbier, Maurice, Illus. by Tibor Gergely. *The Magic Bus.* (New York: Grosset & Dunlap, 1948).

4. Brown, Margaret Wise, and Edith Thacher Hurd. Illus. by Alice and Martin Provensen. *The Little Fat Policeman.* (Racine, WI: Golden Press, 1950).

Chapter Eight

No End

Farewell

Here on this lonely cliff top
Facing the wind and the sea,
I recall many trips to this beachside
And what they have meant to me.

How I loved those walks of a morning
With the crunch of the still-wet sand,
The voice of the restless ocean
And flotsam on every hand.

How I thrilled to the panorama
That colored the morning sky:
The sun's first rays on the surf spray,
The sea gull's haunting cry.

I watched you asleep on the softsand
At the edge of the shade from the bluff
Hoping to get a sun tan
But only just enough.

Those golden summer twilights
After watching the setting sun
The calm, receding ocean
And the end of a day of fun.

How I've loved those walks in this setting
By the ever murmuring sea;
I wonder if even God knows
What they have meant to me.

I watch—the wind stirs sand clouds
And hurries them along.
Is this farewell to this beachside
And the days when we both were strong?

—Ralph M. Zeigler

Community study has no end. In the same way that a culture is an intricate interaction among a people's economic, political, value, and belief systems, a community within that culture is a complex network of people, places, and times. Although parts of a community may not appear connected or even related, each contributes toward shaping the community's unique identity. One aspect relates to another, and to each individual. Exploring one facet of a community inevitably leads to explorations of others: when we see how few public facilities are designed to accommodate very old people, we realize that all people with physical handicaps must face the same obstacles. When we talk to members of the city council about this problem we become curious about how a city government works. So we visit a city council meeting, where we hear a discussion about the costs of constructing a freeway bypass. And then we want to know how roads are built, which makes us conscious of the stereotypes of construction workers. On it goes. One search leads to another; learning leads to learning. Thus at the end of any community study, students are likely to find themselves back at the beginning of the process — examining their attitudes and where they came from.

As children grow up in a community, their awareness and knowledge of the community broadens, regardless of what they learn in school. But by intentionally integrating the community and classroom, teachers can hasten and intensify the process. More importantly, they can help children feel more securely and responsibly connected to the world outside themselves. When the little world of the school room grows, students' language becomes richer, and so do the bonds that unite them with their language community. People and places they meet become a part of their experience just as the young people become real and meaningful to others. Knowledge brings with it a certain responsibility, a sense of ownership. Strangers who become familiar belong to us. They are no longer invisible; we must acknowledge their existence and concerns. We can no longer not see the absence of wheelchair ramps in buildings or the patronizing stereotypes of old people in a television commercial. We can no longer ignore the people sleeping in the park or under the freeway. These people have become part of our lives because we know about them. Similarly, imagined enemies who become friends belong to us in a new way. When we abandon our prejudices and fears we can no longer abuse or deride law enforcement officers or members of a minority group. I may be entitled to an opinion, but I am responsible for a fact.

Whether we recognize it or not, we are the community — all the people, the factories, shops, traffic, skyscrapers, garbage disposal systems, waterways, and playgrounds. Our environments affect our lives for better or worse, just as we have the power to influence and change our environments. We are connected to the community in multiple and various ways. Local business and industry affect employment patterns and perhaps our own incomes. What our neighbors purchase determines what is available in stores. We drive on community streets and enjoy parks, pools, and other neighborhood recreational facilities. The city takes away our trash and sewage, purifies our water, and removes snow in the winter. We are connected to people of all ages, physical and mental abilities, and ethnic backgrounds by the fact that we are human and share common interests and concerns. (Prejudice and ignorance affect all members of a community, not merely the victims.) So when young people explore their environment, they are, in a way, taking a look at themselves. And when they end a community study, they should have a greater sense of connectedness, confidence, power. But as I said before, community study has no end.

Children's Books with Themes of Old Age and/or Significant Older Characters

Most of the works cited here are recent. An excellent bibliography of children's and young adult's literature published before 1980 is included in Catherine Townsend Horner's The Aging Adult in Children's Books & Nonprint Media *(Scarecrow Press, 1982).*

The ages noted in parentheses are general guides only; individual readers vary widely in interests and abilities. Titles for readers age 11 and up are also included in the bibliography of young adult literature.

Aaron, Chester. *Better than Laughter.* New York: Harcourt Brace Jovanovich, 1972. (11–14). Two boys have material advantages but little in the way of attention or love. They meet an old man who runs the town dump and has problems of his own.

Ackerman, Karen. Illus. by Stephen Gammell. *Song and Dance Man.* New York: Knopf, 1988. (4–7). A grandfather shows his grandchildren some of the songs and dances he performed on the vaudeville stage.

Adler, C. S. *Goodbye Pink Pig.* New York: Avon, 1986. (9 and up). An unconventional grandmother is a school custodian.

———. *Fly Free.* New York: Coward-McCann, 1984. (10–14). A kindly older neighbor offers friendship to a lonely 13-year-old girl with an emotionally abusive mother and absent father.

Anders, Rebecca. Photographs by Maria S. Forrai. *A Look at Aging.* Minneapolis: Lerner, 1977. (1–5). Photos showing the pleasures and pains of old age.

Anderson, Susanne, David R. Brower, ed. *Song of the Earth Spirit.* Washington, DC: Friends of the Earth, 1974. (All ages). Photographs of the Navajo families with whom the author lived.

Ancona, George. *Growing Older.* New York: Dutton, 1978. (8–11). A photo-essay of aging, showing old age in a positive light. Shows people from different ethnic backgrounds in different parts of the country.

Bales, Carol Ann. *Tales of the Elders: A Memory Book of Men and Women Who Came to America as Immigrants, 1900–1930.* Chicago: Follett, 1977. (11–14). Stories of 12 naturalized Americans.

Bellairs, John. *The Mummy, the Will, and the Crypt.* New York: Dial, 1983. (9–12). Second in *The Curse of the Blue Figurine* trilogy. A boy and his grandparents are involved in a mystery.

Berenstain, Stan and Jan. *A Week at Grandma's.* New York: Random House, 1986. (5–8). Brother and Sister Bear experience some anxiety when they go to spend a week by themselves at their grandparents so their parents can have a second honeymoon.

Berger, Barbara. *Grandfather Twilight.* New York: Philomel, 1984. (4–8). Grandfather Twilight walks through the woods each evening to perform a special nightly ritual.

Beritner, Sue. *The Bookseller's Advice.* New York: Viking, 1981. (8–10). The customers of an old book seller come to him for advice. Because he is hard of hearing, he misunderstands their questions but his advice still has good results.

Berridge, Celia. *Grandmother's Tales.* Bergenfield, NJ: Deutsch, 1982. (3–7). Grandmother cares for the children when their mother is in the hospital; she sings, cooks, tells stories.

Blos, Joan. Illus. by Stephen Gammell. *Old Henry.* New York: Morrow Junior, 1987. (3–9). An eccentric old artist moves into old, run-down house and has problems with the neighbors who expect him to renovate.

Branscum, Robbie. *The Girl.* Harper Junior Books, 1986. (11 and up). Left in the care of a cruel grandmother and lazy grandfather, five children struggle to survive in an Arkansas sharecropper community.

Bridgers, Sue Ellen. *All Together Now.* New York: Knopf, 1979. (11 and up). A 12-year-old girl spends the summer with her grandparents while her father is fighting in Korea and her mother works. She encounters a number of unusual characters and fights to help a retarded man avoid institutionalization.

Brown, Margaret Wise. Illus. by Geoffrey Hayes. *When the Wind Blew.* New York: Harper & Row, 1977. (4–7). An old woman lives alone by the seashore and derives comfort from her 17 cats, and especially one blue-gray kitten.

Bunting, Eve. Illus. by Lorinda Bryan. *Clancey's Coat.* New York: Viking, 1985. (6–9). Two older men are best friends until the tailor's cow ruins Clancey's garden. When Clancey brings the Tailor a coat to mend, the friendship is patched up as well.

———. Illus. by Charles Mikolaycak. *The Man Who Could Call Down Owls.* New York: Macmillan, 1984. (6–10). An old man is a friend of the owls but an evil stranger tries to take his power.

———. Illus. by Vo-Dinh Mai. *The Happy Funeral.* New York: Harper & Row, 1982. (7–10). A young Chinese-American girl mourns her grandfather's death.

———. Illus. by Allen Say. *Magic and the Night River.* New York: Harper & Row, 1978. (2–5). A Chinese boy fishes with his grandfather using cormorants with rings around their necks. The grandfather's kindness to the birds after several fishing boats collide helps the old man gain new respect.

Burch, Robert. Illus. by Richard Cuffari. *Two that Were Tough.* New York: Viking, 1976. (7−10). An old man tries to preserve his independence while coming to terms with his own aging.

Buscaglia, Leo. Pictures by Carol Newsom. *A Memory for Tino.* New York: SLACK/Morrow, 1988. (7−10). An eight-year-old boy befriends an old woman who lives in the old house on the hill.

Byars, Betsy. Illus. by Rocco Negri. *Trouble River.* New York: Avon, 1978. (8−11). A boy in the old west takes his grandmother down a river to escape from Indians.

Carey, Valerie Scho. Illus. by Arnold Lobel. *The Devil and Mother Crump.* New York: Harper & Row, 1987. (7−11). A cranky, mean old woman gets the best of the devil. Folktale.

Caseley, Judith. *Apple Pie and Onions.* New York: Greenwillow, 1987. (6−9). A girl who loves her grandmother, her stories, and the things she brought from the old country experiences discomfort at her grandmother's exuberance. Grandmother knows how to deal with it.

———. *When Grandpa Came to Stay.* New York: Greenwillow, 1986. (5−8). Benny's grandpa moves in with his family after the death of Grandma. They become great friends, and Benny comes to understand Grandpa's sadness.

Cate, Riki. *A Cat's Tale.* San Diego: Harcourt Brace Jovanovich, 1982. (7−11). A mistaken, wind-blown shout brings Mary the recluse a house full of cats that she hates. They save her from a burglar.

Cazet, Denys. *Great Uncle Felix.* New York: Watts/Orchard/Richard Jackson, 1988. (4−6). Young Rhinoceros meets his great-uncle at the bus station but everything seems to go wrong.

———. *Sunday.* New York: MacMillan/Bradbury, 1988. (6−9). Barney's Sundays with his grandparents are never dull.

———. *December 24th.* New York: Bradbury, 1986. (4−7). Grandfather Rabbit pretends he doesn't know that it's his birthday when his grandchildren bring him a present.

———. *Big Shoe, Little Shoe.* New York: Bradbury, 1984. (4−7). Little Rabbit and his grandfather exchange shoes.

———. *Christmas Moon.* New York: Bradbury, 1984. (4−7). A young rabbit misses his grandfather who has died, but learns from the moon.

Cleaver, Vera and Bill. *Queen of Hearts.* New York: Lippincott Jr. Books, 1987. (10−13). A 12-year-old girl resents having to stay with her grandmother.

Clifton, Lucille. Illus. by Dale Payson. *The Lucky Stone.* New York: Dell/Yearling. (7−10). Four stories told by a great-grandmother bring understanding across several generations.

Cooney, Barbara. *Island Boy.* New York: Viking Kestrel, 1988. (4−8). Four generations of a New England coastal island show strong relationships between old and young.

———. *Miss Rumphius*. (4–8). New York: Viking, 1982. Great Aunt Alice tries to figure out how to honor her grandfather's request to make the world more beautiful.

Dahl, Roald. Illus. by Quentin Blake. *The Witches*. New York: Farrar, Straus & Giroux, 1982. (8–10). A boy is turned into a mouse by the Grand High Witch of the World. He and his grandmother begin a war against all the witches.

Daly, Nike. *Not So Fast Songololo*. New York: Puffin, 1987. (6–10). A South African story of a boy who proudly wears the new sneakers his grandmother buys for him.

Davis, Maggie S. Illus. by Kay Chorao. *Rickety Witch*. New York: Holiday House, 1984. (5–8). A kindly old witch is cleverer than two younger witches. She "treats" the town children on Halloween.

Delton, Judy. Illus. by Marc Simont. *My Uncle Nikos*. New York: Thomas Y. Crowell, 1983. (6–9). Helena visits her uncle's rustic house in a small Greek mountain village during the summer.

Delton, Judy, and Dorothy Tucker. *My Grandma's in a Nursing Home*. Niles, IL: Albert Whitman, 1986. (7–10). A boy learns the value of his visits to his grandmother in a nursing home.

de Paola, Tomie. *Now One Foot, Now the Other*. New York: G. P. Putnam's Sons, 1981. (4–8). A young boy whose grandfather helped him learn to walk returns the favor when his grandfather recovers from a stroke.

———. *Watch Out for the Chicken Feet in Your Soup*. Englewood Cliffs, NJ: Prentice-Hall, 1974. (4–7). Joey is embarrassed by his Italian grandmother's "difference," and angry that she seems to criticize him and praise his friend. He learns that criticism sometimes means special love.

Donnelly, Elfie. Trans. by Anthea Bell. *So Long, Grandpa*. New York: Crown, 1981. (9–12). A boy has a close relationship with his dying grandfather.

Douglass, Barbara. Illus. by Carol Newsom. *The Great Town and Country Bicycle Balloon Chase*. New York: Lothrop, Lee & Shepard, 1984. (5–8). A grandfather and his granddaughter join a bicycle race to reach a hot-air balloon.

———. Illus. by Patience Brewster. *Good as New*. New York: Lothrop, Lee & Shepard, 1982. (4–8). Grandfather fixes a teddy bear that was ruined by a visitor.

Egger, Bettina. Illus. by Sita Jucker. *Marianne's Grandmother*. New York: Dutton, 1987. (4–8). Girl experiences memories of her grandmother after the grandmother's funeral. She realizes that death cannot take away love.

Farber, Norma. Illus. by Trina Schart Hyman. *How Does it Feel to be Old?* New York: Dutton, 1979. (6–10). An old woman explains to her granddaughter some of the pleasures and pains of being old. Poignant, realistic, positive.

Fine, Anne. *The Granny Project.* New York: Farrar, Straus & Giroux, 1983. (11 and up). Four children's efforts to keep their grandmother from being put in a rest home.

Fosburgh, Liza. *Mrs. Abercorn and the Bounce Boys.* New York: Four Winds, 1986. (9–12). Two boys without a father become friends with an old woman.

Fox, Mem. *Wilfrid Gordon McDonald Partridge.* Brooklyn. NY: Kane/Miller, 1984. (5–11). A young boy begins a project to find memories for his favorite friend in the old peoples' home next door.

Gelfand, Marilyn. Illus. with photographs by Rosemarie Hausherr. *My Great Grandpa Joe.* New York: Four Winds, 1986. (4–8). Through a photo album, a young girl learns about her great-grandfather and about aging.

Girion, Barbara. Illus. by Richard Cuffari. *Joshua, the Czar, and the Chicken Bone Wish.* New York: Scribner, 1978. (8–11). A boy who feels awkward and has low self-esteem learns confidence from some friends in the nursing home where his mother works.

Goldman, Susan. *Grandpa and Me Together.* Niles, IL: Albert Whitman, 1980. (4–7). A girl spends a day doing things with her very active grandfather.

Gomi, Taro. *Coco Can't Wait!* New York: Puffin, 1985. (4–7). A girl and her grandmother want to visit but keep missing each other.

Gondosch, Linda. Illus. by Helen Cogancherry. *Who's Afraid of Haggerty House?* New York: Lodestar, 1987. (9–11). An 11-year-old girl befriends an old woman after she becomes alienated from her two best friends.

Gould, Deborah. Illus. by Cheryl Harness. *Grandpa's Slide Show.* New York: Lothrop, Lee & Shepard, 1987. (3–8). Two boys whose grandfather liked to show slides remember him after his death by looking at the slides again.

Graeber, Charlotte. Illus. by Donna Diamond. *Mustard.* New York: Macmillan, 1982. (4–7). A family experiences the decline and death of a beloved cat.

Green, Phyllis. *Uncle Roland, The Perfect Guest.* New York: Four Winds, 1983. (6–10). A disruptive house guest teaches children to play their noses and offers to do their chores.

———. *Grandmother Orphan.* Nashville, TN: Thomas Nelson, 1977. (9–12). An 11-year-old shoplifter is sent to her tough grandmother's house for a week.

Griffith, Helen V. Illus. by James Stevenson. *Grandaddy's Place.* New York: Greenwillow, 1987. (5–8). Prequel to *Georgia Music,* about the first meeting of the grandfather and granddaughter and their growing relationship.

———. *Georgia Music.* New York: Greenwillow, 1986. (6–10). A little girl from the city gets to know her grandfather during a summer at his cabin in rural Georgia. When he must go to the city because of failing health, the girl brings him all the sounds of the cabin.

Griffiths, Helen. *Running Wild.* New York: Holiday House, 1977. (11 and up). A boy lives in the mountains in Spain with his grandparents. His grandfather gives him a dog, but kills the dog's first litter of pups. The boy hides the next batch of puppies, who turn out to be wild.

Guernsey, JoAnn Bren. *Journey to Almost There.* New York: Ticknor & Fields, 1985. (11–14). To escape having her grandfather placed in a nursing home, a girl takes her grandfather and runs away to find her father. The grandfather's health weakens, and the girl must make some difficult decisions.

Guthrie, Donna. Illus. by Katy Keck Arnsteen. *Grandpa Doesn't Know It's Me.* New York: Human Sciences Press, 1986. (5–10). A girl tells about her grandfather and his progression into Alzheimer's disease. She is able to love and understand him even though he is not the same.

Hall, Donald. Illus. by Mary Azarian. *The Man Who Lived Alone.* Boston: Godine, 1984. (7 and up). A wonderful, eccentric old man who lives alone deserves respect and admiration.

Hall, Lynn. *The Seige of Silent Henry.* Chicago: Follett, 1972. (11–14). A selfish, lonely young man, who wants to be rich befriends an old man in order to steal the secret of the valuable Ginseng root beds; both realize their selfishness.

Hamm, Diane Johnston. Illus. by Charles Robinson. *Grandma Drives a Motor Bed.* Niles, IL: Albert Whitman, 1987. (4–8). A young boy's love and concern for his bedridden grandmother and the realities of the physical disabilities of aging.

Havill, Juanita. Illus. by Janet Wentworth. *Leroy and the Clock.* Boston: Houghton Mifflin, 1988. (5–7). A five-year-old boy makes his first solo visit to Grandfather's house with some trepidation; his discomfort is expressed through his feelings about the hall clock.

Hayes, Sheila. *Speaking of Snapdragons.* New York: Lodestar, 1982. (10–14). A lonely, fatherless 11-year-old girl befriends an old gardener.

Hedderwick, Mairi. *Katie Morag and the Two Grandmothers.* Boston: Little, Brown, 1985. (10–13). A girl's two grandmothers are very different.

Heide, Florence Parry. *When the Sad One Comes to Stay.* New York: Bantam, 1976. (11–14). A girl who moves to a new town befriends a poor old woman. The girl's mother, who is conscious of her social position, disapproves.

Henkes, Kevin. *Grandpa and Bo.* New York: Greenwillow, 1986. (6–9). A boy spends the summer with his grandfather and learns about life in the country.

Henriod, Lorraine. Illus. by Christa Chevalier. *Grandma's Wheelchair.* Niles, IL: Albert Whitman, 1982. (3–6). A loving relationship is shared by a four-year-old and his grandmother.

Hest, Amy. Illus. by Karen Gundersheimer. *The Midnight Eaters*. New York: Four Winds Press, 1989. (6–9). A girl's grandmother disregards her doctor's warning and joins her granddaughter for a midnight snack.

———. Illus. by Amy Schwartz. *The Purple Coat*. New York: Four Winds, 1986. (6–9). A girl and her mother go to the city to visit Grandfather, a tailor, who will make her a new fall coat. The girl wants a purple coat instead of her usual blue one.

———. *The Crack-of-Dawn Walkers*. New York: Macmillan, 1984. (3–7). A girl and her grandfather share an early Sunday morning walk.

Hines, Anna Grossnickle. *Grandma Gets Grumpy*. Boston, MA: Houghton Mifflin, 1988. (5–8). The story of a special grandparent-grandchild relationship when five cousins spend the night together.

Holl, Kristi D. *No Strings Attached*. New York: Atheneum, 1988. (10–12). A 12-year-old girl's mother is a paid companion to a "crusty" old man. When they move in with the man, the girl experiences initial resentment.

Hooker, Ruth. Illus. by Ruth Rosner. *At Grandma and Grandpa's House*. Niles, IL: Albert Whitman, 1985. (4–6). The warmth and joy of grandparents' houses.

Hurd, Edith Thatcher. *I Dance in My Red Pajamas*. New York: Harper & Row, 1982. (5–7). Jenny looks forward to dancing noisily with her grandfather when she goes to visit.

Hutchins, Pat. *The Doorbell Rang*. New York: Greenwillow, 1986. (5–8). The children are sharing cookies when Grandma shows up with the best cookies of all.

Jones, Weyman. Illus. by J. C. Kocsis. *Edge of Two Worlds*. New York: Dial, 1968. (11–15). In 1842, circumstances bring together a 15-year-old white boy and an aging Cherokee Indian.

Joose, Barbara. *Jam Day*. New York: Harper & Row, 1987. (5–9). Ben overcomes his loneliness when he discovers his extended family on a trip to visit relatives on a farm.

Jukes, Mavis. Illus. by Thomas B. Allen. *Blackberries in the Dark*. New York: Alfred A. Knopf, 1985. (10–12). A nine-year-old boy visits his grandmother the summer after his grandfather dies, and they try to come to terms with their loss.

Kantrowitz, Mildred. Illus. by Emily McCully. *Maxie*. New York: Four Winds, 1980. (4–8). When Maxie feels so lonely and unwanted that she doesn't get up one morning, her neighbors convince her that she is needed.

Keller, Holly. *The Best Present*. New York: Greenwillow, 1989. (5 and up). A little girl wants to visit her grandmother in the hospital, but her visit is against the rules. Her flowers, however, speak for her.

Kessler, Ethel, and Leonard Kessler. *Grandpa Witch and the Magic Doobelator*. New York: Macmillan, 1981. (5–8). A grandfather witch helps his grandchildren learn Halloween tricks.

Khalsa, Dayal Kaur. *Tales of a Gambling Grandmother*. New York: Crown, 1986. (8–11). The author recalls the advice of his warm, independent grandmother and the strong influence she had on his life.

Kibbe, Pat. Illus. by Jenny Rutherford. *Mrs. Kiddy and the Moonbeams*. New York: Bradbury, 1983. (9–12). Several stories about an old woman's generosity to friends and neighbors.

Klein, Leonore. Illus. by Leonard Kessler. *How Old Is Old?* New York: Harvey House, 1967. (5–9). Shows that old age is relative and differs among the species. Old is also how one feels.

LaFarge, Phyllis. Illus. by Gahan Wilson. *Granny's Fish Story*. Bowling Green, KY: Parents, 1975. (5–8). A grandmother wears jeans and lives in the country. She helps her granddaughter and her friend overcome their fear of thunderstorms.

Langer, Nola. *Freddy My Grandfather*. New York: Four Winds, 1979. (6–9). A girl tells about her Hungarian-born grandfather who lives with her and leads an active life with many friends and things to do.

Lasky, Kathryn. Illus. by Catherine Stock. *Sea Swan*. New York: Macmillan, 1988. (5–9). A 75-year-old woman learns to swim.

———. Illus. by Trina Schart Hyman. *The Night Journey*. New York: Frederick Warne, 1981. (10–14). A young Jewish girl learns about her great-grandmother's escape from persecution in Russia.

LeShan, Eda. Illus. by Tricia Taggart. *Grandparents: A Special Kind of Love*. New York: Macmillan, 1984. (8–12). Explores relationships between grandparents and grandchildren and gives advice about inter-generational conflicts.

LeTord, Bijou. *My Grandma Leonie*. New York: Bradbury, 1987. (4–6). A girl remembers her grandmother.

Levinson, Riki. *I Go with My Family to Grandma's*. New York: Dutton, 1986. (3–7). Five cousins and their families arrive at Grandmother's home by various means of transportation, and the house gets livelier.

Levitin, Sonia. *All the Cats in the World*. San Diego: Harcourt, Brace Jovanovich, 1982. (4–7). Two elderly people become friends and feed stray cats together.

Lloyd, David. *Grandma and the Pirate*. New York: Crown, 1986. (4–7). A boy and his contemporary grandmother go to the beach and he pretends to be a pirate in his sand ship.

Lundgren, Max. Illus. by Fibben Hald. Trans. by Ann Pyk. *Matt's Grandfather*. New York: G. P. Putnam's Sons, 1972. (6–9). A boy visits his grandfather in a nursing home on his 85th birthday. They take a walk in the park and the boy learns about him and his secret.

Lyon, George Ella. *Borrowed Children*. New York: Watts/Orchard, 1988. (11–15). The story of an extended family in Kentucky and Tennessee during the Depression.

McCulley, Emily. *Grandmas at the Lake*. New York: Harper & Row, 1990.

(6–9). Two grandchildren can't have fun when two grandmothers don't agree.

MacLachlan, Patricia. *Cassie Binegar*. New York: Harper & Row, 1987. (9–12). A young girl who feels guilty about the way she talked to her grandfather before he died comes to terms with her feelings through encounters with an insightful grandmother and some eccentric relatives.

———. Illus. by Lloyd Bloom. *Arthur, For the Very First Time*. New York: Harper & Row, 1980. (9–12). A 10-year-old boy spends the summer at the farm of his great aunt and uncle, and discovers in their unconventional, loving household a new way of seeing things.

Martin, Bill Jr., and John Archambault. Illus. by Ted Rand. *Knots on a Counting Rope*. New York: Henry Holt, 1987. (6–9). A blind Indian boy and his grandfather retell the story of his birth and naming.

Mathis, Sharon Bell. Illus. by Leo and Diane Dillon. *The Hundred Penny Box*. New York: Viking, 1975. (7–10). A young boy loves his old aunt, whose habits of saving things irritate his mother.

Mayer, Mercer. *Just Grandpa and Me*. New York: Golden Press, 1985. (4–7). Little Critter and his grandfather go on a shopping expedition.

———. *Just Grandma and Me*. New York: Golden Press, 1983. (4–7). Little Critter and his wise, tolerant grandmother go to the beach.

Mazer, Norma Fox. *A Figure of Speech*. New York: Dell, 1973. (11–15). A 13-year-old girl is a close companion of her aging grandfather and helps him run away when her family plans to put him in a nursing home.

Mills, Claudia. *The Secret Carousel*. New York: Four Winds, 1983. (8–12). A 10-year-old girl finds life with grandparents in a small town monotonous until she discovers an old carousel.

Montaufier, Poupa. *One Summer at Grandmother's House*. Minneapolis: Carolrhoda Books, 1985. (7–10). The author describes the summers spent in Alsace with his grandmother.

Moore, Elaine. Illus. by Elise Primavera. *Grandma's Promise*. New York: Lothrop, Lee & Shepard, 1988. (7–10). A girl learns that no matter how old she gets, there is a place for her a Grandma's.

———. Illus. by Elise Primavera. *Grandma's House*. New York: Lothrop, Lee & Shepard, 1985. (5–9). Kim enjoys the summers she spends with her active, loving grandmother.

Mosel, Arlene. Illus. by Blair Lent. *The Funny Little Woman*. New York: Dutton, 1972. (5–8). Folk tale about a giggling Japanese woman who outwits the wicked underground creatures who capture her.

Myers, Walter Dean. *Won't Know 'Till I Get There*. New York: Puffin, 1988. (10–14). A boy and his friends are caught spray painting a subway train and sentenced to work in an old people's home.

Newton, Suzanne. *A Place Between*. New York: Viking, 1986. (11–15). A

13-year-old girl feels dislocated when she has to move for her father's new job and when her beloved grandfather dies. She is forced to live temporarily with her grandmother, who encourages friendships with only wealthier, sophisticated girls. She plans to run away to her old home.

Nixon, Joan Lowery. *Maggie, Too.* New York: Dell/Yearling, 1988. (9−12). A father who is about to remarry sends his daughter to spend the summer with her grandmother.

―――. Illus. by Andrew Glass. *The Gift.* New York: Macmillan, 1983. (8−12). The story of a boy and his Irish great-grandfather and the tales the old man tells.

Olson, Arielle North. Illus. by Lydia Dabcovich. *Hurry Home Grandma.* New York: Dutton, 1984. (3−7). An explorer, Grandmother races to get home by Christmas Eve.

Oppenheim, Joanne. *Mrs. Peloki's Snake.* New York: Dodd, Mead, 1980. (5−7). Mrs. Peloki's classroom is upset by a snake in the boy's restroom until a girl goes in and sees that it is just a rope.

Oxenbury, Helen. *Grandma and Grandpa.* New York: Dial, 1984. (3−7). A granddaughter's weekend visit is greeted by love, but requires a certain amount of tolerance on the part of the grandparents.

Parsons, Elizabeth. Illus. by Ronald Himler. *The Upside-Down Cat.* New York: Margaret K. McElderry Books, 1981. (9−12). An old lobster fisherman and a boy love a cat they can't have. Set in Maine.

Paterson, Katherine. *Come Sing, Jimmy Jo.* New York: Avon, 1985. (11 and up). A young teen with a musical gift struggles to maintain an identity in the face of a burgeoning career; his grandmother is a central figure.

Paulson, Gary. *Tracker.* New York: Berkley, 1982. (12−14). John deals with his grandfather's impending death as he slowly tracks a doe.

Pearson, Susan. Illus. by Ronald Himler. *Happy Birthday, Grampie.* New York: Dial, 1987. (4−8). A girl makes a special, textured birthday card for her blind grandfather.

Polacco, Patricia. *Rechenka's Eggs.* New York: Philomel, 1988. (5−8). The relationship between a kindly old woman who lives in the country near pre-revolutionary Moscow and a goose that lays decorated eggs.

―――. *The Keeping Quilt.* New York: Simon & Schuster, 1988. (7−10). A quilt made from old clothes is used over four generations, from Russia to America.

Pomerantz, Charlotte. Illus. by Dyanne DiSalvo-Ryan. *The Half Birthday Party.* New York: Ticknor & Fields 1984. (4−8). Daniel plans a half-birthday party for his six-month-old sister and forgets to get a present for her.

―――. Illus. by Yossi Abolafia. *Buffy and Albert.* New York: Greenwillow, 1982. (4−8). Growing old presents problems for a grandfather and his two cats. Humorous, serious, realistic.

Pople, Maureen. *The Other Side of the Family*. New York: Henry Holt, 1986. (11–15). The humorous story of a 15-year-old English girl sent to live in Australia during World War II. She encounters some very interesting, eccentric relatives, including a grandmother.

Pringle, Laurence. *Death is Natural*. New York: Four Winds, 1977. (9–12). Simple discussion of the nature of death.

Raynor, Dorka. *Grandparents Around the World*. Niles, IL: Albert Whitman, 1977. (6–12). Black-and-white photos from 25 countries.

Rice, Eve. *Aren't You Coming, Too?* New York: Greenwillow, 1988. (4–6). A fun-filled trip to the zoo with Grandpa saves Amy from loneliness when everyone else is busy.

Rogers, Paul. *From Me to You*. New York: Watts/Orchard, 1988. (7–10). Grandma traces three generations of the family's history in a story told to her granddaughter.

Rosen, Winifred. Illus. by Kay Chorao. *Henrietta and the Gong from Hong Kong*. New York: Four Winds, 1981. (5–10). A girl learns from her grandmother that her own mother had some problems growing up, too.

Rylant, Cynthia. Illus. by Stephen Gammel. *The Relatives Came*. New York: Bradbury, 1985. (5–11). This story of a family get-together in rustic, rural Virginia is full of fun, family love, and support.

———. Illus. by Thomas Di Grazia. *Miss Maggie*. New York: Dutton, 1983. (5–9). A young boy makes friends with an old woman who lives in an old log house at the end of the pasture.

Schertle, Alice. Illus. by Lydia Dabcovich. *William and Grandpa*. New York: Lothrop, Lee & Shepard, 1989. (4–8). A boy discovers that his grandfather, as a boy, liked to do the same things he does. The two spend a day playing their favorite games.

Schwartz, Amy. *Oma and Bobo*. New York: Bradbury, 1987. (5–7). A grandmother is horrified when her granddaughter brings home and sets out to train a dog. She secretely softens and helps the dog graduate from obedience school.

Segal, Lore. Illus. by Marcia Sewall. *The Story of Old Mrs. Brubeck and How She Looked for Trouble and Where She Found Him*. New York: Pantheon, 1981. (5–9). A grandmother goes out to find trouble so she can keep an eye on it.

Seuling, Barbara. *The Teeny Tiny Woman*. New York: Viking, 1976. (1–5). A ghost story from England about an old woman who lives alone.

Shanks, Ann Zane. *Old Is What You Get: Dialogues on Aging by the Old and the Young*. New York: Viking, 1976. (9 and up). Photos and transcribed comments on different aspects of aging from young and old people. Examines the realities of aging.

Silverstein, Alvin, Virginia Silverstein, and Glenn Silverstein. *Aging*. New York: Franklin Watts, 1979. (9–13). Comprehensive discussion and photographs about the processes of aging. Covers theory, research, and issues related to aging in current society.

Silverstein, Shel. *The Giving Tree.* New York: Harper & Row, 1964. (5 and up). The story of the nurturing relationship between a tree and a boy as they both age.

Skorpen, Liesel Moak. Illus. by Wallace Tripp. *Old Arthur.* New York: Harper & Row, 1972. (5–8). A dog is too old to help on the farm, but not too old to be a good friend to a little boy.

Smith, Robert Kimmel. Illus. by Richard Lauter. *The War with Grandpa.* New York: Dell/Yearling. (9–11). A boy tries to get his room back when Grandpa moves in.

Stevens, Margaret. Illus. by Kenneth Ualand. *When Grandpa Died.* Chicago: Children's Press, 1979. (5–8). A girl is angry when her grandfather dies. She learns to cry and talk about her feelings.

Stevenson, James. *What's Under My Bed?* New York: Greenwillow, 1983. (4–8). A grandfather tells his grandson about his adventures as a boy.

———. *The Worst Person in the World.* New York: Greenwillow, 1978. (5–9). Mean Ms. Worst meets friendly, outgoing Mr. Ugly.

Stock, Catherine. *Emma's Dragon Hunt.* New York: Lothrop, Lee & Shepard, 1984. (6–8). When Emma's grandfather from China comes to live with her, they share many Chinese dragon myths.

Stolz, Mary. Illus. by Pat Cummings. *Storm in the Night.* New York: Harper & Row, 1988. (6–9). When a storm knocks out the power, a boy listens to his grandfather tell stories about a time when he was young, in a storm, and afraid.

Streich, Corrine, comp. Illus. by Lilian Hoban. *Grandparent's Houses: Poems About Grandparents.* New York: Greenwillow, 1984. (6 and up). Poems by well-known and unknown poets from many cultures.

Stren, Patti. *There's a Rainbow in My Closet.* New York: Harper & Row, 1979. (5–8). A girl at first resents her grandmother who comes to stay with her when her mother goes on a trip. She learns to appreciate and value her grandmother and her special qualities.

Taylor, Mildred. Illus. by Max Ginsberg. *The Friendship.* New York: Dial, 1987. (9 and up). A prequel to *Roll of Thunder, Hear My Cry,* about the younger Logan children's encounter with an old man and his struggle for dignity and respect in the face of racism.

———. *Roll of Thunder, Hear My Cry.* New York: Dial, 1976. (11 and up). A black family in the rural south in the 1930s struggles to hold on to its land. The grandmother is a strong woman who teaches 11-year-old Cassie some valuable lessons about survival.

Thomas, Ianthe. Illus. by Ann Toulmin-Rothe. *Hi, Mrs. Mallory!* New York: Harper & Row, 1979. (6–9). A girl stops after school every day to visit and help her friend, old Mrs. Mallory, and her two dogs. One day, Mrs. Mallory is not home, and the girl learns she has died.

Thomas, Jane Resh. Illus. by Marcia Sewall. *Saying Good-bye to Grandma.*

New York: Clarion, 1988. (7–9). A detailed description of a grand-other's funeral.

Thomson, Pat. Illus. by Faith Jaques. *Good Girl Granny*. New York: Dell, 1988. (5–7). A grandmother tells her grandson about the times she got into trouble when she was little.

Tolan, Stephanie. *Grandpa — and Me*. New York: Scribner's, 1978. (10–14). An 11-year-old girl's grandfather becomes increasingly confused. She begins to learn about his past and her family, and about the connections between being young and being old.

Van Leeuwen, Jean. Illus. by Ann Schweninger. *Oliver, Amanda, and Grandmother Pig*. New York: Dial, 1987. (4–8). Oliver and Amanda are annoyed because their grandmother's age keeps her from playing the games they want to play. They learn to value her special qualities.

Vigna, Judith. *Grandma Without Me*. Niles, IL: Albert Whitman, 1984. (4–8). A boy is separated from the grandmother he loves when his parents divorce.

Wagner, Jenny. Illus. by Ron Brooks. *John Brown, Rose, and the Midnight Cat*. New York: Bradbury, 1978. (4–8). An old woman who lives alone with her sheepdog befriends a cat, much to the disgust of the sheepdog.

Walker, Alice. *To Hell With Dying*. San Diego: Harcourt Brace Jovanovich, 1988. (8–11). Two children who loved their elderly neighbor must deal with his death.

Wallace, Barbara Brooks. Illus. by Gloria Kamen. *Hawkins*. Nashville, TN: Abingdon, 1977. (8–11). A 10-year-old boy wins a gentleman's gentleman for a month, and learns, among other things, about the perspective of older people.

Warren, Cathy. *Saturdays Belong to Sara*. New York: Bradbury, 1988. (6–9). A mother and daughter enjoy a visit with Aunt Claire's elderly friend.

Wells, Rosemary. *Good Night, Fred*. New York: Dial, 1981. (4–7). A boy believes his grandmother lives in the telephone and worries when the telephone breaks.

Wilkinson, Brenda. *Ludell*. New York: Harper & Row, 1975. (11 and up). Ludell is a black pre-teen living in the segregated South; she is being raised by a loving, firm grandmother.

Wilkinson, Sylvia. *A Killing Frost*. Boston: Houghton Mifflin, 1969. (11–14). A sensitive 13-year-old girl describes the old age of her grandmother, a tough, stubborn woman who lives in rural North Carolina.

Williams, Vera. *Music, Music for Everyone*. New York: Greenwillow, 1984. (4–9). Rosa and her friends organize a band to play for neighborhood parties to raise money for the care of her grandmother.

Wilson, Forrest. Illus. by David McKee. *Super Gran*. Harmondsworth, Middlesex, England: Puffin Books, 1980. (9 and up). The comic adventures of an old woman with super-powers who vanquishes evil. Also a television program in the U.K. Other books in the series include *Super Gran Superstar, Super Gran is Magic, The Television Adventures of Super Gran, More Television Adventures of Super Gran, Super Gran in Orbit, Super Gran: The Picture Book,* and *Super Gran: Rules OK!*

Wood, Phyllis Anderson. *Then I'll Be Home Free.* New York: Signet, 1988. (12 and up). A girl must deal with her grandmother's death and grandfather's breakdown.

Wright, Betty Ren. *Getting Rid of Marjorie.* New York: Holiday House, 1981. (10–13). A young girl feels threatened and jealous when her grandfather remarries.

Yolen, Jane. Illus. by Nancy Winslow Parker. *No Bath Tonight.* New York: Crowell Jr. Books, 1978. (1–5). A little boy does everything to avoid a bath until Grandmother comes to visit and outfoxes him.

Zim, Herbert S., and Sonia Bleeker. *Life and Death.* New York: Morrow, 1970. (8–11). Straightforward explanation of death and its place in the life cycle. Describes burial customs.

Zolotow, Charlotte. Illus. by James Stevenson. *I Know a Lady.* New York: Greenwillow, 1984. (5–10). The story of an elderly neighbor woman who shares her garden, gives Halloween treats, and knows the names of the children's pets.

——. Illus. by Kazue Mizumura. *River Winding.* New York: Crowell Jr. Books, 1978. (8–11). Poems on the cycles of life and nature.

Young Adult Fiction and Nonfiction with Themes of Old Age and/or Significant Older Characters

Books in this bibliography are for readers age 11 and older. Titles suitable for younger adolescents (ages 11–13) are also listed in the bibliography of children's literature.

Aaron, Chester. *Catch Calico!* New York: Dutton, 1979. A 14-year-old boy faces problems when his grandfather gets sick and his cat dies.

———. *Better Than Laughter.* New York: Harcourt Brace Jovanovich, 1972. Two boys have material advantages but little in the way of attention or love. They meet an old man who runs the town dump and has problems of his own.

Adler, C. S. *Fly Free.* New York: Coward-McCann, 1984. A kindly older neighbor offers friendship to a lonely 13-year-old girl with an emotionally abusive mother and absent father.

Anderson, Susanne, David R. Brower, ed. *Song of the Earth Spirit.* Washington, DC: Friends of the Earth, 1974. Photographs of the Navajo families with whom the author lived.

Bach, Alice. *Mollie Make-Believe.* New York: Dell, 1976. An adolescent girl must deal with the crisis of her favorite grandmother's impending death.

Bales, Carol Ann. *Tales of the Elders: A Memory Book of Men and Women Who Came to America as Immigrants, 1900–1930.* Chicago: Follett, 1977. Stories of 12 naturalized Americans.

Benjamin, Carol Lea. *Nobody's Baby Now.* New York: Berkley, 1985. A young girl is torn by feelings of loyalty to her grandmother, whose mental health is deteriorating, and her desire to spend her time on romance.

Bosse, Malcolm J. *The 79 Squares.* New York: Thomas Y. Crowell, 1979. A 14-year-old boy who hangs around with a gang of toughs becomes drawn to a strange old man. He must defend him against his parents and the gang.

Brancato, Robin. *Sweet Bells Jangled Out of Tune.* New York: Scholastic, 1982. A girl tries to unravel the mystery of her strange grandmother who has become a bag lady shunned by her family.

Branscum, Robbie. *The Girl*. Harper Junior Books, 1986. Left in the care of a cruel grandmother and lazy grandfather, five children struggle to survive in an Arkansas sharecropper community.

Bridgers, Sue Ellen. *Permanent Connections*. New York: Harper & Row, 1987. An angry young man who feels life is against him is sent to a small town in rural Appalachia to care for his cantankerous grandfather, an aunt, and an uncle. He acquires a greater appreciation for his heritage and family.

————. *Notes for Another Life*. New York: Bantam, 1982. A girl and her brother adjust to divorce with the help of their grandmother.

————. *All Together Now*. New York: Knopf, 1979. A 12-year-old girl spends the summer with her grandparents while her father is fighting in Korea and her mother works. She encounters a number of unusual characters and fights to help a retarded man avoid institutionalization.

Bryant, Dorothy. *Miss Giardino*. Berkeley, CA: Ata Books, 1978. After she has been mugged, a retired teacher tells her life story in flashback, from her childhood on up.

Butterworth, W. E. *Leroy and the Old Man*. New York: Four Winds Press, 1980. A high school boy who witnessed a robbery goes to live with his grandfather. During a number of adventures, their relationship grows.

Cavanna, Betty. *Storm in Her Heart*. Louisville, KY: Westminister Press, 1983. A girl whose parents are divorcing lives with her grandmother, a recovering alcoholic. The two survive catastrophes and learn to deal with their respective problems.

————. *The Surfer and the City Girl*. Louisville, KY: Westminister Press, 1981. A girl meets an attractive boy on a visit to her grandmother's, but also discovers that her grandmother is an alcoholic.

Childress, Alice. *Rainbow Jordan*. New York: Putnam's, 1981. A girl who has been abandoned by her mother is cared for by an older woman.

Cleaver, Vera, and Bill. *Queen of Hearts*. New York: Lippincott Jr. Books, 1987. A 12-year-old girl resents having to stay with her grandmother.

Clifford, Eth. *The Rocking Chair Rebellion*. Boston: Houghton Mifflin, 1978. A 14-year-old girl upset by the isolation and loneliness of the residents of a home for elders volunteers to work there in order to make some changes.

Cohn, Anna R, and Lucinda A. Leach, eds. *Generations: A Universal Family Album*. New York: Pantheon/Smithsonian Institution, 1987. Photographs, folklore, poetry, autobiography, and journalism by well-known writers about families in different cultures. Based on a Smithsonian exhibit.

Cookson, Catherine. *Mrs. Flannagan's Trumpet*. New York: Lothrop, Lee & Shepard, 1980. A fifteen-year-old boy must go to live in Northumberland with his grandmother, who disowned his mother many years ago for marrying "beneath" her. He finds her deafness and constant nagging to be most unpleasant, until he and his sister are faced with great danger and he and his grandmother must team up to save the day.

Corcoran, Barbara. *Faraway Island.* New York: Atheneum, 1977. A 14-year-old girl stays with her grandmother when her family goes to Belgium. Her grandmother seems old and forgetful, and requires a great deal of care.

Culin, Charlotte. *Cages of Glass, Flowers of Time.* New York: Laurel-Leaf Library, 1983. A girl must deal with a mother who becomes abusive when drunk, and with her grandmother who shares the tendency.

Cummings, Betty Sue. *Let a River Be.* New York: Atheneum, 1978. An old woman tries to save the river area from developers; in the process, she helps a retarded man.

Dorris, Michael. *A Yellow Raft in Blue Water.* New York: Holt, 1987. Stories of three generations of Indian women. A 15-year-old girl who wishes she had a suburban life is left on the Montana reservation with a grandmother whom she doesn't know and who doesn't want her.

Easton, Patricia Harrison. *Summer's Chance.* San Diego: Harcourt Brace Jovanovich/Gulliver, 1988. A 14-year-old girl whose mother died when she was young visits her grandmother whom she hardly knows. The grandmother appears to be cold and brusque—a shield for her own grief.

Eige, Lillian E. *The Kidnapping of Mister Huey.* New York: Harper & Row, 1983. A 14-year-old boy tries to save an old friend from a nursing home.

Fine, Anne. *The Granny Project.* New York: Farrar, Straus & Giroux, 1983. Four children try to keep their grandmother from being put in a rest home.

Garcia, Ann. *Spirit on the Wall.* New York: Holiday House, 1982. This story of cave-people times includes an interesting grandmother.

Graber, Richard. *Doc.* New York: Harper & Row/Charlotte Zolotow Books, 1986. A boy must learn to accept and deal with his grandfather's Alzheimer's disease—a disease that has forced the grandfather to quit his medical practice.

Green, Phyllis. *Grandmother Orphan.* Nashville, TN: Thomas Nelson, 1977. An 11-year-old shoplifter is sent to her tough grandmother's house for a week.

Griffiths, Helen. *Running Wild.* New York: Holiday House, 1977. A boy lives in the mountains in Spain with his grandparents. His grandfather gives him a dog, but kills the dog's first litter of pups. The boy hides the next batch of puppies, who turn out to be wild.

Guernsey, JoAnn Bren. *Journey to Almost There.* New York: Ticknor & Fields, 1985. To escape having her grandmother placed in a nursing home, a girl takes her grandfather and runs away to find her father. The grandfather's health weakens, and the girl must make some difficult decisions.

Hall, Lynn. *Tin Can Tucker*. New York: Ace, 1984. A 16-year-old girl whose parents abandoned her at birth joins the rodeo and is befriended by a kindly older couple.

——. *The Seige of Silent Henry*. Chicago: Follett, 1972. A lonely young man who wants to be rich befriends an old man in order to steal the secret of the valuable Ginseng root beds; both realize their selfishness.

Hamilton, Virginia. *A Little Love*. New York: Philomel, 1984. A girl living with loving grandparents searches for her father, who disappeared when she was young.

Hayes, Sheila. *Speaking of Snapdragons*. New York: Lodestar, 1982. A lonely, fatherless 11-year-old befriends an old gardener.

Hedderwick, Mairi. *Katie Morag and the Two Grandmothers*. Boston: Little, Brown, 1985. A girl's two grandmothers are very different.

Heide, Florence Parry. *When the Sad One Comes to Stay*. New York: Bantam, 1976. A girl who moves to a new town befriends a poor old woman. The girl's mother, who is conscious of her social position, disapproves.

Hobbs, Will. *Bearstone*. New York: Atheneum, 1989. A Ute Indian boy who had been rebellious at boarding school goes to live with an aging rancher whom he learns to respect.

Hoffman, Alice. *Illumination Night*. Putnam's, 1987. Two families on Martha's Vineyard have similar problems. Once family includes a teenage girl and her grandmother, who becomes increasingly reclusive because of her failing eyesight. In the other family are a small boy, his attractive father, and his agoraphobic mother.

Howker, Janni. *The Nature of the Beast*. New York: Greenwillow, 1987. Three generations of males — a boy, his father and his grandfather — try to take care of each other.

——. *The Badger and the Barge and Other Stories*. New York: Greenwillow, 1985. Five short stories, each about a young person who is helped in some way by an old person. Set in New England.

Huyck, Margaret Hellie. *Growing Older*. Spectrum, 1974. Dist. by Social Studies School Service, 10,000 Culver Blvd., Culver City, CA 90230. Articles on issues and problems of aging.

Irwin, Hadley. *What About Grandma?* New York: Margaret K. McElderry Books, 1983. A daughter and her mother spend the summer at the house of the girl's dying grandmother, where they learn about themselves and each other.

Johnston, Norma. *The Potter's Wheel*. New York: Morrow, 1988. A girl's mother goes off to England, leaving her with her father. At a family reunion she encounters, among group of interesting relatives, a strong, enigmatic grandmother.

Jones, Weyman. Illus. by J. C. Kocsis. *Edge of Two Worlds*. New York: Dial,

1968. In 1842, circumstances bring together a 15-year-old white boy and an aging Cherokee Indian.

Korman, Gordon. *A Semester in the Life of a Garbage Bag.* New York: Scholastic, 1987. Two boys scheme to win a trip to Greece and get some help from a zany grandfather who appreciates the unconventional.

Lasky, Kathryn. Illus. by Trina Schart Hyman. *The Night Journey.* New York: Frederick Warne, 1981. A young Jewish girl learns about her great-grandmother's escape from persecution in Russia.

L'Engle, Madeleine. *Ring of Endless Light.* New York: Dell, 1986. A 15-year-old girl and her family spend the summer with the grandfather, who is dying. The girl confronts the meaning of death and its place in life.

Levin, Betty. *The Trouble with Gramary.* New York: Greenwillow, 1988. Set in a New England coast town, the story concerns a girl and her grandmother, a tough, independent woman whose welding yard ruffles the feathers of some residents.

Lingard, Joan. *Odd Girl Out.* New York: Elsevier/Nelson, 1979. A 14-year-old Scottish girl, whose mother divorces and remarries, becomes friends with a 70-year-old Czechoslovakian pianist, who gives her piano lessons in exchange for cooking.

Lyon, George Ella. *Borrowed Children.* New York: Watts/Orchard, 1988. The story of an extended family in Kentucky and Tennessee during the Depression.

Magorian, M. *Good Night Mr. Tom.* New York: Trophy, 1986. Willie is evacuated from London to the countryside before the outbreak of World War II. Kind, old Mr. Tom helps him overcome the terror of his abused childhood.

Mahy, Margaret. *Memory.* New York: Margaret K. McElderry Books, 1988. A 19-year-old boy who is having trouble coming to terms with his sister's death takes up with an old woman with Alzheimer's disease. Set in New Zealand.

Majerus, Janet. *Grandpa and Frank.* Philadelphia: Lippincott, 1976. A girl and her friend try to keep her uncle from putting grandpa in a nursing home by taking the grandfather to Chicago.

Mazer, Norma Fox. *After the Rain.* New York: Morrow, 1987. A girl who always felt uncomfortable around her grandfather is forced to care for him during his terminal illness and develops a close relationship with him.

————. *A Figure of Speech.* New York: Dell, 1973. A 13-year-old girl is a close companion of her aging grandfather and helps him run away when her family plans to put him in a nursing home.

Meyer, Carolyn. *Denny's Tapes.* New York: Margaret K. McElderry Books, 1987. A gifted young musician who is the product of an interracial marriage journeys West and learns about his roots. His two grand-mothers, both of whom rejected their children for marrying out of their race, play important roles in helping Denny learn his heritage.

Miller, Jim Wayne. *Newfound*. New York: Orchard, 1989. A boy who grows up in his grandparents' house in Appalachia learns from their stories about the people and town.

Myers, Walter Dean. *Won't Know 'Till I Get There*. New York: Puffin, 1988. A boy and his friends are caught spray painting a subway train and sentenced to work in an old age home.

Naylor, Phyllis Reynolds. *Faces in the Water*. New York: Atheneum, 1981. A boy whose father is deteriorating with Huntington's disease goes to spend the summer with his grandmother and meets a ghost — from his past or future?

Newton, Suzanne. *A Place Between*. New York: Viking Kestral, 1986. A 13-year-old girl feels dislocated when she has to move for her father's new job and when her beloved grandfather dies. She is forced to live temporarily with her grandmother, who encourages friendships with only wealthier, sophisticated girls. She plans to run away to her old home.

———. *M. V. Sexton Speaking*. New York: Viking, 1981. An orphan girl who feels as though she does not fit in and who has trouble communicating with her great aunt and uncle, with whom she lives, finds that a job in a bakery brings a number of rewards.

———. *Rubella and the Old Focus Home*. Philadelphia: Westminster, 1978. Three intelligent, active old women move to a small town on the coast of North Carolina and become involved with a teenage girl, her father, and the town. The association is mutually beneficial.

Oliphant, Robert. *A Piano for Mrs. Cimino*. New York: Prentice-Hall, 1980. A 19-year-old girl is able to help her grandmother, who has become mentally confused, get placed in a rehabilitative nursing home instead of a custodial one. There, the grandmother is able to recover her faculties and her life.

Paterson, Katherine. *Come Sing, Jimmy Jo*. New York: Avon, 1985. A boy with a musical gift struggles to maintain an identity in the face of a burgeoning career; his grandmother is a central figure.

———. *Jacob Have I Loved*. New York: Avon, 1980. This book about the struggle of a less-favored twin to find her own identity contains a caustic, difficult grandmother.

Paull, Irene. *Everybody's Studying Us: The Irony of Aging in the Pepsi Generation Cartoons by Bulbul*. Volcano, CA: Volcano Press, 1976. Dist. by Volcano Press, P.O. Box 270, Volcano, CA 95689. The difficulties of aging in a youth-oriented society is told from the perspective of elders.

Paulson, Gary. *The Winter Room*. New York: Orchard, 1989. A boy describes the scenes around him and recalls his old Norwegian uncle's stories about his past as a logger.

———. *Tracker*. New York: Berkley, 1982. John deals with his grandfather's impending death as he slowly tracks a doe.

―――. *The Night the White Deer Died*. New York: Delacorte, 1978. A teenage girl and an old Indian share the same haunting dream.

Pollowitz, Melinda. *Cinnamon Cane*. New York: Harper & Row, 1977. A junior-high girl begins to discover her own life and to neglect her aging grandfather, only to become reacquainted with him after he suffers a stroke.

Pople, Maureen. *The Other Side of the Family*. New York: Henry Holt, 1986. The humorous story of a 15-year-old English girl sent to live in Australia during World War II. She encounters some very interesting, eccentric relatives, including a grandmother.

Porter, Barbara Ann. *I Only Made Up the Roses*. New York: Greenwillow, 1987. The story of a girl with black and white relatives finds her identity in their stories.

Provost, Gary, and Gail Levine-Freidus. *Good If It Goes*. New York: Bradbury, 1984. A boy's Bar Mitzvah and other plans are interrupted by the dying of his grandfather.

Sebestyen, Ouida. *IOU's*. New York: Dell/Laurel-Leaf Books, 1985. A 13-year-old boy tries to reconcile his dying grandmother, whom he had not previously met, and his mother, whom the grandfather once refused to help.

Shanks, Ann Zane. *Old Is What You Get: Dialogues on Aging by the Old and the Young*. New York: Viking, 1976. Photos and transcribed comments on different aspects of aging from young and old people. Examines the realities of aging.

Shannon, George. *Unlived Affections*. New York: Harper & Row, 1989. When his grandmother dies, a boy finds a box of old letters that reveal family secrets.

Silverstein, Alvin, Virginia Silverstein, and Glenn Silverstein. *Aging*. New York: Franklin Watts, 1979. Comprehensive discussion and photographs about the processes of aging. Covers theory, research, and issues related to aging in current society.

Smith, Robert Kimmel. Illus. by Richard Lauter. *The War with Grandpa*. New York: Dell/Yearling. A boy tries to get his room back when Grandpa moves in.

Sobol, Harriet. *Grandpa: A Young Man Grown Old*. New York: Coward, McCann & Geoghegan, 1980. The reminiscences of a 17-year-old's grandfather. Includes pictures.

Strang, Celia. *Foster Mary*. New York: McGraw-Hill, 1979. A family of itinerant fruit pickers includes two older people and all the orphaned, mistreated children they've taken in.

Taylor, Mildred. *Let the Circle Be Unbroken*. New York: Dial, 1981. The sequel to *Roll of Thunder, Hear My Cry* continues the saga of the Logan family.

————. *Roll of Thunder, Hear My Cry.* New York: Dial, 1976. A black family in the rural south in the 1930s struggles to hold on to its land. The grandmother is a strong woman who teaches 11-year-old Cassie some valuable lessons about survival.

Tolan, Stephanie S. *Grandpa — and Me.* New York: Scribner's, 1978. An 11-year-old girl's grandfather becomes increasingly confused. She begins to learn about his past and her family and about the connections between being young and being old.

Voigt, Cynthia. *Dicey's Song.* New York: Fawcett Juniper, 1982. A grandmother takes in four grandchildren whose mother cannot care for them.

Wersba, Barbara. *The Dream Watcher.* New York: Atheneum, 1969. An adolescent boy who feels like a misfit is befriended by an aging actress and comes to find an identity.

Wilkinson, Brenda. *Ludell and Willie.* New York: Harper & Row, 1977. Sequel to *Ludell.* Ludell is now 17 and planning to marry Willie, despite her aging grandmother's disapproval. Ludell must cope with the mental deterioration and death of her grandmother,

————. *Ludell.* New York: Harper & Row, 1975. Ludell is a black pre-teen living in the segregated South; she is being raised by a loving, firm grandmother.

Wilkinson, Sylvia. *A Killing Frost.* Boston: Houghton Mifflin, 1969. A sensitive 13-year-old girl describes the old age of her grandmother, a tough, stubborn woman who lives in rural North Carolina.

Wood, Phyllis Anderson. *Then I'll Be Home Free.* New York: Signet, 1988. A girl must deal with her grandmother's death and grandfather's breakdown.

Zindel, Paul. *A Begonia for Miss Applebaum.* New York: Harper Junior Books, 1989. A high-school boy and girl learn that their favorite former teacher is dying. The three share the teacher's last days and learn the importance and depth of life.

————. *The Pigman's Legacy.* New York: Harper & Row, 1980. In this sequel to *The Pigman*, John and Lorraine befriend another old man.

————. *The Pigman.* New York: Harper & Row, 1968. A teenage boy and girl who do not get along with their respective parents make friends with a lonely old man and in the process, learn about responsibility.

Resources for Teachers

On Aging

Arluke, Arnold, and Jack Levin. "Another Stereotype: Old Age as a Second Childhood." *Aging*: 7–11; August/September, 1984.

Armour, Richard W. *Going Like Sixty, A Lighthearted Look at the Later Years*. New York: McGraw-Hill, 1976.

Barnum, Phyllis W. "The Aged in Young Children's Literature." *Language Arts* 54(1): 29–32; January, 1977.

Blank, Ruth, comp. *Aging in North America: Projections and Policies*. Washington, DC: National Council Aging, 1982.

Bradbury, Wilbur, *et al. The Adult Years*. Waltham, MA: Little, Brown, 1975.

Butler, Robert N., and Myrna I. Lewis. *Aging and Mental Health*. St. Louis: Mosby, 1977.

———. *Why Survive? Being Old in America*. New York: Harper & Row. 1975.

Cameron, Marcia J. *Views of Aging: A Teacher's Guide*. Ann Arbor, MI: Institute of Gerontology, 1976.

Coles, Robert. *The Old Ones of New Mexico*. Photographs by Alex Harris. San Diego: Harcourt Brace Jovanovich, 1984.

Constant, Helen. "The Image of Grandparents in Children's Literature." *Language Arts* 54(1): 33–40; January 1977.

Cunningham, Imogen. *After Ninety*. Seattle: University of Washington Press, 1977. (Photographs of elders.)

Davis, Richard H. "TV's Boycott of Old Age." *Aging*: 12–17; August/ September, 1984.

Fact Book on Aging: A Profile of America's Older Population. Washington, DC: National Council on Aging, 1978.

Fisher, David H. *Growing Old in America*. New York: Oxford University Press, 1977.

Forrai, Maria S. *A Look at Old Age*. Minneapolis: Lerner, 1976. (Photographs.)

Fusco, Esther. "Adopting a Grandparent: A Rewarding Language Experience." *English Journal* 78(1): 56–59; January, 1989.

Gillis, Candida. "English Education and Aging." *English Journal* 72(5): 62–66; September, 1983.

Gold, Don. *Until the Singing Stops: A Celebration of Life and Old Age in America*. New York: Holt, Rinehart & Winston, 1979.

Grambs, Jean. "Grow Old Along With Me—Teaching Adolescents About Age." *Social Education* 44(7): 595–598, 560; November/December, 1980.

Hess, Beth B, and Elizabeth W, Markson. *Growing Old in America.* 4th ed. New Brunswick, NJ: Transaction Books, 1990.

Huyck, Margaret Hellie. *Growing Older.* Englewood Cliffs, NJ: Prentice Hall, 1974. Distributed by Social Studies School Service (10,000 Culver Blvd., Culver City, CA 90230).

Instructor and Teacher. Winter, 1986 (special issue).

Jacob, Norma. *Growing Old: A View from Within.* Wallingford, PA: Pendle Hill, 1981.

Jantz, Richard K., *et al. Curriculum Guide—Children's Attitudes Toward the Elderly.* Department of Early Childhood/Elementary Education, College of Education, University of Maryland and Center on Aging, Division of Human Resources, University of Maryland, 1976.

Kaminsky, Marc, ed. *Uses of Reminiscence: New Ways of Working with Older Adults.* (Journal of the Gerontological Social Worker Series 7 [1, 2].) Binghamton, NY: Haworth Press, 1984.

————. *What's Inside You It Shines Out of You.* New York: Horizon Press, 1974.

Kart, Cary. *The Realities of Aging.* Boston: Allyn & Bacon, 1981.

Knopf, Olga. *Successful Aging: The Facts and Fallacies of Growing Old.* New York: Viking, 1975.

Kubler-Ross, Elisabeth. *Death: The Final Stage of Growth.* Englewood Cliffs, NJ: Prentice-Hall, 1975.

————. *On Death and Dying.* New York: Macmillan, 1969.

L'Engle, Madeleine. *The Summer of the Great-Grandmother.* New York: Farrar, Straus & Giroux, 1974.

Louis Harris and Associates. *The Myth and Reality of Aging in America.* Washington, DC: National Council on Aging, 1976.

McKenzie, Sheila C. *Aging and Old Age.* Glenview, IL: Scott Foresman, 1980.

Madison, John P. "Teaching About Age and Aging: Selected Resources for Elementary and Secondary Teachers." *Social Education* 44(7): 599–603; November/December, 1980.

Media and Methods. February 1980 (special issue: *Getting to Know the Elderly*).

Moss, Gordon, and Walter Moss. *Growing Old.* Senate Committee on Long-Term Care of the Aging, 1975. Distributed by Social Studies School Service (10,000 Culver Blvd., Culver City, CA 90230).

Murphey, Milledge *et al.* "Attitudes of Children Toward Older Persons: What They Are, What They Can Be." *The School Counselor.* 281–288; March, 1982.

National Crime Prevention Council, *Reaching Out: School-based Community Service Programs*. Washington, DC: National Crime Prevention Council (733 15th St. N.W., Suite 540, Washington, DC 20005), 1988.

Paull, Irene. *Everybody's Studying Us: The Ironies of Aging in the Pepsi Generation*. Cartoons by Bulbul. Volcano, CA: Volcano Press, 1976 (distributed by Volcano Press, P.O. Box 270, Volcano, CA 95689).

Percy, Charles, and Charles Mongel. *Growing Old in the Country of the Young*. New York: McGraw-Hill, 1974.

Peterson, David A., and Elizabeth L. Karnes. "Older People in Adolescent Literature." *Gerontologist* 16(3): 225–31; June, 1976.

Pratt, Francis E. *Teaching About Aging*. ERIC Clearinghouse for Social Studies/Social Science Education and Social Science Education Consortium, Inc., Boulder, Colorado (n.d.).

———. "Teaching Today's Kids—Tomorrow's Elder's." *Aging*, 19–26; August/September, 1984. (Contains excellent list of sources of curriculum materials, information agencies.)

Raynor, Dorka. *Grandparents Around the World*. Chicago: Albert Whitman, 1977.

Saxe, Adele. *The Young Look at the Old: Curriculum Building in the Area of Aging*. San Jose, CA: Gerontology Education and Training Center, 1977.

Shanks, Ann Zane. *Old Is What You Get: Dialogues on Aging by the Old and the Young*. New York: Viking, 1976.

Smith, Bert Kruger. *Aging in America*. Boston: Beacon, 1973.

Ulin, Richard O. *Teaching and Learning About Aging*. Washington, DC: National Educational Association, 1982.

Understanding and Appreciating The Aging: A Handbook for Elementary Teachers. Sister Mary Austin Schirmer, Project Director, Catholic Church Office for Services to the Aging, Archdiocese of Kansas City, Kansas (229 South 8th St., Kansas City, KS, 66101), 1983. (Contains excellent bibliographies of children's books and information sources.)

Understanding and Appreciating the Aging: A Handbook for Secondary Teachers. Sister Mary Austin Schirmer, Project Director. Catholic Church Office for Services to the Aging, Archdiocese of Kansas City, Kansas (229 South 8th St., Kansas City, KS, 66101), 1984. (Also contains excellent bibliographies.)

Van Tassel, David D. *Aging, Death, and the Completion of Being*. Philadelphia: University of Pennsylvania Press, 1979.

Young, Margaret. "We're All Growing Older." *Forecast for the Home Economist*: 21–23, 47; April, 1987.

Writing Ideas

Bryant, Jean. *Anybody Can Write*. Mill Valley, CA: Whatever Publishing,

1985.

Fletcher, William. *Recording Your Family History.* Berkeley, CA: Ten Speed Press, 1989.

Goldberg, Natalie. *Writing Down the Bones.* Boston: Shambhala, 1986.

Jackson, Jacqueline. *Turn Not Pale, Beloved Snail.* Boston: Little, Brown, 1974.

Kirby, Dan, and Tom Liner. *Inside Out: Developmental Strategies for Teaching Writing.* Portsmouth, NH: Boynton/Cook, 1981.

Koch, Kenneth. *I Never Told Anybody—Teaching Poetry Writing in a Nursing Home.* New York: Vintage, 1977.

Stillman, Peter. *Families Writing.* Cincinnati, OH: Writer's Digest Books, 1989.

———. *Writing Your Way.* Portsmouth, NH: Boynton/Cook, 1984.

Thomas, Frank P. *How to Write the Story of Your Life.* Cincinnati, OH: Writer's Digest Books, 1984.

Ueland, Brenda. *If You Want to Write.* St. Paul, MN: Graywolf Press, 1987.

Wiggington, Eliot. *Sometimes a Shining Moment.* Garden City, NY: Anchor Press/Doubleday, 1985.

Wood, Pamela. *You and Aunt Arie: A Guide to Cultural Journalism Based on "Foxfire" and Its Descendants.* Washington, DC: Institutional Development and Economic Affairs Service, 1975.

Bibliographies

Berman, Lorna, and Irina Sobkowska-Ashcroft. *Images & Impressions of Old Age in the Great Works of Western Literature (700 B.C.–1900 A.D.)* Lewiston/Queenston: St. David's University Press, (n.d.).

Books For You: A Booklist for Senior High Students Richard F. Abrahamson and Betty Carter, Co-Chairs. Urbana, IL: NCTE, 1988.

Guide to Play Selection. Compiled by the NCTE Liaison Committee with the Speech Communication Association and the American Theater Association, Joseph Mersand, Editorial Chairman. Urbana, IL: NCTE, and New York: Bowker, 1975.

Horner, Catherine Townsend. *The Aging Adult in Children's Books and Nonprint Media.* Metuchen, NJ: Scarecrow Press, 1982.

Monson, Dianne L., ed. *Adventuring with Books: A Booklist for Pre-K-Grade 6.* Urbana, IL: NCTE, 1985.

Your Reading: A Booklist for Junior High and Middle School Students. Jane Christensen, Chair. Urbana, IL: NCTE, 1989.

Writing By Elders

Ancona, George. *Growing Older.* New York: Dutton, 1978.

Bales, Carol Ann. *Tales of the Elders*. Chicago: Follett, 1977.

Blythe, Ronald, ed. *A View in Winter: Reflections on Old Age*. New York: Penguin, 1979.

Cowley, Malcolm. *The View from 80*. New York: Viking, 1980.

de Beauvoir, Simone. *Old Age*. London: Deutch, 1972.

George, Phil. *Kautsas (Grandmothers)*. Spalding, ID: Phil George, 1978.

Kloontz, Tom, and Thom Tammaro, eds. *The View from the Top of the Mountain: Poems After Sixty*. Daleville, IN: Barnwood Press Cooperative, 1981.

Koch, Kenneth. *I Never Told Anybody: Teaching Poetry Writing in a Nursing Home*. New York: Vintage, 1977.

Martz, Sandra, ed. *When I Am an Old Woman I Shall Wear Purple*. Manhattan Beach, CA: Papier Mache Press, 1988.

NIMROD: Old People: A Season of the Mind 20 (2); Spring/Summer, 1976. Humanities Council of Tulsa, Oklahoma.

Sarton, May. *At Seventy*. New York: Norton, 1984.

———. *As We Are Now*. New York: Norton, 1973.

Schulman, L. M., ed. *Autumn Light — Illuminations of Age*. New York: Thomas Y Crowell, 1978.

Shanks, Ann Zane. *Old Is What You Get: Dialogues on Aging by the Old and the Young*. New York: Viking, 1976.

Sobol, Harriet Langsam. *Grandpa: A Young Man Grown Old*. New York: Coward, McCann & Geoghegan, 1980.

Wagner, Linda W., ed. *Interviews with William Carlos Williams*. New York: New Directions, 1976.

Zeidenstein, Sondra., ed. *A Wider Giving: Women Writing after a Long Silence*. Goshen, CT: Chicory Blue Press, 1988.

Film Distributors

Benchmark Films, 145 Scarborough Rd., Briarcliffe, NY 10510

BFA Educational Films, 2211 Michigan Avenue, P.O. Box 1795, Santa Monica, CA 90406

Carousel Films, 1501 Broadway, New York, NY 10036

CINE 16 Films, 2233 40th Place, NW, Washington, DC 20007

Center for Southern Folklore, 1216 Peabody Avenue, P.O. Box 4081, Memphis, TN 38104

Entertainment Marketing Corp., 159 West 53 St., New York, NY 10019

Films Incorporated, 733 Green Bay Road, Wilmette, IL 60091

Kane-Lewis Productions, 811 Enderby Drive, Alexandria VA 22302

Learning Corporation of America, 1350 Avenue of the Americas, New

York, NY 10019

MTI Teleprograms, Inc., 4825 N. Scott Street, Suite 23, Schiller Park, IL 60176

New Day Films, P.O. Box 315, Franklin Lakes, NJ 07417

New Dimension Films, 85895 Lorane Highway, Eugene, OR 97405

Perspective Films, 369 West Erie Street, Chicago, IL 60610

Phoenix Films, 470 Park Avenue South, New York, NY 10016

Sunburst Films, Inc., 7466 Beverly Boulevard, Los Angeles, CA 90036

Time-Life Multimedia, Time & Life Building, 1271 Avenue of the Americas, New York, NY 10020

Sources of Information on Aging and Aging Education

On Aging

Administration on Aging (AoA), 4760 Wilber J. Cohen Bldg., 330 Independence Ave. SW, Washington, DC 20201

American Association of Retired Persons and National Retired Teachers Association, 1909 K Street NW, Washington, DC, 20049

Catholic Church Office for Services to the Aging, Archdiocese of Kansas City in Kansas, 229 South 8th St., Kansas City, KS 66101

Catholic Golden Age, National Headquarters, 400 Lockawanna Ave, Scranton, PA 18503

Federal Council on the Aging, 4545 Wilber J. Cohen Bldg., 330 Independence Ave. SW. Washington, DC 20201

Federal Information Program, General Services Administration, Washington, DC 20405

Gray Panthers, 311 S. Juniper St., Suite 601, Philadelphia, PA 19107

Jewish Association for Services for the Aged, 40 W. 68th St., New York, NY 10023

National Asociation for Hispanic Elderly (Asociacion Nacional Pro Personas Mayores), 2727 W. Sixth St., Suite 270, Los Angeles, CA 90057

National Clearinghouse on Aging, c/o Administration on Aging, 4760 Wilber J. Cohen Bldg., 330 Independence Ave, SW, Washington, DC, 20201

National Council of Senior Citizens, 925 15th St., NW, Washington, DC 20005

National Council on Black Aging, Box 51275, Durham, NC 27717

National Council on the Aging, 600 Maryland Ave. SW, W. Wing 100, Washington, D.C. 20024

National Pacific-Asian Resources Center on Aging, 2033 Sixth Ave., Suite 410, Seattle, WA 98212

National Retired Teachers' Association, 1909 K Street, NW, Washington, DC 20049

Older Women's League, 730 11th St. NW, Suite 300, Washington, D.C. 20001

Retired Senior Volunteer Program/ACTION, 806 Connecticut Avenue NW, Rm. M-1006, Washington, DC 20525

On Aging Education

The Teaching and Learning About Aging (TLA) Project, McCarthy-Towne School, Acton, MA 01720

The Center on Aging at the Presbyterian School of Christian Education, 1205 Palmyra Ave., Richmond, VA 23227

Clearinghouse for Elementary and Secondary Aging Education, Tennessee Technological University, Box 5112, Cookeville, TN 38501